Junior Certificate
Technology

Course Material, Activities and Exam Preparation

Gráinne Enright

Editors
Kristin Jensen and Ciara McNee

Design and layout
Artwerk Limited and Melanie Gradtke

Cover Design
Karen Hoey

© 2005 Gráinne Enright

ISBN 1-84131-705-5

Folens Publishers,
Hibernian Industrial Estate,
Greenhills Road,
Tallaght,
Dublin 24.

Produced by Folens Publishers.

All rights reserved. No part of this publication may be reproduced or transmitted in any form or by any means, electronic, mechanical, photocopying, recording, or otherwise without prior written permission from the Publisher.

The Publisher reserves the right to change, without notice, at any time the specification of this product, whether by change of materials, colours, bindings, format, text revision or any other characteristic.

TABLE OF CONTENTS

Acknowledgements iv

About the Author iv

Preface v

Student Introduction vii

CHAPTER 1 Health and Safety 1

CHAPTER 2 Technology in Society 5

CHAPTER 3 Energy 16

CHAPTER 4 Materials 22

CHAPTER 5 Equipment and Processes 30

CHAPTER 6 Structures 47

CHAPTER 7 Mechanisms 57

CHAPTER 8 Computers 71

CHAPTER 9 Electricity and Electronics 76

CHAPTER 10 Technical Graphics 100

CHAPTER 11 Project 115

CHAPTER 12 The Junior Certificate Exam 125

CHAPTER 13 Revision 127

CHAPTER 14 Symbols 139

Glossary 146

Index 151

ACKNOWLEDGEMENTS

Thanks to all the people who helped to bring this book together, in particular, Kristin Jensen, Don Harper and Ciara McNee.

Thanks also to all the fantastic staff and students in the Loreto Secondary School, Balbriggan, who help to make my job so great.

Finally, thanks to my husband Paul for his help and support.

ABOUT THE AUTHOR

Gráinne Enright is a qualified practising, secondary school teacher with a background in engineering, IT and technical training. This book is based on her practical experience of helping all levels of students enjoy and gain from the Junior Certificate Technology course, as well as achieving great results.

PREFACE

PURPOSE

This book is for students and teachers of Junior Certificate Technology. For the first time, it brings together course and project material for the Junior Certificate Technology syllabus at the right level in one easy-to-use book. It covers the Junior Certificate syllabus as outlined by the Department of Education and Science and is specifically written with a strong exam focus.

This book provides excellent preparation for the Junior Certificate exam because the structure and focus of and level of detail in the book are based on previous exam papers. It includes a specific chapter on the exam and previous exam questions. It also provides additional questions and quizzes for revision and class exams.

This book also provides valuable assistance to students in choosing and carrying out their Technology project work, which counts for either 50 or 60 per cent of the course result, depending on the level.

The objectives of the book are to:

- Cover the syllabus.
- Explain technology in a simple explanatory style that is aimed at its audience, using lots of illustrations.
- Provide a useful glossary of technology terms.
- Help students to research, design, implement and document their Technology projects.
- Provide suggested activities, project ideas, revision questions and games that assist in learning.
- Link project and coursework together so that the theory and practice reinforce each other.
- Help students prepare for the Junior Certificate Technology exam.
- Include past exam questions as guidelines.

STRUCTURE OF THE BOOK

This book uses a separate chapter for each section of the syllabus. Further chapters are added for project work, revision, exam preparation and a glossary.

Chapters are presented in a sequence that takes account of the dependencies between the subject matter, as well the student's broadening knowledge and interest. Some chapters, such as Health and Safety, Technical Graphics and Project, are relevant every year, while other chapters, such as Mechanisms, may be dealt with in isolation. Teachers may adapt the sequence and the depth to which to cover each chapter for each year of the Junior Certificate programme.

Each chapter is divided into three sections – course material, activities and previous exam questions. The course material section provides information relevant to the Technology syllabus and previous exam papers. The activities section gives suggestions for classroom work that will provide a practical reinforcement of the information discussed in the course material section. To relate the course material to the exam, sample past papers are included in a previous exam questions section at the end of each chapter.

EXAM PREPARATION

Chapter 12 provides a guide to the Junior Certificate exam itself, in terms of how it is structured and how best to approach it.

Chapter 13 provides revision questions, quizzes and word searches that can be used for classroom revision and homework. They are also helpful for exam preparation.

PROJECT WORK

As an important focus of the Junior Certificate course is to get students managing practical activities and projects, one chapter of the book has been devoted to project work. The Junior Certificate project counts for 50 per cent of the higher level result and 60 per cent of the ordinary level result.

Students should start with simple, safe projects early in the first year, e.g. making toys from cardboard or building bridges from art straws, and should progress in to more complex projects over the years. With each project, the student's confidence and competence should increase. The student should be encouraged to spend time unhurriedly contemplating a variety of solutions to problems.

Students should also be encouraged to source information on practical activities themselves. It is indispensable to have a variety of reference books available. Computers should also be available for students' work.

STUDENT INTRODUCTION

TECHNOLOGY IN OUR WORLD

Technology means designing and using materials, tools and machines. It also refers to the tools and machines themselves. Computers, cars, tin openers and cameras are all examples of technology.

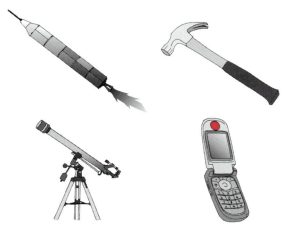

We use technology at home, at school and when we travel from place to place. At work, technology helps people to do their jobs more quickly and easily. Some technology is very complicated. Some is very simple.

Computer technology is everywhere in offices and in homes nowadays. This technology can make all kinds of tasks much easier to do than they were in the past. For instance, it can help people with disabilities who may have difficulty writing or talking.

Building technology is used to design houses, tunnels, dams and bridges. Choosing the right materials and making the design strong and safe are important parts of building technology.

Food technology helps to improve the quality, safety, taste or shelf life of food.

Technology has changed more over the last 100 years than in any other period of time before that. Modern technology began towards the end of the 1700s. Who knows what the future of technology holds?

USES AND BENEFITS OF TECHNOLOGY

Technology is not 'good' or 'bad'. However, it can be used in good or bad ways. Used well, technology has many benefits – it saves lives, improves the quality of lives, helps us make money, improves our education and has many more benefits. Used badly, it pollutes, destroys, makes us unhealthy and can even kill.

Understanding technology is your first step to using it to your benefit and the benefit of the world around you.

CAREERS IN TECHNOLOGY

Almost every career is at least touched by technology. Some have greater emphasis than others, but you will use at least some of the skills covered in this book in your future career.

Careers in technology can be very interesting and rewarding. Some highly technical careers include:

- engineer, e.g. electrical, electronic, chemical, mechanical, civil
- software programmer/computer technician
- mechanic/technician
- architect
- carpenter.

JUNIOR CERTIFICATE TECHNOLOGY

During the years that you will be studying Junior Certificate Technology, you will be shown how to use the stages in the design process to progress from an initial idea or problem to a finished product. All project work that you do will relate back to other sections of the course.

Among other things, you will:

- Realise the role of technology in our society.
- Be introduced to a range of materials, tools and processes.

JUNIOR CERTIFICATE TECHNOLOGY

- Learn about computers, electronics and mechanisms.
- Know how to draw your ideas carefully and accurately.

TECHNOLOGY ROOM

The Technology Room is not like other classrooms. As well as having ordinary tables and chairs, there is a range of benches, tools and equipment. In addition, there are storage areas to store materials, equipment and projects.

All Technology Rooms are different, each with its own range of tools and equipment. You will see tools in this book that you have not seen before, and you will have tools in your Technology Room that are not in this book. The main tools that you need to know about are covered. In the Technology Room, always follow the safety precautions outlined in Chapter 1.

SAFETY SYMBOLS

Wear safety glasses.

Can be fatal.

Flammable.

Wear face guard.

Electrical hazard.

Wear breathing apparatus.

1 HEALTH AND SAFETY

INTRODUCTION

Safety is always the first priority in technology and in the Technology Room. The Technology Room is potentially one of the most dangerous places in your school.

Note that Health and Safety is also an examinable section of the Junior Certificate Technology exam.

HEALTH AND SAFETY PRECAUTIONS

The general safety precautions outlined below should *always* be observed in the Technology Room. Also, depending on the task you are doing, there may be extra safety precautions to be observed. Read through all the safety precautions now, at the beginning of your Technology course, and make sure that you know and understand the general safety precautions well. As you carry out different tasks as part of your projects, read back over the safety precautions specific to the task to refresh your memory.

GENERAL SAFETY PRECAUTIONS

- Follow the teacher's instructions. Ask if you are unsure about anything.
- Wear protective clothing suitable for your work. Do not wear loose clothes or bulky jackets.
- Remove loose jewellery.
- Wear a face mask if dust or fumes are a problem.
- No horseplay in the Technology Room. Walk – do not run.
- Clamp work securely when possible.
- Clean up tools and waste material as you work. Untidy areas are a safety hazard.
- Only one person should use each tool or machine at a time.
- Do not interfere with others' work.
- Double check everything before starting a machine.
- Do not leave a machine switched on.
- Observe safety notices.
- Do not enter the Technology Room without a teacher.
- Never eat or drink in the Technology Room.
- Keep away from sharp or moving parts. Handle sharp tools with extreme care.
- Use the right tool for the job. Never force a tool.
- Do not carry tools around unless absolutely necessary.
- Only use machines or tools you have been trained to use.
- Watch the teacher's demonstrations carefully.
- Dangerous power tools must only be used under careful teacher supervision.

INJURIES

- Report injuries to your teacher.
- Know where the first aid kit is.
- If burned, place the burn in cold water for 10 minutes.
- If bleeding, elevate and apply pressure to the wound.
- For fainting, lay the patient down.
- If something gets in your eyes, use the eye bath to wash it out. *Do not rub* your eyes.
- For electric shock, turn off the power immediately.

TIDINESS IN THE TECHNOLOGY ROOM

- Keep the benches tidy.
- Do not leave tools or materials lying around when you are not using them.
- Brush the bench top clean of dust and shavings at the end of class. Use a brush, not your hand.
- Keep the areas between benches and around machines clear and tidy.

JUNIOR CERTIFICATE TECHNOLOGY

- Keep the bench vices closed, with the handles in a vertical position.
- Store tools, clothes, chemicals and equipment as instructed by your teacher.
- Report breakages and spillages to your teacher.
- Store your work in the storage area assigned to you.

GENERAL PRECAUTIONS WHEN USING ELECTRICITY

- Take special care when using mains electricity. Touching electricity can be fatal.
- Do not touch plugs and sockets with wet hands.
- Switch off the socket before inserting or removing a plug.
- Select and use the correct fuse.
- Replace all cut, frayed or damaged cables immediately.

EXTRA PRECAUTIONS WHEN USING ELECTRIC POWER TOOLS

- Use only with your teacher's permission and if you have been trained in its use.
- Only one person per tool.
- Know how to use and locate all STOP buttons. Get a friend to 'guard' the STOP button when you are working.
- Hold the work firmly. Clamp it in if possible.
- Use guards and goggles.
- Keep hands away from moving or sharp parts.
- Unplug the tool if changing bits, blades, belts or abrasive paper.

EXTRA PRECAUTIONS WHEN SAWING

Remember: If it can cut through wood, it can cut through you!

- Keep your hand away from the cutting line, unless you are starting a cut.
- Never force a saw blade.
- Select the correct saw for the work that is to be completed.
- Sharpen, clean and replace blades before they become damaged or dull.

EXTRA PRECAUTIONS WHEN DRILLING

- Wear safety glasses.
- Use a centre or dot punch to mark where you want the hole.
- Hold the work firmly, using a vice or G clamp.
- Ensure the drill bit is in tight.
- Remove the chuck key. (If you start drilling with the chuck key in place, it will fly across the room.)
- Use a timber support when drilling through acrylic so that the acrylic does not shatter.
- Choose the correct speed drill as instructed by your teacher.

EXTRA PRECAUTIONS WHEN PLANING

- Never force the plane.
- Keep your hands away from the cutting edge.
- Never remove shavings from the mouth of the plane with a chisel.

EXTRA PRECAUTIONS WHEN HAMMERING

- Use the correct sized hammer for the job.
- Do not use if the head of the hammer is loose.
- Only use the centre of the striking face of the hammer.
- Clean the head of the hammer regularly by rubbing it with a piece of emery paper.
- Wear safety glasses to protect against flying nails.

EXTRA PRECAUTIONS WHEN CHISELLING

- Wear safety goggles.
- Strike the chisel gently with the centre of the mallet face.
- Always chisel away from your body.

EXTRA PRECAUTIONS WHEN USING ADHESIVES

- Follow the manufacturer's instructions.
- Do not inhale. Use a face mask for adhesives with strong smells.
- Do not touch the adhesive. Use gloves or barrier cream if necessary. If adhesive comes into contact with skin, wash thoroughly.
- Do not put adhesive near your eyes.
- Use adhesives in well-ventilated conditions away from flames.
- Wear protective clothing.
- Take care when using superglues, as they stick very quickly.

HEALTH AND SAFETY

EXTRA PRECAUTIONS WHEN SOLDERING

- Do not touch the hot soldering iron.
- Keep the sponge damp, but not wet.
- Put the hot soldering iron in the stand when resting.
- Turn the iron off and allow it to cool down when your work is finished.
- When many students are soldering over a period of time, ventilation is needed to clear the fumes.
- Flux is a corrosive paste. Do not let it come into contact with skin if you are using it.

HEALTH AND SAFETY IN DESIGN

When you are designing something, safety should always be the main concern. For example, some things to be considered if designing a child's toy include:

1. All parts should be tightly attached so that they cannot fall off or be pulled off by a child.
2. If your design is something that the child sits on, the centre of gravity should be low so that it cannot topple over easily.
3. There should be no sharp edges that children could cut themselves on, e.g. from a tin plate.
4. There should be no toxic paint (e.g. containing lead) or materials used in the construction of the item.

HEALTH AND SAFETY ACTIVITIES

1. Fill in the blanks in these statements.
   (a) One of the most dangerous rooms in your school is the _____ Room.
   (b) If you are unsure about anything in the Technology Room, you should ask your _____.
   (c) To help deal with injuries, your teacher has a _____ _____ kit.
   (d) At the end of class, you must _____ up.
   (e) The most important button on a power tool is the _____ button.
   (f) When drilling, you must remember to remove the _____ key before starting.
   (g) When using power tools, you must wear _____ _____.
   (h) If adhesives smell strong, you must wear a _____ _____.
   (i) Ventilation is needed if many students are _____ at the same time.
   (j) When designing something, your most important concern is for _____.

2. Design an A3-size safety rules poster for your Technology Room.

3. What would you do if you had a burn?

4. What would you do if you got some sawdust in your eye?

5. What is the student in the picture doing wrong?

6. What about this one? Can you see any mistakes he is making?

PREVIOUS HEALTH AND SAFETY EXAM QUESTIONS

HEALTH AND SAFETY SYMBOLS

1. What does each of the symbols shown indicate?
   (a)
   (b)
   (c)
   (d)
   (e)
   (f)

JUNIOR CERTIFICATE TECHNOLOGY

HEALTH AND SAFETY USING EQUIPMENT

1. Identify two safety precautions which should be taken by a student using the pillar drill.

2. State two safety precautions which should be taken when drilling thin material.

3. State two safety precautions that should be taken when working with power tools.

4. State two safety precautions which should be taken when using adhesives.

5. List one safety rule which must be observed when soldering.

6. List two safety precautions which must be taken when using an electric drill.

7. Give two examples of when safety glasses should be worn in the workshop.

8. Name two safety rules which must be followed when drilling acrylic sheet.

9. Name one safety rule to be observed when using any hand tool with a sharp edge.

HEALTH AND SAFETY IN DESIGN

1. Name two safety features a bicycle manufacturer should include on a child's tricycle.

2. Many toys produced in the early 1900s were made of tin plate and used lead-based paints for decoration. State two reasons why these materials are no longer used in toys.

3. If you were designing a safety helmet for cyclists, name two important points that should be included in the design.

2 TECHNOLOGY IN SOCIETY

INTRODUCTION

It is important to understand how technology affects our lives and our world. Materials, machines, processes and communications all impact on society.

This section will help you to understand the impact and effects of technology in the home, school and workplace and on transport, industry and leisure. A selection of materials, tools, processes and systems are discussed with regard to their impact on society. This section also contains an introduction to forms of pollution and its control. The impact of good design practice on waste generation and disposal is also discussed.

INVENTIONS AND DISCOVERIES

Inventions are new ways of doing things. Discoveries means finding something that already exists. Some have made life more comfortable or have improved our health. Some have helped us to travel further and faster. Some have changed how we talk to one another. Not all inventions have changed our world for the better, however.

COMMUNICATION

- Alexander Graham Bell: Invented the telephone.
- Guglielmo Marconi: Sent the first radio signals.
- John Logie Beard: Invented the TV.

TRANSPORT

- The Wright brothers: Invented aeroplanes.
- Gottleib Daimler and Karl Benz: Invented the car.
- Henry Ford: Mass produced cars.
- George Stevenson: Invented the first steam train engines.
- John Dunlop: Invented the pneumatic tyre.
- Rudolf Diesel: Invented the diesel engine.
- John P. Holland: Invented the submarine.

HEALTH

- Marie Curie: Discovered radiation.
- Louis Pasteur: Invented pasteurisation, now used in pasteurised milk.
- Wilhelm Conrad Rontgen: Discovered X-rays.

HOUSEHOLD

- Thomas Edison: Invented the filament light bulb.
- George Eastman: Invented the camera.
- Michael Faraday: Invented the electric motor.
- James Spangler: Invented the vacuum cleaner.

TECHNOLOGY IN HEALTH CARE, SPECIAL NEEDS AND FOR THE ELDERLY

There have been huge improvements in health care over the years, such as the following:

- Anaesthetics: Allow people to be put asleep, pain free, for surgery.
- Antibiotics: Fight bacterial infection.
- Radiation: Used in cancer treatment.
- Laser surgery: More accurate than cutting with knives.
- Anti-AIDS drugs.
- Prosthetic limbs and organ transplants are now possible.
- Incubators protect sick and premature babies.
- A microscope makes things look much bigger than they really are. Scientists use microscopes to examine germs that cause disease.
- Antiseptics kill germs. Before them, people often died from infections after operations.
- X-rays are waves that pass through flesh but not through bones. They are used in hospitals to check for broken bones.
- Vaccinations are available that help prevent the spread of disease.

Further technological improvements benefiting people with special needs include:

- pacemakers
- plastic surgery
- glasses
- hearing aids
- electric wheelchairs.

Technological improvements benefiting the elderly include:

- panic alarms
- house alarms
- stairs lifts.

FOOD TECHNOLOGY

FOOD ADDITIVES

Additives are put in food to improve the flavour or smell, change the colour or preserve it, i.e. keep food fresh for longer. However, some food additives have been linked to cancer, food allergies and hyperactivity in children.

FOOD PRESERVATION

Using fridges and freezers, vacuum packing (which removes air from food), tinning and drying food all keep food fresh for longer.

FOOD SAFETY

- Better food preservation means there is less likelihood of eating food that has gone off.
- Pasteurisation of milk and other products kills many germs.
- Modern testing in laboratories gives us vital information about food safety, e.g. it is easy to test for *E. coli*, salmonella, etc.
- Heat probes allow us to tell what temperature meat is inside, so that we can know when the meat is fully cooked.
- Air sterilisers kill germs in the air and are often used in kitchens.
- Electric fly killers kill germ-carrying flies where food is being prepared.

GENETIC MODIFICATION

In genetically modified (GM) crops, scientists extract a gene from a living plant, animal or person and place it into a different food. This creates new varieties of plants that could not have been created by nature.

GM crops are made for many different purposes, the main purpose being to create plants that are more resistant to disease or pests. This means that more food can be produced from a given piece of land. GM crops create plants that can survive being sprayed with harmful chemicals like pesticides and herbicides. They also produce food that will stay fresh for longer or look or taste better.

However, many people are not in favour of GM crops because they say it is unnatural. They argue that the full effect of genetically modified crops may not be known for some time. Also, some people are suspicious of the companies that produce GM crops because they can own the GM seeds and charge farmers lots of money to use them.

Below is a list of some of the advantages and disadvantages claimed of genetic modification.

Advantages of genetic modification:

- ✔ There are increased yields and tolerance to cold, drought or salt levels.
- ✔ GM crops are faster to grow and cheaper, as there is less work needed by growers.
- ✔ There is a longer shelf life of produce.
- ✔ Possibly better flavour, colour and texture of food.
- ✔ Possibly more environmentally friendly, as less weed-killers and pesticides need to be used.
- ✔ It can boost immunity and develop inbuilt vaccines for animals.

Disadvantages of genetic modification:

- ✘ Nature has always fought back when interfered with. GM crops may be shown to be unsafe in the future.
- ✘ Vegetarians do not agree with putting animal genes into plants.
- ✘ World starvation has more to do with wealth distribution than the inadequate production of food.
- ✘ Sometimes GM crops have allergenic effects.
- ✘ There may be a loss of nutritional value.

TECHNOLOGY IN SOCIETY

TECHNOLOGY IN TRANSPORT

Technology has vastly changed the way people get around over the years.

Year	Transport Methods
0	By foot, horse, donkey, cart or wooden or animal-skin boats.
1900	Wooden bicycles, electric trams, steam engines, steam-powered ships.
1950	Diesel trains, electric trains, petrol and diesel cars, aeroplanes, helicopters.
Today	As in 1950, but more advanced, faster and safer. We also have rockets and shuttles for space transport. Some cars run on different fuels than before, e.g. gas, electricity or solar power.

TRAINS
Steam trains used coal or wood to make steam to drive their wheels. Many modern trains run on electrified rails and carry people through tunnels under cities. Some trains travel as fast as 300 km per hour.

CARS
Some modern electric cars have an electric motor instead of a petrol engine. The electricity for the motor comes from rechargeable batteries inside the car.

BOATS
Boats have been used for thousands of years. Early boats were log rafts. Boats use sails, oars or engines to push them through the water. The Vikings built strong wooden longboats that had square sails and were rowed with oars. The biggest ships in the world are oil tankers. They can be 500 m long and are so heavy that they take 20 minutes to stop. A speedboat has a powerful engine. The front lifts up so the boat can skim quickly across the top of the water. Huge passenger ships, which are like floating hotels, are called cruise liners.

FLYING MACHINES
There are all kinds of different flying machines, like hot air balloons, gliders, helicopters and passenger planes. Passenger planes now often carry more than 400 people and travel very fast. An aircraft's wings are specially shaped to lift the aeroplane when it is speeding through the air at speeds up to 3,500 km per hour. Unfortunately, aeroplanes have very high fuel needs, which contribute to carbon dioxide emissions and global warming.

SPACE VEHICLES
Humans landed on the moon in 1969. Since then, scientists have learned a lot about other planets and stars from unmanned space craft called space probes.

IMPROVEMENTS IN CARS OVER THE YEARS

- Vehicle bodies that crumple more in an accident, absorbing shock.
- Safer brakes, like ABS (anti-lock braking system).
- Cars now use unleaded petrol. In the past, leaded petrol caused heavy pollution.
- Pollution-free hydrogen-powered cars are now possible.
- Special parts reduce pollution.
- Electric windows.
- Central locking.
- Alarms and immobilisers.
- Air conditioning.
- Radios/CDs/TVs.

Advantages of public transport over private transport:

✔ Less petrol is used when people take public transport and so less pollution is caused.
✔ Less time would be spent in traffic if lots of people switched to public transport.
✔ There would be less obesity, diabetes and heart disease if people did not use private cars so often.

Disadvantages of advances in transport:

✘ Very high carbon dioxide emissions from all vehicles mean more pollution.
✘ Higher rates of heart disease, diabetes and obesity.

JUNIOR CERTIFICATE TECHNOLOGY

TECHNOLOGY IN COMMUNICATION

Over the years technology has greatly changed the way people communicate.

Year	Communication Methods
0	Mostly oral, from person to person.
1900	Telegram, telegraph, post, newspaper.
1950	As before, also television, telephones, radio.
Today	More advanced, cheaper, faster versions of what was available in 1950. Also mobile phones, interactive TV, the Internet, e-mail.

TELEPHONES

Early telephones had no buttons or dials. You asked the operator to connect you to the number you wanted.

The modern phones we use do not really look or act like the one invented by Alexander Graham Bell. Phones now have functions such as:

- texting
- phone book
- calculator
- organiser
- calendar
- ring tones
- clock.

FAX MACHINES

A fax machine plugs into a telephone line. It has a scanner that turns words and pictures into electrical signals. The fax sends these to another fax machine, which turns the signals back into printed words and pictures.

COMMUNICATION SATELLITES

A satellite is an object in space that travels around another object, such as a planet. Some satellites watch the weather, some are used for communications, some are used for GPS car navigation systems and some investigate outer space. Communication satellites carry telephone messages through space around the world. The Hubble Space Telescope is a satellite that takes pictures of objects in space and sends them back to Earth.

RADIO WAVES

Radio waves are used to send signals from radio and television stations and to carry messages to and from mobile telephones.

MICROWAVES

As well as being used in cooking, microwaves can carry messages and signals through space. Satellite television programmes and international telephone calls are carried by microwaves. Ships and aircraft use radar to detect objects. A radar dish sends out beams of microwaves. If these strike an object, they bounce back to the dish and the object shows up on a screen.

NEWSPAPERS

There were some newspapers even 300 years ago, but they had very little access to any news from beyond the area in which they were printed. They were also slow and expensive to make. Nowadays, newspapers have instant access to news from all around the world. They are printed on big, fast printing machines, and can print photographs.

TECHNOLOGY IN SPORTS, MUSIC AND PHOTOGRAPHY

ADVANCES IN SPORTS

- Speakers built into athletes' starting blocks so athletes will hear the starting gun at the same time.
- Very accurate stopwatches.
- Laser beams across finishing lines.
- Underwater cameras for watching swimming and diving.
- Full TV coverage available of events.
- TV cameras built into racing cars.
- Steroids and performance-enhancing drugs are now available, but so is drug testing.
- Better shoes – air-cushioned soles, more appropriate materials, better grips and lighter.

TECHNOLOGY IN SOCIETY

ADVANCES IN MUSIC

- Many electric musical instruments are now available, e.g. electric pianos, drum machines, guitars, violins and harps.
- More advanced digital recording systems are available.
- We now listen to CDs instead of LPs and audio tapes. On a CD, sounds are recorded as a pattern of tiny pits in the surface. A laser beam in the player reads this pattern and turns it into electrical signals and then into sound.
- We have surround sound and Dolby sound systems.

ADVANCES IN PHOTOGRAPHY

- Photography is now regularly done with digital cameras, which means photos can be checked directly from the camera as soon as they are taken.
- Photos can be put on computer and e-mailed.
- Digital photos can be changed, e.g. cut to size, have people cut out, have light 'softened', etc.

When you take a photograph of an object with a non-digital camera, light bounces in through the camera's lens to hit the film inside. The light changes chemicals in the film. Behind the lens there is a shutter that opens and shuts very fast. The shutter lets just enough light into the camera for a picture to form on the film. When the film is processed (treated with more chemicals), the pictures appear.

With a digital camera, the picture is divided up into millions of tiny dots called pixels. Digital pictures can be saved on your PC or sent as e-mails.

ADVANCES IN BOOKS

The first books were written by hand. Each book was unique. Then a machine called a printing press was invented over 500 years ago so that multiple copies of books could be made. Today most books are made of paper and cardboard and printed in enormous numbers on fast machines. Books are also all composed on computers before they are sent for printing.

TECHNOLOGY IN THE HOME, SHOPS AND OFFICE

TECHNOLOGY IN THE HOME

- There is now electricity and running water in probably every home in Ireland.
- Houses are full of modern appliances, e.g. washing machines, hoovers, irons, dishwashers, tumble dryers, food processors. This has cut down on the number of hours people spend doing housework.
- Prepared food is available from supermarkets. Not everything is cooked from raw ingredients any more.
- Houses have advanced communication devices, e.g. phones, radios, computers, TVs.

TECHNOLOGY IN THE SHOPS

- Bar codes are placed on supermarket items so that the price of the item is automatically added to your bill when the bar code is scanned in. Customers can sometimes do their own bar code scanning.
- The information entered at the till is more accurate. Many mistakes occurred when people entered information or did calculations by hand.
- You can pay for your items using your debit or credit card. The credit card machine dials up a computer and checks if you can make purchases with your card.

TECHNOLOGY IN THE OFFICE

- All offices and most desks have telephones.
- Most PCs have e-mail and Internet access.
- Offices have fax machines.
- Offices often have intercom systems.
- Paper work used to be done using pen and paper. This was replaced by typewriters, but now is mostly computerised, i.e. typing is done on word processing packages on PCs. This means:
  ▲ Mistakes are easier to correct.
  ▲ Documents can be stored for future reference.
  ▲ Parts of documents can be copied and pasted for reuse.
  ▲ Spell checkers and different languages are available on word processors, which helps people write more accurately.
  ▲ There is a wide range of fonts and styles available on word processors, which makes work look better.
  ▲ When somebody rings up, you can find their file and all their details quickly on the computer. With a paper office, you would have to search through many filing cabinets.

TECHNOLOGY IN SECURITY

- Security alarms are common on buildings. These can be activated by movement, heat, doors or windows opening or by someone crossing a laser beam.
- PINs (personal identification numbers) are used at ATMs (automatic teller machines) as a security measure.
- X-rays are used at airports to check people's baggage.
- Code access locks: The lock is released by a computer recognising a code entered.
- Swipe card access locks: The lock is released by a computer recognising a swipe card.
- Key fob access locks used instead of keys: These are often operated by infrared light or radio waves – the infrared light or radio waves trigger the locks to release.
- Voice recognition locks: A lock that opens when a particular voice triggers it.
- Fingerprint recognition locks: A lock that opens when a particular fingerprint triggers it.

TECHNOLOGY AND THE WEATHER

ADVANCES TECHNOLOGY HAS BROUGHT TO WEATHER FORECASTING

- Satellites watch weather patterns and send the information to computers on Earth to help predict weather changes and future climates.
- Thermometers, barometers and other tools tell us what the weather is like. Using computers and information collected from these tools at weather stations around the world, the weather can be predicted.

WEATHER PROBLEMS TECHNOLOGY HAS CAUSED

- The misuse of technology and burning of fossil fuels cause global warming, which affects our weather (see the 'Technology and the Environment' section on p. 11 for more information).

GENERAL

Other everyday items have changed due to technological advances.

CHANGES IN HOW WE TELL THE TIME

In the past, people used candle clocks to tell the time. Candle clocks were marked in sections. The candle burned away one section every hour. People could tell the time by the number of sections left.

Modern clocks may have some or all of the following features:

- digital display
- date
- stopwatch
- 24-hour clock or 12-hour clock
- times in different countries
- increased accuracy.

TECHNOLOGY IN SOCIETY

CHANGES IN HOW WE SPEND MONEY

We now use 'plastic cash' – debit cards, credit cards and store cards – more often.

Advantages of this include:

✔ Less cash being carried around reduces the number of street robberies.

✔ You do not have to remember to go to the ATM to get enough cash for your shopping.

✔ You can buy more expensive purchases on 'plastic cards', which means you do not need to have lots of cash on you.

✔ You can get interest-free credit on 'plastic cards'.

Disadvantages include:

✘ Most people spend more than they had intended to.

✘ If you do not pay your bill on time, a high interest rate is charged and you have to pay back more than you originally paid for the item.

MODERN CURRENCY CHANGES

- Euro notes have a watermark on them and a metal strip in the middle of the notes, which makes them hard to forge, i.e. to create an illegal copy.
- Coins are also complicated. They are made from a mixture of different materials with a number of distinguishing marks, again to make it difficult and expensive to forge them.

CHANGES IN HOUSEHOLD ITEMS

Many things are being controlled by computers now. Even a sewing machine can be controlled by a computer, the advantages being:

- It is more accurate.
- It is more even, i.e. all the stitches look the same.
- It is faster and, therefore, cheaper.
- It can be programmed to do different types of stitches using different thread.
- It is safer, as hand stitching can be hard on the user's fingers and eyes.
- It can stitch hard material like denim and leather.

TECHNOLOGY AND THE ENVIRONMENT

Always use technology in such a way that it causes as little damage as possible to the environment.

POLLUTION

Everyone can do something to reduce pollution – you should not always leave it to someone else. Do not waste hot water. Turn off lights that are not needed, turn down your central heating, walk or use public transport and recycle.

Air Pollution

Causes:
- Waste gas from engines in cars and other vehicles from burning fuel.
- Industrial heating and cooling.
- Deforestation, i.e. cutting down trees that absorb carbon dioxide.

Effects:
- Cancer.
- Asthma.
- Global warming → rise in sea levels → coastal flooding.

Steps to reduce air pollution:
- Take public transport where possible.
- Make your home energy efficient.
- Reduce, reuse, recycle.

Acid Rain

Causes:
- Acid rain is caused by air pollutants like sulphur dioxide (emitted by traffic and coal-burning power stations) combining with rain and snow.

Effects:
- Animals and plants are being killed.
- Farmland is less suitable for growing crops.
- Human health is harmed.
- Old limestone buildings are being damaged.

Steps to reduce acid rain:
- The same as for reducing air pollution.

River Pollution

Causes:
- River pollution has many causes, e.g. farmers not following correct dumping procedures, chemical dumping and sewage.

Steps to reduce river pollution:
- Careful farm management.
- Proper drainage systems in farms so that contaminated liquids do not drain into rivers.
- Properly contained slurry tanks.

Litter

Steps that may help reduce littering:
- The problem of litter may be avoided by better education of young people, providing more litter bins and more cleaning up.
- Teaching people about the basics of reducing, reusing and recycling.

RECYCLING

Recycling occurs when materials are broken down and reused. For example, when you put your bottles in the bottle bin for recycling, they may be used again or the glass may be melted down to make new bottles.

The recycling symbol.

Recycling uses less energy and causes less pollution than using raw materials. It reduces the demand for new materials and greatly decreases the amount of waste generated. For every tonne of waste produced, an extra 20 tonnes was created at the point where the raw material was extracted.

The best way to deal with our waste is to stop creating so much of it. Landfill sites and incinerators (furnaces for burning waste) have environmental problems related to them. For example, landfill sites attract rats and cause pollution to seep into ground water. Incinerators release toxic gases into the air.

Use recycled paper so fewer trees have to be cut down. More trees growing means more oxygen and less carbon dioxide, as trees take in carbon dioxide and give out oxygen. One tonne of recycled paper saves 12 trees and 7,000 gallons of water.

Some things may need to be dismantled so that some parts can be recycled, e.g. batteries are taken apart for scrapping and recycling. Cars should be dismantled before scrapping. Some parts could be reused, e.g. seats, radios, mirrors; some parts recycled, e.g. aluminium shell; some parts disposed of safely, e.g. chemicals in batteries; and some parts dumped.

What Can Be Recycled?

- Glass: Bottle banks accept white, green and brown glass for recycling.
- Paper: Recycling banks accept newspapers, magazines, cardboard, junk mail, milk and beverage cartons. Some of these require different recycling processes.
- Aluminium and steel cans: Many bottle banks have can banks for aluminium and steel cans. Flatten beverage cans before recycling.
- Plastic: Plastic is difficult to recycle. Some local authorities accept some types.
- Organic waste: Compost food and garden waste. Otherwise it will rot, producing methane, which contributes to global warming.
- Electrical, electronic and computer equipment: There are few facilities for recycling this kind of waste. Check with your local authority.
- Batteries: Batteries are varied and complex, so are difficult to sort and recycle. Some local authorities provide facilities for battery recycling.

Disposable Products

Many things nowadays are designed to be disposable, i.e. once they are used or broken they are designed to be thrown out, not fixed.

Advantages of disposable products:

✔ Convenient.
✔ Cheap.

Disadvantages of disposable products:

✘ More waste from old things being disposed of.
✘ More waste of raw materials to make replacement products.

TECHNOLOGY IN SOCIETY

When disposing of products, recycle whatever you can, even if it means dismantling the products to get out parts that can be recycled.

Biodegradable Materials

Biodegradable materials are better for the environment because they decompose naturally over time and will eventually be recycled into the earth. People are being discouraged from using non-biodegradable products, as they are littering the earth.

Even biodegradable materials can take a while to decompose, but this is still much quicker than other materials.

HOW LONG WILL OUR WASTE BE HERE?

Banana skin/orange peel	1–2 years
Cigarette butts	1–5 years
Plastic-coated paper	5 years
Nylon fabric	30–40 years
Tin cans	50 years
Aluminium cans and tabs	500 years
Glass bottles	1,000 years
Plastic bottles	Indefinitely

FIRST WORLD VERSUS THIRD WORLD ENVIRONMENTAL EFFECTS

Advanced industrialised counties, such as those in Europe, North America and some parts of Asia, are said to be in the First World. Poor, developing countries, such as most countries in Africa, are said to be in the Third World.

Most of the damage to the environment is caused by highly developed First World countries and newly developing countries, such as China and India. Reasons for this include the following.

- There is very little heavy industry in the Third World. Factories account for a huge amount of our environmental problems.
- There are very few cars in the Third World. The developed world relies heavily on private cars for transport and this is causing big problems for the environment.
- There is very little packaging of food, as people usually produce their own. The developed world dumps millions of euro in packaging every day.
- The Third World often does not have running water, heated water or central heating.
- In the Third World there is less money to buy products that eat up the earth's energy resources.

Even though the First World is by far the bigger cause of the environmental problems, the Third World does not escape the negative effects. The impact is global.

All these environmental issues are dealt with in detail at Enfo's website, www.enfo.ie.

TECHNOLOGY IN SOCIETY ACTIVITIES

1. Fill in the blanks in these statements.

   (a) Alexander Graham Bell, Guglielmo Marconi, the Wright brothers and George Stevenson were all _____.

   (b) _____ can be preserved for longer now than it could in the past. It also often has _____ added to it to enhance flavour, smell or taste.

   (c) Cars, diesel trains, aeroplanes and rockets are all examples of technology in _____.

   (d) There is very little heavy industry, cars or heating in the _____ World. Their use of technology and their environmental impact is far less than the First World's.

   (e) Telephones, e-mail and satellite TV are all examples of technology in _____.

   (f) In the home, technology has cut down on the number of hours spent doing _____.

   (g) Chemical dumping, burning fossil fuels and sewage all contribute to _____ _____, which affects limestone structures.

   (h) Items designed to be thrown out once they are used or broken are called _____.

   (i) Banking has been changed greatly by technology, e.g. _____ and _____ cards are often used instead of cash to pay for things.

JUNIOR CERTIFICATE TECHNOLOGY

(j) Many appliances nowadays are controlled by _____. This makes them faster and more reliable and means they can be pre-programmed.

2. Choose one inventor mentioned in this chapter and research him/her on the Internet.

PREVIOUS TECHNOLOGY IN SOCIETY EXAM QUESTIONS

INVENTIONS AND DISCOVERIES

1. Name two people who have made a contribution to the development of technology and state their contribution.

2. Name one person who has made a contribution to the development of modern transport. State the contribution.

3. Name one inventor who has made a contribution to the development of communication systems and name the invention.

4. Mass production was developed by Rudolf Diesel/Karl Benz/Henry Ford. Circle the correct answer.

5. The light bulb was invented by Thomas Edison/Alexander Graham Bell/John Logie Baird. Circle the correct answer.

6. Alexander Graham Bell invented the aeroplane/telephone/television. Circle the correct answer.

7. In the case of any two of the people named below, state the technological contribution they made to society. J.L. Baird, H. Ford, G. Eastman, A.G. Bell.

8. Marconi invented the television/radio/electric light bulb. Circle the correct answer.

TECHNOLOGY IN HEALTH CARE, SPECIAL NEEDS AND FOR THE ELDERLY

1. State two ways technology might be used in the home to assist people with a disability.

2. State one way technology might be used to assist elderly people in their homes.

3. Name two developments that have improved health care in recent years.

FOOD TECHNOLOGY

1. State two ways technology has helped prolong the shelf life of foodstuff.

2. In relation to food, state the meaning of the abbreviation 'GM'.

3. Advances in food technology have resulted in the production of genetically modified (GM) crops. State one advantage and one disadvantage of GM crops.

4. Name two ways technology has improved food hygiene in a restaurant or supermarket.

TECHNOLOGY IN TRANSPORT

1. State two advantages of using public transport in large cities instead of private cars.

2. Name two ways technology has improved the family car in the past 30 years.

TECHNOLOGY IN COMMUNICATION

1. Name two functions found on a mobile phone not found on a home phone.

2. State one way technology might have helped in (a) producing a newspaper and (b) making a phone call.

3. Name two ways technology has improved communications between people in different countries.

4. Identify two ways technology has improved communications in a modern office.

TECHNOLOGY IN SPORTS, MUSIC, ENTERTAINMENT AND PHOTOGRAPHY

1. State two advances technology has brought to photography in recent years.

TECHNOLOGY IN SOCIETY

2. In the case of one named sport, state two changes technology has brought to the sport in recent years.

3. State two ways technology has changed international sporting events in the last 30 years.

4. New musical instruments have been developed as a result of advances in electronics technology. Name two modern musical instruments developed from these advances.

5. Name two features which have improved the modern training shoe.

TECHNOLOGY IN THE HOME, SHOPS AND OFFICE

1. Name two household objects that can be recycled.

2. State two advantages of the use of bar codes in supermarkets.

3. State two benefits to the consumer arising from the use of bar code scanners in supermarkets.

4. Give two examples of technology in the home that has helped to reduce the number of hours spent at housework.

5. Why are paper bags a better alternative to plastic bags in supermarkets?

6. State two reasons why word processors have replaced typewriters in the modern office.

GENERAL

1. This sign indicates an electrical hazard/a fire hazard/recycling. Circle the correct answer.

2. State two ways technology is used to help prevent the forgery of currency.

3. State two advantages of using 'plastic cards' in place of cash.

4. State two advantages of using a sewing machine over hand stitching.

5. Give a use for a periscope.

6. What does each of these symbols indicate?

7. Name two features of a modern digital watch not found in an older pocket watch.

8. Name two modern technologies used to open doors instead of keys.

TECHNOLOGY AND THE ENVIRONMENT

1. Identify two harmful effects of acid rain.

2. Name one source of river pollution and state how this could be avoided.

3. How can using recycled paper help to improve our environment?

4. Why does the First World consume more of the earth's energy resources than the Third World?

5. List two sources of air pollution and state how each one can be avoided.

3 ENERGY

INTRODUCTION

We all use the word 'energy' regularly. Did you ever wonder what energy really means? Where is it? Can you touch it, feel it, hear it or see it? Can you change it? What would happen without it?

WHAT IS ENERGY?

Energy is what gets you out of bed in the morning. It is what makes birds fly, lions roar, wind blow, factories make things, cars drive and light bulbs glow. When something or somebody moves, jumps, falls, explodes, breathes, thinks, dances or does anything, they do it by using energy. Without energy, there would be nothing – no life, no movement, no heat…nothing!

Energy is the ability to do work, i.e. it causes movement. It is measured in joules (J). Power is the rate of doing work. It is measured in watts (W).

The energy you use comes from the food you eat. A car gets energy from the petrol, diesel or gas it burns. A cooker gets its energy from the gas or electricity it uses. So food, petrol, diesel, gas and electricity must all contain energy.

Energy is important – never waste it.

TYPES OF ENERGY

There are many different types of energy, including:

- mechanical
- chemical
- electrical
- heat
- light
- sound.

MECHANICAL ENERGY

There are two types of mechanical energy – potential and kinetic. **Potential energy** has the capacity to do work. For example, a tightly wound spring can do work when it is released. After the spring is released, it has no potential energy. A rock on the edge of a high cliff has the potential to cause damage if it falls. The higher the cliff, the more potential energy the rock has. After the rock has fallen, its potential energy is gone. **Kinetic energy** is the energy a moving object has, e.g. a moving car has the kinetic energy to cause damage, but when it is stationary it does not.

CHEMICAL ENERGY

Chemical energy is energy stored in a chemical form, such as in food, coal, oil, petrol, wood or electric batteries. Energy is released from food when it combines with oxygen in the body. Energy is released from coal, oil, petrol and wood when they burn.

ELECTRICAL ENERGY

Electrical energy is the movement of electrons through an electrical conductor. Electrical energy is convenient and widely used. Electricity powers most things in your home – lights, television, radio and so on. When you press a button or turn a knob on an electrical device, you are controlling electrical energy.

HEAT ENERGY

Heat energy is a type of energy we can use for warming our houses and cooking our food.

LIGHT ENERGY

Light energy is the energy given out by light bulbs, candles, etc. It is energy that we can see.

SOUND ENERGY

Sound energy is carried through the air by vibrating the air. You can feel this if you stand in front of a powerful loudspeaker.

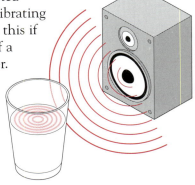

The sound energy causes the water in the glass to move.

ENERGY

HOW DO WE USE ENERGY?

Nearly all the energy we use originally came from the sun. Green plants use the sun's energy to make their own food. The plants are then eaten by animals or humans and give them energy, or they are left to decay and eventually become fossil fuels.

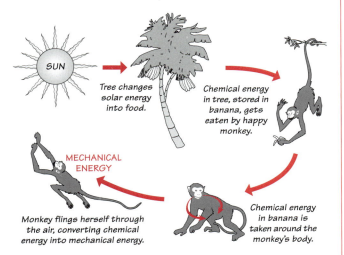

How a monkey uses energy to leap from tree to tree.

SOURCES OF ENERGY

Energy is said to be **renewable**, i.e. the source of the energy is still there after energy is taken from it, or **non-renewable**, i.e. the source of the energy is gone after energy is taken from it. It is better to choose renewable energy sources.

Renewable energy sources will not run out. They include sun (solar), wind, wood (if replanted), water (waves/tidal, river flow) and plants. A problem with renewable energy sources is generating enough reliable energy to meet all our requirements. A lot of research is being done to find practical ways of using these 'alternative' sources for the future.

Non-renewable energy sources are fossil fuels, i.e. oil, gas, coal, peat or nuclear. They are usually easier to get energy from and store, but have a bigger environmental impact.

Five of the most common sources we get energy from are:

1. wind energy (renewable)
2. solar energy (renewable)
3. hydroelectric energy (renewable)
4. nuclear energy (non-renewable)
5. fossil fuel energy (non-renewable).

WIND ENERGY (RENEWABLE)

Wind is air with mechanical energy. The blades of wind turbines catch the mechanical energy from the air, and the turbines turn the mechanical energy into electrical energy.

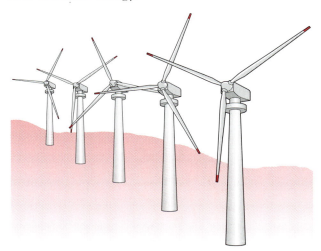

Turbines are on high masts so that they catch lots of wind and do not hurt anyone.

Advantages:
- ✔ Renewable.
- ✔ No pollution.
- ✔ Free.
- ✔ Ireland is a suitable location.

Disadvantages:
- ✘ The energy is difficult to store.
- ✘ Weather dependent – only windy areas of the world are suitable for wind power generation.
- ✘ Takes a lot of wind and wind generators (and therefore land) to generate a small amount of energy.
- ✘ Expensive to maintain.
- ✘ Environmental impact on hillside where the turbines are located.

SOLAR ENERGY (RENEWABLE)

Solar power from sunlight can be trapped and converted into useful energy.

Advantages:
- ✔ Endless fuel source.
- ✔ No pollution.
- ✔ Can be used for many different things, like solar cars and satellites.

Disadvantages:

✘ Many solar panels (and therefore a lot of land) are required.

✘ Only areas of the world with lots of sunlight are suitable for solar power generation.

HYDROELECTRIC ENERGY (RENEWABLE)

A special kind of water wheel, called a turbine, is turned by water. This turns a machine called a generator, which changes the mechanical energy in the water to electrical energy. This source of energy is very suited to islands.

Moving water provides energy, which can be converted into electricity.

Advantages:

✔ Water power is reasonably easy to store (in a reservoir).

Disadvantages:

✘ A lot of water is needed for a small amount of power.

✘ Large areas need to be flooded.

NUCLEAR ENERGY (NON-RENEWABLE)

Everything that exists is made up of atoms. An atom is made up of a nucleus surrounded by electrons. If a nucleus breaks apart, a huge amount of energy is released. This is called nuclear energy. In a nuclear power station, this is used to make electricity.

Advantages:

✔ A huge amount of energy is produced relatively cleanly and cheaply.

✔ You do not get air pollution that you get from fossil fuels.

Disadvantages:

✘ The materials used are highly dangerous and remain extremely dangerous for up to billions of years.

✘ The washing of equipment involved in the process pollutes the water, e.g. Sellafield has polluted the Irish Sea.

✘ Nuclear energy is non-renewable, using atoms of the metal uranium, which is a metal mined in various parts of the world.

✘ The price of uranium is high.

FOSSIL FUEL ENERGY (NON-RENEWABLE)

We get a lot of energy from burning coal, oil, gas and peat. These lie under the ground or under the sea bed. They formed over millions of years from the remains of plants and animals, i.e. fossils.

Advantages:

✔ They are convenient to use and can be stored cheaply until required.

Disadvantages:

✘ They are non-renewable. There is a limited amount of coal, oil and natural gas in the world. These sources are running out.

✘ Fossil fuels have a negative effect on the environment, e.g. smog, acid rain, oil spillages, greenhouse gas, global warming, etc.

✘ Oil is often found deep under the sea bed. To get it out, a deep hole has to be drilled and the oil is pumped up through long pipes. This damages the environment.

Fossil Fuel Use in Ireland

Fossil fuels provide the majority of our energy in Ireland because:

- We have supplies of peat and natural gas.
- Due to our weather, solar energy is not suitable as a main energy source.
- Capturing wind energy has not reached its full potential here yet.
- Most people in Ireland are opposed to nuclear energy.

ENERGY CONVERSION

Energy can change rapidly from one form to another. The principle, or law, of conservation of energy states that energy can change from one type to another, but it cannot be created or destroyed.

You can easily make energy change its form – rub your hands together quickly, and they will soon produce heat. You are converting chemical energy

ENERGY

you got from food into mechanical energy for movement that then gets converted into heat energy. In a gas cooker or fire, the chemical energy stored in the gas is changed into heat energy when it is burned. Electrical energy goes along a wire into a light bulb and is changed into light and heat energy.

Below are some more examples of energy conversions.

- TV: Electrical energy → light and sound energy.
- Electric fire: Electrical energy → light and heat energy.
- Coal fire: Chemical energy → light, heat and sound energy.
- Solar heating: Solar energy → heat energy.
- Light bulb: Electrical energy → light and heat energy.
- Battery radio: Chemical energy → electrical energy → sound energy.
- Electric motor: Electrical energy → mechanical energy.
- Loudspeaker: Sound energy → electrical energy → sound energy in speakers.
- Relay/solenoid: Electrical energy → magnetic energy → mechanical energy.
- Dynamo: Mechanical energy → electrical energy.
- Turbine: Mechanical energy → electrical energy.
- Electric pump: Electrical energy → mechanical energy.

N.B. Relays and solenoids are explained in detail on page 83.

ENERGY LOSS IN THE HOME

Much energy is lost in a house. Most houses could greatly cut their energy bill by taking simple measures.

REDUCING HEAT LOSS IN THE HOME

- Only put the heating on when necessary.
- Close windows and doors when the weather is cold.
- Insulate the attic.
- Use double-glazed windows.
- Insulate around door-frames and windows.
- Use thick curtains on the windows.
- Don't have open fireplaces.
- Insulate around the hot water cylinder.

REDUCING ELECTRICAL LOSS IN THE HOME

- Put electrical appliances on timers and only turn them on when you need to.

ENERGY ACTIVITIES

1. Fill in the blanks in these statements.

   (a) Energy is the ability to do _____.

   (b) Mechanical, chemical, electrical, heat, light and sound are all _____ of energy.

   (c) The two types of mechanical energy are _____ and _____ energy.

   (d) _____ energy will not run out. _____-_____ energy will run out.

   (e) Another term for renewable energy is _____ energy.

   (f) Wind, solar, hydroelectric, nuclear and fossil fuel are all _____ of energy.

   (g) The principle or law of _____ of energy states that energy can change from one type to another, but it cannot be _____ or _____.

   (h) When an electric bulb is turned on, _____ energy is converted into _____ energy.

   (i) In a battery, _____ energy is converted into _____ energy.

   (j) The most effective thing we can do to cut down on heat loss in our houses is to add _____, especially in attics and around hot water cylinders.

JUNIOR CERTIFICATE TECHNOLOGY

ENERGY CROSSWORD

Across

3. Most energy originally comes from this. (3)
4. Energy allows this to be done. (4)
8. Energy that does not run out. (9)
10. Convenient energy used at home. (10)
12. Unit of power. (4)

Down

1. Lots of water can be stored in this. (9)
2. Reduces heat loss in the home. (10)
5. Moving energy. (7)
6. Energy released by splitting atoms. (7)
7. Type of energy stored in batteries. (8)
9. Energy with capacity to do work. (9)
11. A type of dark fossil fuel we burn. (4)

PREVIOUS ENERGY EXAM QUESTIONS

SOURCES OF ENERGY

1. Which one of the following is a renewable form of energy? (a) Natural gas (b) Wood (c) Coal

2. Water is one form of renewable energy. Name two other forms of renewable energy.

3. Name two renewable sources of energy which could generate electricity for an island community during the winter months.

4. State one advantage and one disadvantage in using wind energy to generate electricity.

5. Give two reasons why wind turbines are always placed on tall masts.

6. Identify which one of the following is a renewable source of energy. (a) Coal (b) Solar (c) Oil

7. Oil is referred to as a non-renewable energy source. Name two other non-renewable energy sources.

ENERGY CONVERSION

1. State two energy conversions taking place when current flows through a light bulb.

2. State the energy conversion taking place in each of the following: (a) hair-dryer (b) microphone (c) bonfire.

3. This dynamo converts mechanical energy into electrical energy/mechanical energy into potential energy/mechanical energy into wind energy. Circle the correct answer.

4. Wind turbines convert wind energy into mechanical energy and then into electrical energy. Complete this chart by matching the type of energy conversion with the device. Select your answers from the second table.

Device	Energy Conversion
Motor	Electrical → mechanical
Bulb	
Battery	
Microphone	
Speaker	

Electrical → mechanical
Sound → electrical
Chemical → electrical
Electrical → sound
Electrical → light

ENERGY LOSS IN THE HOME

1. Heat loss is a big problem in our homes. List two ways in which this heat loss can be reduced.

2. Identify two areas where energy loss might occur in your home. For each, name one step you could take to conserve energy loss.

4 MATERIALS

INTRODUCTION

Materials are what all things are made of. Look around your classroom. You can see clothes, shoes, chairs, tables and books. What are these things made of? Some are made of plastic and others are made of metal, wood or fabric. These are all materials. Different materials have different uses.

Your choice of materials will be determined by the function of the finished product. For example, shoes are often made from leather or plastic because these materials are strong and flexible. Tables need to be made from harder material, often wood or maybe different parts made of wood, plastic and metal. Parts that will need to be small but strong may have to be made of metal or a very hard plastic.

The most common materials are:

- fabric
- metal
- wood
- plastic
- ceramic
- composite.

It is good to use a wide range of materials instead of ones that can be cut, shaped and formed relatively easily.

PROPERTIES OF MATERIALS

Properties of materials refer to such things as:

- appearance, e.g. colour, shininess
- weight, density
- strength, toughness, hardness, brittleness (how easily it shatters)
- feel, texture
- resistance to heat and resistance to corrosion
- conductivity/insulation (electrical or heat)
- flexibility
- ability to see through: opaque (light cannot pass through); translucent (some light can pass through); transparent (see through)
- elasticity (how much it can stretch without being damaged), plasticity
- malleability (how easily it can be hammered into shape)
- ductile (how easily it can be drawn into wires).

CHOOSING THE RIGHT MATERIAL

Many products could be made from any one of a number of types of material. The product has to be looked at closely and the chosen material justified. Materials also follow fashion trends – today's trendy material may not be in style tomorrow.

For example, a lampshade could be made from lots of different materials, with advantages to each. Paper is cheap, cotton is pretty and emits a nice light and steel and acrylic are trendy.

FABRIC (CLOTH)

Fabrics are made by weaving fibres (thin strands) together. Natural fibres are fibres that occur naturally, i.e. they come from animals or plants. Synthetic fibres, such as nylon, are made from chemicals.

- Natural fabrics from animals: Silk (from silkworms), wool (from sheep), leather (from cows), mohair (from goats).
- Natural fabrics from plants: Cotton (from the cotton plant), linen (from the flax plant).
- Synthetic fabrics: Nylon, polyester, acrylic. Synthetic fabrics are also called 'manufactured' or 'man-made' fabrics.
- Modern processes that can be applied to fabrics: Dying, stone washing, dry cleaning, fireproofing and printing.

Advantages of natural fabrics:

✔ Natural fabrics usually look better, e.g. leather shoes look better than plastic ones and wool jumpers look nicer than acrylic ones.

✔ Natural materials let skin 'breathe', e.g. in a leather shoe, moisture and air can pass

MATERIALS

through the material so feet do not get hot and sweaty. Cotton is cooler in warm weather than nylon.

✔ Using natural fabrics means using up less non-renewable resources, e.g. nylon, polyester and acrylic all use up oil, a non-renewable resource.

Disadvantages of natural fabrics:

✘ Natural fabrics may require killing animals, e.g. cows are killed for leather and minks are killed for fur.

✘ The plants and animals used for a supply of natural fabrics require feeding and care, which is time consuming and expensive, e.g. silkworms, cows and sheep all need feeding and care. Cotton plants require care.

✘ Natural fabrics may be more expensive, e.g. leather is more expensive than plastic, wool is more expensive than polyester and real fur is more expensive than fake fur.

Symbols used for fabrics include:

The Woolmark symbol indicates that the product is made from 100 per cent pure wool.

This symbol means do not hand wash

SHAPING FABRICS

Common tools for shaping fabric are scissors, sewing machines, needles, thread, iron-on hemming, fabric glue, knitting machines and looms.

USE OF FABRICS APPROPRIATE TO THE PRODUCT

It is important to use fabrics that are appropriate to the finished product.

For example, the material used to make a tent must be waterproof and must be strong enough to withstand rain and wind. Tents are usually made from nylon. The fabric used to make the sails on a yacht must be able to catch enough wind to move the boat but not enough to topple it. It must also be strong enough to withstand rain and wind without tearing.

If choosing materials for a kite, remember that a kite must be light enough to fly but strong enough not to tear in the wind. Many kites' frames are made from thin garden cane covered in plastic sheeting or cotton. The string to run with is often light, strong, plastic fishing line.

Fire-fighters wear special fire-resistant clothes which protect them from heat and smoke.

METAL

SOURCE

Most metals are hard and shiny. They can be bent or hammered into different shapes and sharpened to make knives and tools. Many metals are strong and can get very hot before they melt. This means they are a good material for making cooking pots and pans.

Most metals are extracted from the earth by mining. Rock called ore contains a mixture of metal and rock. The ore is dug out of the ground and the metal is separated from the rock by heating it to a very high temperature.

Aluminium is used for making foil, cans and pipes; copper for saucepans; steel for scissors and paperclips; and gold and silver for jewellery.

TYPES OF METAL

All metals can be classified as either **ferrous** or **non-ferrous**. Ferrous metals contain iron, e.g. iron and steel. Ferrous metals are attracted to magnets and rust from contact with water. Non-ferrous metals contain no iron, e.g. aluminium, copper and zinc. Non-ferrous metals are not attracted to magnets and do not rust.

ELECTRICAL CONDUCTOR

A conductor is a material that allows an electric current to pass through it easily. Conductors are usually metals. Good conductors of electricity are copper, brass, aluminium and silver.

ELECTRICAL INSULATOR

An insulator is a material that does not allow electricity to pass through it easily. Insulators are usually plastic. Good electrical insulators are rubber, paper, plastic and glass.

ALLOY

An alloy is a substance made up of two or more metals. Different metals can be mixed to make tough new metals, which may be more suitable to its use than a pure metal.

For example, brass is an alloy of copper and zinc. Solder is an alloy of lead and tin, which usually contains a core (centre) of a chemical called flux.

USE OF METALS APPROPRIATE TO THE PRODUCT

As with fabrics, it is important to use metals appropriate to the finished product. For example, aluminium is suitable for use in window frames and garden furniture because it is hardwearing, does not

23

rust and withstands a wide range of temperatures. Brass is a suitable material for the pins on plugs as brass is a good conductor of electricity. Tungsten is a suitable material for the filament in a light bulb because it is strong, cheap and has a very high melting point. Plastic is a good material to use for the casing on electrical equipment as it is an insulator, and so is very safe.

In the past, the wrong metals were often used in making products. For example, tin plate and lead were used in the making of toys, but tin plate is not suitable as it can cut children easily and lead is not suitable as it is toxic (poisonous).

Metals should never be used for casings of electrical equipment, as metals conduct electricity and so would not be safe.

MODIFICATIONS THAT MAY BE NECESSARY

Sometimes the most suitable metal may still not be totally suitable for the product, so some design modifications may be necessary. For example, steel is a suitable metal for bridges, as it is strong. However, metals expand when hot, so a steel bridge needs room for this expansion. The steel may be put on rollers to allow for this expansion, otherwise it would buckle.

WOOD
SOURCE

Wood comes from trees. Wood is a natural material that has been used for many centuries by builders and carpenters. Until recently there has been a seemingly endless supply. However, it takes trees between 30 and 100 years to produce wood suitable for human use. If trees are cut down at a faster rate than they are planted, soon there will be little wood to use. This is happening today in the rainforests, where a lot of our wood comes from.

Trees reduce dust, air and sound pollution and are nice to look at.

CHARACTERISTICS OF WOOD

- Pleasant to look at and to touch.
- Insulator of heat.
- It is strong.
- It is quite rigid, but will bend and usually springs back into shape when released. This property of wood is used in sporting equipment like spring boards, bows and hurleys.
- There is no such thing as a perfect piece of wood. All wood contains some type of natural defect, e.g. knots, rot, resin or cracks.

TYPE OF TREES

There two types of trees, hardwoods and softwoods.

The terms 'softwoods' and 'hardwoods' are used to describe the leaves, seeds and structure of the trees, not the type of wood produced. Some hardwoods are soft and light, e.g. balsa, while some softwoods are heavy and hard, e.g. yew.

Hardwood

Hardwood trees take a long time to grow and are therefore quite expensive. These can be native, i.e. they grow in Ireland, or non-native, i.e. they do not grow in Ireland. Hardwoods are generally harder than softwoods and come from broad-leafed deciduous trees (which lose their leaves in autumn).

Native hardwoods include oak, elm, beech and ash. Non-native hardwoods include mahogany, teak and ebony. They are the darker, more expensive hardwoods. It is not environmentally friendly to choose these, as they often come from rainforests that are not replanted.

Softwood

Softwood trees have small, waxy leaves, or sometimes needles. They are often referred to as 'pine' or 'deal', rather than the actual tree name. Examples of softwoods include Scots pine, cedar, spruce, yew and red deal. Softwoods come from conifers, i.e. evergreen trees that keep their needles all year round. Softwoods are generally softer, easier to cut and not as hardwearing as hardwoods. They grow faster and are usually lighter in colour. They are not usually as heavy as hardwoods.

MANUFACTURED WOOD

There is a third type of wood we use, called manufactured wood. Use of this has become more common in recent times due to its relatively low cost and the lack of availability of other wood. Manufactured boards include MDF (medium-density fibre), plywood, blockboard, chipboard and hardboard.

MDF is made from fine wood fibres glued together to make a smooth, stable board. The fibres run in all directions, so there is no grain and the wood is equally strong in all directions. MDF dust is very fine and can damage lungs if inhaled. Cover your mouth, nose and eyes when working with MDF.

Plywood is made by sticking together thin layers of wood called **veneers.** Each layer has its grain in the opposite direction to the layer next to it. This keeps the boards flat and makes them very strong. Plywood is used for things like drawer bottoms, toys and interior doors. It is often very thin.

Blockboard is made by gluing strips of softwood side by side and then sticking a thin veneer on each side. It is very strong and is often used for making modern furniture.

Chipboard is made by gluing and compressing together thousands of tiny pieces of wood. It is cheap, not very strong and is difficult to join. It can crumble and break. It is often used with a veneer facing for modern furniture.

Hardboard is made by gluing and compressing pulped wood. It has one rough and one smooth side. It comes in thin sheets and is used to cover large areas cheaply, such as cupboard backs. It is not very strong.

A **veneer** is a very thin sliver of hardwood or softwood, used to either coat a manufactured wood or to make plywood. When used to coat manufactured wood, the veneer is usually an expensive wood, e.g. oak for a kitchen press or laminate floor.

Advantages of manufactured boards:

✔ They are flat, cheap and can be strong.
✔ They can be machined and cut easily.
✔ They do not have any knots.
✔ They do not rot when damp.
✔ Their width is not limited to the width of the tree.
✔ They are more environmentally friendly, as they are used instead of natural timber and they are made from the waste products of cutting other wood.

Disadvantages of manufactured board:

✘ They do not look as nice.
✘ They may contain a lot of glue or chemicals.
✘ They may irritate the eyes and lungs, therefore they must be machined in a well-ventilated area.

USE OF WOODS APPROPRIATE TO THE PRODUCT

The use of the final wood product must be looked at before choosing a suitable wood for it. Ash is an elastic wood, so is suitable for making hurleys. We often use wood for outdoor furniture, doors and window frames, as it looks good and can be treated to withstand weather. Chipboard may be suitable where cost is important, but it would not be suitable for use outdoors. Beech is a suitable material for workbenches, as it is strong and does not scratch easily.

PLASTIC

SOURCE

Most plastics are made from oil. Plastics are man-made materials. They are a useful invention because they are waterproof, easy to shape and tough. They have taken the place of traditional materials like wood and metal in many products. It is bad to waste plastic, as it is made from non-renewable resources and takes a very long time to decay.

EXAMPLES OF PLASTICS

Examples of plastic include PVC, acrylic, polystyrene, expanded polystyrene (aeroboard), man-made rubber, polythene (or polyethylene, or PET) and nylon.

CHARACTERISTICS OF PLASTICS

- Most plastics are synthetic and are made from oil.
- Plastics are good insulators, which makes them safe for casing of electrical equipment and for coverings on wires. Many plug tops are made from man-made rubber, particularly for outdoor use, as rubber is such a good insulator.
- They are waterproof.
- They are light.
- Most plastics can be made in different colours or can be clear.
- Plastics are non-corrosive and non-toxic.
- They wash well.
- They are relatively cheap.
- They do not biodegrade and cannot be easily recycled.
- There are two main types – thermoplastic and thermosetting.

THERMOPLASTIC

Thermoplastics can be heated, moulded and shaped in various ways *lots of times*. You have probably shaped these in the vacuum former or strip heater in your Technology Room.

Each time a thermoplastic is heated, it tries to return to the shape it first was, usually a flat sheet. This is called **plastic memory**.

THERMOSETTING

Thermosetting plastics are generally strong and resistant to heat, but they melt the first time they are heated to a high enough temperature and harden (set) permanently when cooled. They can never be melted or reshaped again. They are used in situations where resistance to heat is important, e.g. on kitchen work surfaces, good-quality plastic cups, saucepan handles and plug casings.

USE OF PLASTICS APPROPRIATE TO THE PRODUCT

Expanded polystyrene (aeroboard) is used as white foam-like packaging to prevent damage to fragile goods in transit. As it is a good insulator, it is also used as a hot drinks container. It keeps the heat in the drink and away from your hands.

Acrylic, or Perspex, is ideal for signs outside shops, cassette boxes and aeroplane windows, but is too hard for plastic bottles. It does not look as good as glass and is not suitable for things that should not be scratched.

Polythene (or polyethylene, or PET) is ideal for use in plastic bottles.

Rubber is an insulator, which makes it safe for use with outdoor electrical appliances. Even if the rubber gets wet, it will not conduct electricity.

Thermoplastics are usually softer than thermosetting plastics and usually melt at lower temperatures, so are not as suitable for casings of electrical equipment.

CERAMIC

Clay is a kind of soft earth that can be formed into different shapes. When clay is baked it becomes very hard. Things made from clay are called ceramics, e.g. tiles, mugs and cups.

COMPOSITES

Composites are man-made materials with a high strength-to-weight ratio. They consist of two or more materials, with the different fibres bonded together. Examples of composites are paper, cardboard, concrete, Plasticine, plaster and Kevlar.

Paper is made from wood. It is used everywhere – in the home, the office, school and shops. The advantages of paper are that it is cheap, readily available and easy to work with. The disadvantages are that it is not strong, not resistant to corrosion and wastes trees.

Cardboard is common in packaging. Card and paper are made from fibres extracted from wood pulp and recycled waste paper. Wood pulp is the raw material that comes from trees.

Kevlar is a very strong and very light composite. Among other things, it is used in making bullet-proof vests, canoes, sails of boats, trampolines and tennis rackets.

Composite materials are very useful, but can be expensive to make.

MATERIALS ACTIVITIES

1. Fill in the blanks in these statements.

    (a) Paper, fabric, plastic, metal, wood and ceramics are all types of _____.

    (b) Appearance, weight, texture, feel, density and elasticity are all _____ of materials.

    (c) Fabric from plants or animals is called _____ fabric, and man-made fabric is called _____ fabric.

    (d) Metals containing iron are _____. Metals that do not contain iron are _____-_____.

    (e) Materials that allow electrical current to flow easily through them are called _____.

    (f) An _____ is a mixture of two or more metals.

    (g) The two types of wood are _____ and _____.

    (h) Plastic that can be remoulded lots of times is called _____. Plastic that sets after heating and cannot be remoulded is called _____ plastic.

    (i) Mugs and cups are examples of _____.

    (j) A man-made material consisting of two or more materials is called a _____.

2. How have plastics changed our lives for the better? How have they changed our lives for the worse?

3. The table below shows a number of fabrics and a suggested use. List two properties for each fabric that makes it suitable for the use suggested.

Fabric	Use	Properties
Silk	Shawl	(i) (ii)
Cotton	Shirt	(i) (ii)
Wool	Carpet	(i) (ii)
Acrylic	Sofa upholstery	(i) (ii)
Polyester	Yacht sail	(i) (ii)
Leather	Shoes	(i) (ii)

4. The table below shows a number of metals and a suggested use. List two properties for each metal that makes it suitable for the use suggested.

Metal	Use	Properties
Cast iron	Garden furniture	(i) (ii)
Stainless steel	Cutlery	(i) (ii)
Aluminium	Bean tins	(i) (ii)
Silver	Jewellery	(i) (ii)
Brass	Musical instruments	(i) (ii)
Copper	Electricity wires	(i) (ii)

5. The table below shows a number of woods and a suggested use. List two properties for each wood that makes it suitable for the use suggested.

Wood	Use	Properties
Pine	Kitchen table	(i) (ii)
Oak	Laminate on wooden floor	(i) (ii)
MDF	Kitchen presses (under laminate)	(i) (ii)
Mahogany	Furniture	(i) (ii)
Teak	Garden seat	(i) (ii)
Rosewood	Boat building	(i) (ii)
Fir	Christmas tree	(i) (ii)
Birch	Crates	(i) (ii)

6. The table below shows a number of plastics and a suggested use. List two properties for each plastic that makes it suitable for the use suggested.

Plastic	Use	Properties
Acrylic	Lunchbox	(i) (ii)
Expanded polystyrene	Packaging around a new television	(i) (ii)
Nylon	Plastic gear wheels	(i) (ii)
PVC	Garden hose	(i) (ii)

JUNIOR CERTIFICATE TECHNOLOGY

PREVIOUS MATERIALS EXAM QUESTIONS

FABRIC

1. Indicate if the materials listed are natural or synthetic by ticking the appropriate box.

Material	Natural or Synthetic	
Silk	☐	☐
Nylon	☐	☐
Linen	☐	☐
Polyester	☐	☐

2. Name two synthetic fabrics.

3. Which two of the following are natural materials? (a) Wool (b) Nylon (c) Linen (d) Polyester

4. Name one fabric derived from animal fibres and one fabric derived from plant fibres.

5. What is the difference between wool and nylon?

6. A natural material suitable to make a shirt is polyester/nylon/cotton. Circle the correct answer.

7. State one advantage and one disadvantage to the use of leather in shoemaking.

8. Name the source for leather and state one characteristic of leather.

9. List two properties of a fabric used to make tents.

10. Fabrics are used to make the sails on a yacht. What two properties of fabrics make them suitable for this purpose?

11. What does this symbol indicate?

12. What does this symbol indicate?

13. Name two modern processes that can be applied to fabrics.

14. State two advantages of using plastic to make a cheese dish.

15. State two ways to reduce the amount of plastic shopping bags we use.

METAL

1. Bronze and solder are alloys. Explain the word 'alloy'.

2. Copper is a ductile metal. Explain 'ductile'.

3. Solder, used in electronics, contains a core of lead/flux/tin. Circle the correct answer.

4. Solder is an alloy of two metals. Name these metals.

5. Steel girder bridges rest on rollers at one end. What property of steel makes this necessary?

6. Name two properties which make aluminium suitable for use in window frames.

7. Pins on a plug are made from nylon/steel/brass. Circle the correct answer.

8. Many toys produced in the early 1900s were made of tin plate and used lead-based paints for decoration. State two reasons why these materials are no longer used in toys.

9. The filament in this bulb is made from tungsten/steel/lead. Circle the correct answer.

10. What is the difference between ferrous and non-ferrous metals?

11. Name the raw material from which metals are commonly obtained.

12. Why is stainless steel a suitable material for a steel rule?

WOOD

1. Name one native and one non-native hardwood.

2. MDF, chipboard and blockboard are manufactured boards. State two advantages of using manufactured boards instead of natural timber.

3. Which one of the following is a manufactured board? (a) Plywood (b) Balsa (c) Teak

4. Which one of the following is a manufactured board? (a) Red deal (b) Plywood (c) Oak

5. In relation to wood, what is a veneer?

6. Which one of the following is a property of ash (wood) which makes it suitable for sporting equipment? (a) Malleable (b) Ductile (c) Elastic (d) Brittle

MATERIALS

PLASTIC

1. PVC is a(n): (a) animal fibre (b) synthetic fibre (c) vegetable fibre.

2. State two reasons why the casing of a modern portable music centre is made of plastic.

3. State two advantages of using plastic cooking tools over traditional wooden tools.

4. Name the raw material from which plastics are commonly obtained.

5. Plastic bottles are made from (a) expanded polystyrene (b) polythene (c) acrylic.

6. What property makes polystyrene suitable for hot drinks containers?

7. What is a thermoplastic material?

8. Rubber plug tops are recommended for outdoor electrical appliances. What property of rubber makes it suitable for this purpose?

9. Clear acrylic is used as a glass substitute. State one advantage and one disadvantage of acrylic in this situation.

10. Which one of the following is a property of plastic? (a) It is a good conductor. (b) It is easily formed when heated. (c) It is corrosive.

11. State one advantage and one disadvantage of using plastics for drink bottles.

GENERAL

1. Select one of the following objects: window frame, tent, garden chair. Name a suitable material for its manufacture and state a reason for your choice.

2. Name a suitable material for the manufacture of a saucepan handle and give a reason for your choice.

3. Name a suitable material which could be used to make a lampshade and give a reason for your choice.

4. Why is oil used to coat the moving parts in a mechanism?

5. List four different materials that can be recycled.

6. Why are certain modern materials designed to be biodegradable?

7. Which one of the following is best suited as a casing material on a hairdryer?
(a) Thermoplastic (b) Thermosetting plastic (c) Aluminium

8. Which of the following materials would make the best workbench surface?
(a) Acrylic sheet (b) Chipboard (c) Red deal

9. Draw a line from each material to one product in the table opposite that it can be made from.

Material	Product
Wood	Kite
Cotton fabric	Hurley
Acrylic sheet	Cassette box

10. Name one synthetic fibre and one natural fibre.

11. State one reason why new materials are required for space exploration.

12. Name one suitable material for manufacturing each of the objects shown and give one reason for your selection.

    (a) Food container

    (b) Key

13. Match the correct visual property with the named materials. Visual property:
(a) transparent (b) translucent (c) opaque.

Material	Visual Property
Wood	
Glass	
Red acrylic	

5 EQUIPMENT AND PROCESSES

INTRODUCTION

This chapter describes common tools and equipment used in technology and how to use them properly. You will use most of these tools and equipment in the Technology Room. The information in this chapter explains how to turn your design into a real product.

Before you can make anything, you must know what each tool or piece of equipment does and how to use it properly. This will reduce the risk of accidents, improve the quality of your work and decrease the time it takes to make your item.

Identify each tool from this section in your Technology Room. Ask your teacher if you are not sure. Read back over the safety rules for each type of tool or process in Chapter 1.

The pictures in this chapter are quite general – they should allow you to easily identify the tools, but do not be surprised if yours look a bit different.

HAND TOOLS

Hand tools are tools that are operated by hand. They can be categorised as follows:

- measuring and marking-out tools
- handsaws and cutting tools
- chisels
- planes
- tools for holding materials
- tools for hitting materials
- abrasive tools
- boring tools
- tools for joining materials
- threading tools.

MEASURING AND MARKING-OUT TOOLS

'Measure Twice, Cut Once'

Measuring and marking your material properly is the key to a successful project. The following is a selection of marking-out and measuring tools you have probably seen in your Technology Room.

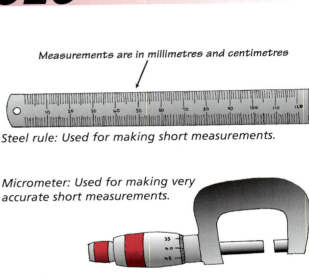

Steel rule: Used for making short measurements. (Measurements are in millimetres and centimetres)

Micrometer: Used for making very accurate short measurements.

Vernier callipers: Used for making very accurate short measurements.

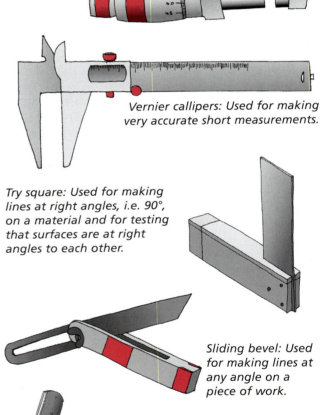

Try square: Used for making lines at right angles, i.e. 90°, on a material and for testing that surfaces are at right angles to each other.

Sliding bevel: Used for making lines at any angle on a piece of work.

Marking knife: Used to cut fine, accurate lines on the surface of wood, veneer, leather or cardboard before chiselling or sawing.

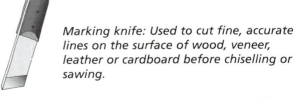

Tape measure: Used for making long and short measurements.

Marking gauge: Used to mark an accurate line parallel to the edge of a piece of timber or plastic by dragging the step of the marking gauge along with a pin embedded in the stem.

EQUIPMENT AND PROCESSES

For marking circles, convenient tools include a compass and dividers. Dividers look similar to a compass but have two points instead of one point and one pencil. They are used to mark circles on wood, metal and plastic.

HANDSAWS AND CUTTING TOOLS

Power saws can be used, but you should use simpler handsaws whenever possible. A handsaw is a cutting tool that has a thin steel blade with small, sharp teeth along the edge. It is designed to cut wood, plastic, metal and other materials. Some saws are designed for cutting straight and others are designed for cutting curves.

Tenon Saw

A tenon saw (sometimes spelled tennon) is good for cutting straight lines in wood or acrylic. The stiff metal (usually brass) strip on the saw keeps the blade flat and straight and strengthens the saw while you cut. Saws with stiff backs on them, like the tenon saw, are sometimes called back saws.

Hold the tenon saw with your outstretched index finger along the handle to stop it from twisting. It cuts on the push stroke.

Coping Saw

A coping saw is used for cutting curves and intricate shapes in thin sheet material. The narrow, flexible blade is kept tightly stretched by the sprung metal frame. You can point the blade in a different direction if you need to. The blades are too narrow to sharpen, so throw them out when blunt or broken.

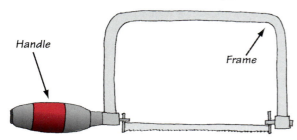

The teeth of the coping saw should face the handle. Pull the saw towards you to cut. Hold it with both hands for better control.

Fret Saw/Scroll Saw

A fret saw is used for cutting curves and circles in thin sheet material. Its frame is tall and deep, which allows it to reach further in from the edge of the material. This saw is used similarly to a coping saw.

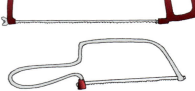

Scroll saw blades: These can be pointed in different directions if needed.

Dovetail Saw

A dovetail saw is particularly suitable for cutting dovetail joints in wood.

Hacksaw

A hacksaw, occasionally called a senior hacksaw, is used for cutting straight lines in metal and plastic. A junior hacksaw is a smaller version of a hacksaw and is especially good for getting into awkward places. The blade can be turned in different directions if necessary. The hacksaw leaves a ragged edge, which needs further finishing.

The strong teeth in these hacksaws can cut through metal.

Snips

Snips, or tin snips, are used to cut thin sheet metal, e.g. sheet aluminium. They can be straight or curved. They are also sometimes called shears because they cut using a shearing force. (There is more about shearing force in the Structures section, p. 49.) Snips act like scissors, but more force is needed because they are cutting metal.

Guillotine

A guillotine uses a shearing action to cut heavy sheet materials.

Hot Wire Cutter

A hot wire cutter uses the heat of a thin wire to cut/melt through materials such as polystyrene (aeroboard) by pressing a hot wire along it and melting it at that point.

31

JUNIOR CERTIFICATE TECHNOLOGY

CHISELS

Chisels come in various types and sizes, but the firmer and bevel edge are the most commonly used types and are the best for general use.

Some of the many different jobs chisels are used for include:

- paring
- making slots, notches, recesses and mortises
- light chopping and cutting
- reaching into awkward corners
- removing small amounts of waste between two cuts.

Push the chisel with your hand or hit it with a mallet. Keep your hands safely behind the cutting edge.

(a) Bevel chisel.
(b) Firmer chisel.
(c) Paring chisel.

PLANES

Planing is a way of removing waste wood when the amount is too thin to be cut with a saw. It is also used to smooth a surface before sanding and polishing it.

Jack plane.

The plane is made from cast iron with plastic or hardwood parts. The cutting parts are made from treated steel.

The jack plane is used to remove waste wood and square up rough timber. The smoothing plane is smaller and lighter and is used for cleaning and smoothing your work before you sand it. The try plane is a smoothing plane for extra-long surfaces.

Always lie the plane on its side, and not touching anything, when not in use. This will protect the cutting edge from damage.

TOOLS FOR HOLDING MATERIALS

It is important to hold materials you are working on, for three reasons:
1. To keep you and others safe.
2. To give you control over your work.
3. To keep materials firmly in position.

Vice

A vice is used to hold materials firmly. A vice has two smooth metal jaws brought together by a screw thread.

A **bench vice** is attached securely to the workbench. Fibre grips can be attached to a vice to protect plastic and delicate metals from being damaged by the jaws of the vice.

Bench vice.

A **hand vice** is held in the hand.

Cramps

Cramps, also called clamps, are used for holding two pieces of material together while glue sets or for securing materials to the bench.

G-cramp.

The G-cramp is the most widely used type of cramp.

Pliers

Pliers, long-nose pliers and snipe-nose pliers are gripping hand tools with two hinged arms and serrated jaws.

Long-nose pliers.

Tongs

Tongs are used to hold hot material.

TOOLS FOR HITTING MATERIALS

Hammer

A hammer is made of a head and a shaft or handle. On the head is a striking face, made from hard steel. The claw hammer is the most common type of hammer, but smaller hammers are used for smaller nails, e.g. in furniture making and light hammering.

Claw Hammer

The claw hammer gets its name from its strong claw, which is used to pull nails out. When pulling nails out, protect the surface of your material with waste wood, plywood or card.

Centre Punch/Dot Punch

The centre punch and dot punch are used to mark the centre of a hole to be drilled. The dot punch is lighter, thinner and more accurate.

32

EQUITMENT AND PROCESSES

Nail Punch

A nail punch is for driving a nail head below the surface of wood.

Pincers

Pincers are used to pull out small nails and pins that a claw hammer cannot grip, and also to cut the heads off small nails. As with the claw hammer, you should protect your material surface when using pincers.

Mallet

A mallet is generally used for jobs where your hand is not strong enough or where it is safer not to use your hand, e.g. for hitting the handle of a chisel, for knocking pieces of wood together or apart and for knocking metal parts together without damaging them.

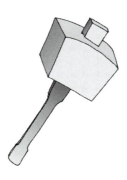

ABRASIVE TOOLS

Abrasive tools are used for shaping wood, plastic and metal using an abrasive (rubbing/grating) action. They leave the surfaces rough, so further smoothing is needed.

There are four abrasive tools commonly used in the Technology Room:

- files
- surforms (less common)
- rasps
- abrafile.

Files

Files are used to shape wood, plastic or metal and to smooth edges, curves and holes. They come in many shapes and sizes, with rough and smooth teeth. They give a relatively smooth finish.

Flat file: Used to file a flat edge.

Half-round file: Used to file a concave (curving inwards) curve.

Round file: Used to file a convex (curving outwards) curve.

Square file: Used to remove a square or rectangular section from inside a piece of material.

Choose the best file for the job:

- If you are filing a long, flat edge, choose a large flat file.
- If you are filing out a small, rectangular shape, choose a small square file.
- If you want to remove a lot of waste material, choose a file with rough teeth.

Clean your file with a little brush called a file card.

There are two ways of using a file: cross-filing and draw-filing. These are covered in the Processes section (see p. 38).

Surforms

The surform is a cross between a file and a plane. It is a light, strong tool with a plastic handle. It removes material with a two-handed pushing action, roughly shaping curved surfaces. The blades can vary in coarseness.

Rasp

Similar in appearance to a file, a rasp is harder to hold than a surform. The rasp works more quickly, but gives a rougher finish. If a lot of wood has to be cut away, a rasp should be used first, followed by a file. It may also be used on leather and soft metal.

Abrafile

An abrafile looks a bit like a coping saw, but uses a filing action to cut through metal.

Sanding

A sanding block is a block of wood or cork around which abrasive paper is wrapped or glued to aid efficient smoothing.

Always working with the grain, sand the object with a rough piece of sandpaper. Repeat the process

33

JUNIOR CERTIFICATE TECHNOLOGY

with a fine piece of sandpaper. Finally, use the back of a sheet of sandpaper to give a really smooth finish.

When checking sanding, run your finger over the surface, as it is easier to feel a rough spot than see one.

Glass Paper

Glass paper is quite like sandpaper, but is made from ground glass stuck onto strong backing paper.

Steel Wool

Steel wool is used to finish an edge of acrylic.

Abrasive Tool	Uses	Finish
File	Shaping wood, plastic and metal.	Smooth or rough, depending on file chosen.
Surform	Shaping wood, plywood, chipboard, fibreglass, soft metals and plastic.	Smooth or rough.
Rasp	Shaping wood quickly.	Rough.
Abrafile	Cutting metal.	Rough.
Sandpaper/ glass paper	For sanding and smoothing wood.	Smooth.
Steel wool	For finishing acrylic.	Smooth.

BORING TOOLS
Bore

'To bore' means to make a hole in a material.

Bradawl

A bradawl has a very sharp point that is used to make small holes in wood before screws are put in and before drilling. This provides a guide hole for the screw or drill bit and helps to prevent the wood from splitting.

Press and twist the bradawl in both directions.

Hand Drill

A hand drill bores holes in wood, plastic and soft metals by turning a handle. Its operation is based on bevel gears (see more information on bevel gears on p. 63). Different 'bits' fit into the hand drill, depending on the material being drilled, e.g. wood, metal, concrete. The 'bit' is the part that does the drilling. The 'chuck' is the piece that holds the bit in the drill.

Rotate the handle clockwise to drill in, and anticlockwise to pull the drill out.

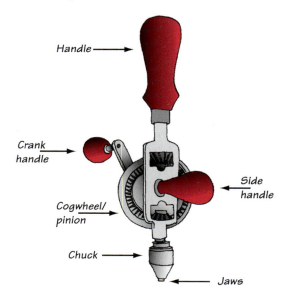

Brace

A brace is a boring tool that turns the bit by hand. To drill with a brace, rotate the cranked handle clockwise.

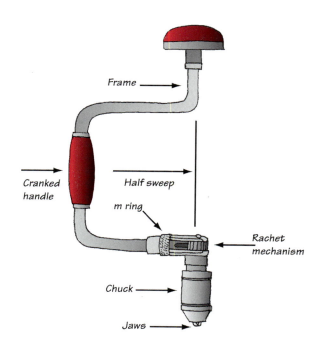

34

EQUIPMENT AND PROCESSES

Pilot Hole

A pilot hole is a tiny drill hole that is made in material to aid the accurate insertion of a screw or nail and to prevent splitting. It can also be easier to drill a large hole by first drilling a small pilot hole. The pilot hole for a screw should be the width of the screw if it did not have a thread.

TOOLS FOR JOINING MATERIALS

Nails

Nails are usually made of mild steel (an alloy of iron and carbon) and come in many shapes and sizes. Some common nails are:

- **Round wire nails:** The heads stick out above the surface.
- **Oval wire nails:** Used for better-quality work, as their smaller heads can be punched below the surface.
- **Panel pins:** Very small nails used for fixing thin sheet wood. They can easily be punched below the surface.

Screws

Screws are all the same basic shape, but they have different types of head and are made from different metals. Three common types of screw head are countersunk (or flat head), round head and pan head.

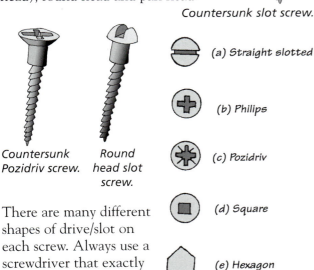

Countersunk slot screw.

Countersunk Pozidriv screw. *Round head slot screw.*

(a) Straight slotted
(b) Philips
(c) Pozidriv
(d) Square
(e) Hexagon

There are many different shapes of drive/slot on each screw. Always use a screwdriver that exactly matches the slot shape.

Countersunk Hole

To insert a countersunk screw, you must drill a countersunk hole in the material. This is done by using a countersunk drill bit.

Self-tapping screws

Self-tapping screws are very hard screws that cut in their own thread as they are screwed in.

Advantages of using nails over screws:
✔ Nails are quicker and easier to insert.
✔ Nails are cheaper.
✔ Nails are permanent.

Advantages of using screws over nails:
✔ Screws provide a better, stronger grip than nails.
✔ Screws pull the two pieces of material closer together.
✔ Screws can be removed more easily than nails.
✔ Screws look better.
✔ Screws do not bend or rust like nails can.

Nuts and Bolts

A bolt is a screw with no point. A nut screws onto the bolt. Nuts and bolts are often used to attach metals together.

Riveting

If you need a joint that allows movement, i.e. a pivot, a riveted joint may suit. Rivets are small metal pins with a head at one end.

Use round head riveting when you have access to both sides of the material. The rivet is placed through drilled holes. The other end is hammered into a head after insertion. Pop riveting is quicker and easier and can be used when there is access to only one side. A rivetting pliers causes the pin to form a head on the other side of the material.

Place a piece of paper between the two materials. Pass the rivets through holes in two or more material pieces. Rivet them together. Tear the paper out. The gap from the paper allows the joint to pivot perfectly.

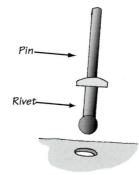

Pop rivet.

Split Pins/Cotter Pins

Split pins are easy to use and effective. The legs of the split pin are put through the hole. The legs are then bent back, holding the split pin in place.

35

JUNIOR CERTIFICATE TECHNOLOGY

Washers

Washers are metal discs with holes in the centre. They are used under screw and bolt heads to protect the material surface from any damage that may be caused when tightening nuts, bolts or screws. Washers are also useful on axles for keeping wheels away from the sides of a toy and reducing friction.

Spanners

There are two types of spanner commonly used – an open-ended or C spanner and a ring spanner with an enclosed head.

This has a C spanner on one end (right) and a ring spanner on the other (left).

Hinges

Hinges attach items to one another and allow them to pivot. They are used to attach lids, doors and gates.

THREADING TOOLS

Threading tools are used to cut threads on materials.

- **Thread:** The raised spiral ridge that goes round the outside of a bolt or screw and the inside of a nut.
- **Tap:** A tool used to cut threads on the inside of a hole to enable it to receive a bolt or screw.

- **Die:** A tool used to cut threads on the outside of a bolt or screw.

POWER TOOLS

Power tools can be categorised as follows:

- **Portable electric tools:** Tools that can be carried by hand from place to place.
- **Machine tools:** Tools that have a fixed position.

PORTABLE POWER TOOLS

A power drill is a tool in which the bit is turned using electricity. There are various forms of power drill, including hand-held drills and bench or pillar drills.

Portable electric drill.

Portable electric jigsaw.

Electric screwdriver.

MACHINE TOOLS

- **Band saw:** A circular-toothed steel band passing over two wheels.

- **Electric scroll/fret saw:** A power version of the hand tool.

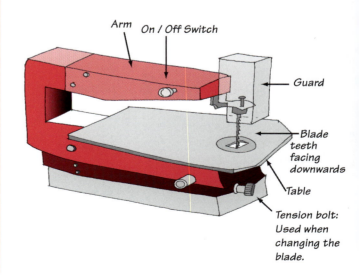

EQUITMENT AND PROCESSES

- **Bench drill**: Useful in the Technology Room.

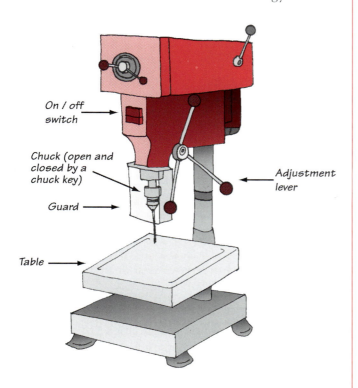

- **Pillar drill**: Can drill larger pieces of materials and produce larger holes.

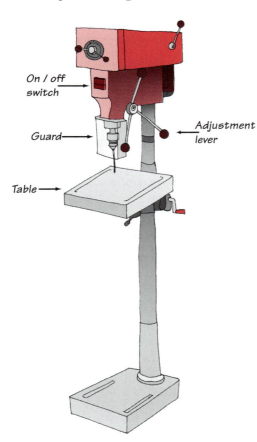

- **Sanding machine**: Use the belt or disc sander. Portable reciprocating sander is also available for use where the material is in a fixed position.

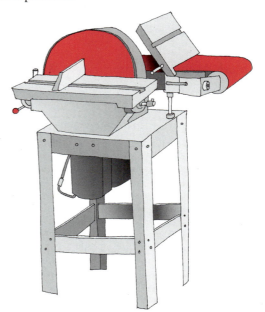

Lathe

A lathe is a machine that holds and rapidly turns cylindrical material while a cutting tool is slowly brought close to cut it. The most common lathe is the centre lathe.

Milling Machine

A milling machine uses spinning cutting pieces to cut stationary material.

PROCESSES

Now that you understand the tools, we can have a look at some of the processes (jobs) they can be used for.

The processes that are carried out in the Technology Room are generally:

- shaping
- forming
- joining
- finishing, i.e. doing something to the surface of the material.

SHAPING

Shaping means to change the shape of material by removing small amounts of the material with tools designed for the purpose.

JUNIOR CERTIFICATE TECHNOLOGY

The most common shaping processes used in the Technology Room are sawing, drilling, planing and filing.

Sawing

The same basic method applies to all materials and saw types:

1. Mark the line you want to saw. Wood is easier to cut across the grain than along the direction of the grain.
2. Hold the work firmly in a vice or clamp or with your free hand, protecting its surface from being scratched. Materials that break more easily, e.g. acrylic, need to be held very close to the cut.
3. Keep your eye (usually the right eye) in line with the saw blade.
4. Make a saw cut lightly towards you two or three times, 2 mm to the waste side of the marked line. (The waste side is the side of the material that you are not using.)
5. Continue sawing, going very gently as you near the end so that the work will not break.

Drilling

Drilling is used to make various sized circular holes.

1. Wear safety glasses.
2. Mark the hole clearly on the material.
3. For metal or plastic, use a centre or dot punch to make a small guide hole or dent. This will stop the drill bit slipping around on the material before it 'catches'. Drilling wood is easier because wood is softer than metal or plastic, and you can use a bradawl to make a small guide hole in wood.
4. Hold the work firmly, using a vice or G-cramp. Put scrap wood under it.
5. Select the size of the drill bit you want and fix it firmly in the chuck. Tighten it with a chuck key, then remove the chuck key.
6. Switch on the machine.
7. Bring the drill bit to the work. On a pillar drill, this is done by rotating the handles towards you.
8. Check that the work is in the correct position.
9. Press steadily on the handles until the hole is drilled.
10. Release the handle and switch off the machine.
11. If you only want to drill in part of the way, measure the correct distance from the tip of the drill bit before you start. Turn off the drill or unplug the hand drill before you do this. Put a piece of sticky tape on the drill bit at that height and stop drilling when you reach the sticky tape.

Planing

1. Hold the wood in a vice or pushed against a bench stop. Plane with the grain.
2. Grip the plane with both hands.
3. Press down at the front of the plane.
4. Push from the back. Move your body to move the plane.
5. As the plane gets to the end of the work, press down at the back.

Cross Filing

Cross filing is used to remove waste material and to file down to a line. To cross file:

1. Hold both ends of the file.
2. Push the file forwards at right angles to the line of the work (it cuts when going forwards).
3. Slide the file back.
4. Repeat.

Draw Filing

Draw filing is done with a smooth file to give a smooth, shiny finish to the work. To draw file:

1. Hold both ends of the file.
2. Push the file backwards and forwards along the line of the work until all the scratches are out.

FORMING

Forming means to change the form of the material without any loss of the material.

The most common shaping processes used in the Technology Room are line bending, vacuum forming and moulding. Less common are the potting wheel, weaving, macramé, knitting, patchwork, metal casting and plaster casting.

Bending Metals

Sheet metal can be bent by folding or beating it into shape. Shaping metal by heating and hammering it into shape is called forging. The source of heat is called a forge.

Line Bending Plastics

Thermoplastics, such as acrylic, can be easily bent, pressed or blown into shape at temperatures of around 160°C. Line bending is done on a strip heater as follows:

38

EQUIPMENT AND PROCESSES

1. Mark the position of the bend.
2. Switch on the strip heater and allow to heat fully.
3. Place the 'bend line' over the heat. Turn the work over every few seconds.
4. The work soon gets soft along the bend line. Once it is soft, place the work on some sort of former or mould and hold it there until it cools.

Strip heater: One of the post popular methods of shaping plastic.

Vacuum Forming Plastics

Vacuum forming is a way of shaping thermoplastic sheets (acrylic, polystyrene or PVC), i.e. it allows them to be moulded into complicated 3-D shapes such as casings, storage trays, etc. Vacuum forming is done as follows.

1. Buy or make a mould/former for the shape you need out of plywood, hardwood, clay, MDF, steel or lead. Put it on the base, which has holes drilled in it to allow air to be sucked through it.

2. A sheet of thermoplastic held by clamps is heated until it becomes malleable, i.e. soft and flexible.

3. The air is then sucked out from underneath the plastic using the machine vacuum. The plastic sheet takes the shape of the mould.

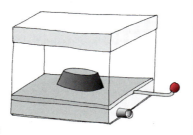
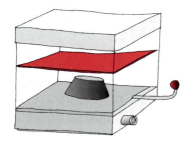
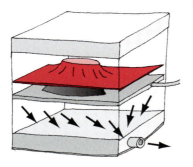

4. Set the vacuum to pump in the opposite direction. Allow the work to cool and then remove the formed sheet from the machine.

5. A thin plastic film is applied on a new sheet of acrylic or PVC. This prevents the sheet from getting scratched when it is being cut, drilled or sanded. It also allows the user to write on it. This is to be removed when the product is finished or before gluing.

Press Moulding Plastics

Press moulding is a process for shaping plastic by pressing it into shape. The plastic is heated and pressure is applied to make it take a shape.

Blow Moulding Plastics

Blow moulding is a process for shaping plastic by blowing it into a mould. It is usually used in the manufacturing of plastic bottles.

JOINING

Joining means to attach two or more pieces of material together.

The most common joining processes used in the Technology Room are nailing, screwing, sticking and soldering.

When you are deciding what kind of joint you need, ask yourself the following questions:

- What are the materials being joined?
- Does the joint need to be permanent (glued) or semi-permanent (using screws or other fittings)?
- Does the joint need to allow for movement, e.g. hinge or slide?
- How important is the appearance of the joint?

There are several types of joints:

- **Fixed/permanent joints:** Joints that make use of adhesives are considered permanent.
- **Moveable joints:** Joints that need to move, e.g. pivot, are moveable joints.
- **Temporary joints:** These are joints that will only be kept temporarily and then separated again.

Nailing (Particularly Suitable for Wood)

1. Choose the correct type of nail for the job. The nail should be two or three times as long as the thickness of the top piece of material.
2. Do not nail too close to the edge of a piece of material, as the material could split.
3. Knock the nails into the top piece of wood until you see the tips coming through.
4. If you are going to glue the joint, do so now.
5. Place the two parts of material together and hammer in the nails fully.
6. If your nails can be punched below the surface, do so using a nail punch.
7. If nailing wood, fill the holes that are left using wood filler.

Screwing

1. Choose the correct screw length. The screw should be two or three times as long as the thickness of the top piece of material. Fatter screws provide stronger joints.
2. If you are using a countersunk head screw, drill the countersink to let the screw head go just below the surface.
3. Make a pilot hole in the lower piece of material. In softwood, make the hole with a bradawl. In hardwood, plastic or metal, drill it.
4. Insert the screw with a screwdriver that fits the head well.

Sticking

Sticking means joining together by the use of adhesives, i.e. glues. Adhesives are supplied in liquid, paste, solid and powder form.

Advantages of adhesives:

✔ Very strong, usually stronger than the material being joined.
✔ Permanent.
✔ Ready to use.
✔ Can be used where it is difficult to use screws or nails.

Disadvantages of adhesives:

✘ They need to be held in position until set.
✘ If you change your mind, you cannot undo them.
✘ Changes in temperature and humidity can affect their strength.
✘ Bacteria and fungi can weaken the adhesive.

There are several types of adhesives:

- **PVA** (polyvinyl acetate) is a thick, white liquid that comes ready to use from a squeeze bottle or tube with a nozzle. PVA is often just called 'wood glue' and is the most popular glue you will see in the Technology Room.
- **Hot-melt glues** are rods that melt when heated in an electrically heated glue gun. They are convenient to use and bond in 90 seconds or less.
- **Epoxy adhesives** are chemical glues that are very strong, can bond different types of material together and can sometimes set very fast. Because of this, care is needed.

Soldering

Soldering is a permanent method of connecting components in an electrical circuit using solder. Soldering is done onto copper stripboard or printed circuit board (PCB).

The steps involved in soldering are as follows:

1. Clean everything to be soldered with a wire brush or sandpaper and fine wire wool.
2. If you are not using solder with a flux core, apply flux to both the areas on the surfaces that are to receive solder.
3. Heat both parts of the joint with a soldering iron.
4. Apply the solder, allowing it to melt and run into the joint.
5. Remove the iron and allow the joint to cool without moving.
6. Use a heat sink when soldering transistors, diodes and LEDs, e.g. pliers held to the LED leg will take some heat away. (For more information on transistors, diodes and LEDs see p. 80.)
7. Use chip holders to hold integrated circuits (for more details on integrated circuits, see p. 83).
8. Cut off any loose wires or component legs.

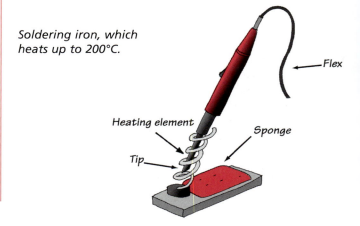

Soldering iron, which heats up to 200°C.

EQUIPMENT AND PROCESSES

Joining Plastic

Plastics like acrylic can be joined to wood and metal using screws or nuts and bolts. Acrylic can be fixed to a softer plastic like PVC with self-tapping screws. Acrylic is usually fixed to acrylic using a glue such as epoxy resin or Tensol cement.

Joining Metals

Metals can be joined by soldering, welding, screwing with self-tapping screws, or gluing with adhesives. Adhesives can be used to create a strong bond for metal.

Joining Wood

Joining wood involves cutting the most appropriate type of joint and then gluing, screwing or nailing it.

There are many types of wood joints. Some of the more common ones are listed below.

- **Butt joint:** This is the simplest joint. Two pieces of wood are just pushed (butted) together with no interlocking parts. This type of joint relies entirely on adhesives and nails or screws for strength.

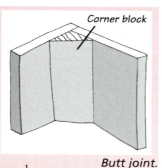

Butt joint.

- **Lap joint:** This joint has a shoulder, which makes it a bit more rigid than the butt joint, but it still relies on glue and nails for its strength.

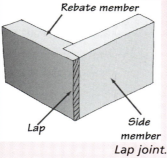

Lap joint.

- **Dowel joint:** A dowel is a circular wooden peg available in various sizes. They are used for axles, pegs and handles and for reinforcing joints. A dowel joint has mechanical strength because a dowel goes into both pieces of wood. The holes are drilled while both pieces of wood are held in place. Glue makes the joint stronger.

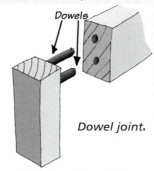

Dowel joint.

- **Finger joint/comb joint:** A comb joint is an interlocking joint that is very strong if well made and glued.

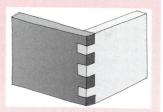

Finger joint/comb joint.

- **Dovetail joint:** This is a strong joint where the interlocking pieces are shaped like doves' tails so that they cannot slip past each other. This type of joint is commonly used in high-quality furniture.

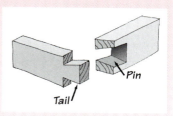

Dovetail joint.

- **Halving joint:** This connects two pieces of wood so that both pieces cross without a break and finish flush on the top and the bottom (i.e. the surfaces join up). Half the thickness of the wood is cut from each piece. A cross-halving is a common type of halving joint.

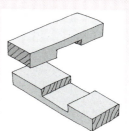

Cross halving joint.

Joining Fabric

Fabric is joined using needle and thread, staples, fabric glue and fasteners.

FINISHING

Most products have a finish. The finish may sit on top of the surface or soak in and become part of the material. All sawing, cutting, drilling and sanding must be complete before adding a finish.

A finish is needed to:

- Protect materials from corrosion and decay. Outdoor materials can be damaged by weather, insects and fungi. Other products may have constant wear and tear, e.g. friction. Wood is not very durable and can get very stained and dirty if it does not have some kind of finish.

- Improve the material's appearance.

41

JUNIOR CERTIFICATE TECHNOLOGY

Finishing Plastic

Apart from edges that have been cut, plastics usually just need a rub or a polish to finish them. To finish cut edges:

1. Plane them.
2. File them smoothly.
3. Rub them with steel wool, wet and dry.

Finishing Metal

- Copper and brass are polished.
- Metal can be painted with oil or acrylic paint to protect it from corrosion.
- Electroplating or anodising means putting a thin coat of one metal on another so the new surface looks nicer and protects the metal underneath, e.g. chrome plating protects steel in many bathroom taps.

Finishing Wood

- Wood preservative protects woods that are to be used outdoors to:
  ▲ Lengthen the life span of the wood.
  ▲ Protect the wood from being attacked by fungi and insects.
  ▲ Guard against weathering.
- Paint is suitable for indoors or outdoors. Paint for wood is usually oil based. Give wood a number of coats of paint and rub down between each coat with a fine abrasive paper.
- Varnish is a type of colourless paint which provides a hard waterproof finish for wood. The varnish shows the grain and natural colour of the wood. As with paint, usually two or more coats of varnish are applied, rubbing down between coats with a fine abrasive paper.
- Wood stain soaks into the wood and can be used to darken and highlight the natural beauty of the wood. If wood is stained, it is usually varnished afterwards to provide a more durable finish.
- Some hardwoods in particular can be kept durable and good looking by applying special kinds of wood oils.
- Wood can be waxed with special wood waxes, which are often based on beeswax, to provide a nice shine.

Finishing Ceramic

Ceramics are finished by covering them with a smooth, glossy surface. Mugs and tiles are finished this way.

EQUIPMENT AND PROCESSES ACTIVITIES

1. Fill in the blanks in these statements.
   (a) Hand-operated tools not run by electricity are called _____.
   (b) _____ twice, _____ once.
   (c) Tools used for cutting are called _____.
   (d) _____ are used for making mortises, slots, notches, recesses and reaching into awkward corners.
   (e) A tool used to remove a thin sliver of waste wood before sanding and polishing is called a _____.
   (f) Vices, clamps, cramps, pliers and tongs are all used to _____ material.
   (g) A convenient tool for putting nails in and taking nails out is a _____.
   (h) Tools that use a rubbing or grating action to shape wood are called _____ tools.
   (i) Tools used to put holes in things are called _____ tools.
   (j) _____ are essential for putting in and taking out screws.
   (k) Tools that are powered by electricity are called _____ tools.
   (l) Power tools that can be carried from place to place are called _____ tools.
   (m) Power tools that are fixed in position are called _____ tools.
   (n) A permanent method of fixing electronic components to an electric circuit is by _____. This is done by melting an alloy called _____.
   (o) To shape metal or plastic, you must first _____ it.

42

(p) Vacuum forming, blow moulding and press moulding are three common ways of shaping _____.

(q) Attaching two or more pieces of material together is called _____.

(r) To protect a material from corrosion and decay and to improve the appearance of something, we usually apply some kind of _____ to it.

(s) A common finish we apply to wood, usually to protect it and give it a nice colour, is _____.

2. Find the following tools in your Technology Room and draw neat, labelled freehand sketches of them: (a) tape measure (b) try square (c) sliding bevel (d) marking gauge (e) tenon saw (f) mallet (g) plane (h) a selection of hammers (i) a selection of chisels (j) a selection of files (k) nail punch (l) pincers.

3. What purpose is served by the brass strip on the top edge of the blade of a back saw, e.g. a tenon saw?

4. Why is your index finger placed along the handle of a tenon saw when sawing?

5. List four safety precautions you would tell someone using a saw for the first time.

6. Name four materials that can be cut with a coping saw.

7. State which direction the teeth should face when using a coping saw.

8. When starting the saw cut, cut on the _____ side of the marked line.

9. What safety precautions should you take when planing?

10. What precautions should be taken to prevent the cutting edge of a plane from being damaged when not in use?

11. Describe the steps that are taken to plane a short, flat surface smooth. What type of plane would you use?

12. Where does a claw hammer get its name?

13. What kind of hammer would you use for hitting large nails?

14. Name a hammer, other than a claw hammer, that can be used for hitting small nails or pins.

15. State two safety precautions you should use when hammering.

JUNIOR CERTIFICATE TECHNOLOGY

EQUIPMENT AND PROCESSES CROSSWORD

Across
2. Type of former that shapes plastic. (6)
4. To chip away small bits of waste wood. (6)
6. Use this to dent before drilling. (11)
7. Used like scissors to cut thin metal. (5)
9. Tool for drawing circles. (7)

Down
1. Small hacksaw. (5)
3. Type of saw with a stiff back. (5)
4. Name of key for removing drill bits. (5)
5. Punches holes in wood before screwing. (7)
8. Used to remove waste wood and smooth. (5)
9. Used to hold materials in place. (5)
10. Type of heater that bends plastic. (5)

EQUIPMENT AND PROCESSES

PREVIOUS EQUIPMENT AND PROCESSES EXAM QUESTIONS

EQUIPMENT

1. This tool is a tenon saw/hacksaw/coping saw. Circle the correct answer.

2. This tool is a marking gauge/G-cramp/hand vice. Circle the correct answer.

3. This tool is a marking gauge/sliding bevel/marking knife. Circle the correct answer.

4. This tool is a guillotine/vice grips/tin snips. Circle the correct answer.

5. This tool is a wire strippers/side cutters/long-nose pliers. Circle the correct answer.

6. Part X is a drill bit/chuck/chuck key. Circle the correct answer.

7. This screw is a cheese head screw/countersunk screw/pan head screw. Circle the correct answer.

8. Name and state one use of this tool.

9. Which tool is best suited to shaping expanded polystyrene (aeroboard)?

10. Which one of the following should be used to draw a line at 90° to a straight edge on a piece of wood? (a) A set square (b) A try square (c) A tee square

11. Select a material from the list below that should be shaped with the named tools.
    Materials: (a) Perspex (b) Copper sheet (c) Plywood (d) Aeroboard
    Tools: Strip heater, snips.
    A strip heater is used to shape _____
    Snips are used to shape _____

12. Which one of the following tools should be used to finish the curved edge on a piece of Perspex? (a) Drill (b) File (c) Chisel

13. Select which hand tool you would use to shape sheet aluminium: (a) chisel (b) snips (c) plane.

14. Name a material which should be cut with a hot wire cutter.

15. Name a tool which cuts using a shearing action.

16. Name a tool which shapes using an abrasive action.

17. Why is a centre punch used when drilling certain materials?

18. Briefly explain when each of these tools is used in the Technology Room: (a) hacksaw (b) plane.

PROCESSES

1. This wooden joint uses pop rivets/panel pins/bolts. Circle the correct answer.

45

2. Why is a new sheet of Perspex covered with a thin plastic skin?

3. Briefly explain the difference in finish between cross filing and draw filing.

4. Name the type of drill hole shown and state its purpose.

5. With a toy acrylic sheet puppet the toy's legs are moved by pulling a string. Sketch details of a joining method that could be used to attach the legs to the body of the toy.

6. List four stages in the manufacture of an acrylic bracket.

7. State the function of the plastic film on a new sheet of acrylic.

8. From the list, select the most suitable finish for (a) a brass plate (b) a ceramic container. Finish: varnishing, glazing, painting, anodising, polishing.

6 STRUCTURES

INTRODUCTION

This chapter is about how materials can be formed into different shapes (or structures) to support loads and withstand pressures. Did you know you can make strong structures from fairly weak materials? Most structures are designed to support heavy loads. A bridge is an example of an everyday structure. Can you think of others?

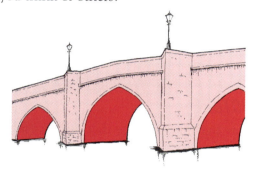

When you think of structures, you probably think of things like bridges, mobile phone masts and tall buildings. There are also other examples that we use every day, like chairs, tables, windows and presses.

The two main kinds of structures are:
- frame structures
- shell structures.

These structures may be man-made or may occur naturally.

FRAME STRUCTURES

Frame structures are structures that have a 'frame' or skeleton associated with them. They may or may not have a 'skin' on them. If they have no 'skin' on them, they are called 'open frame'. For example, our bodies and leaves are natural frame structures with skin on them. A spider's web is a natural open-frame structure without a skin. Man-made skyscrapers have a skeleton, or frame, made of steel, usually strong I-beams. The 'skin' is the walls that are made of glass panels and thin concrete sheets.

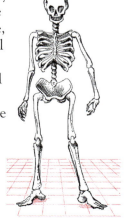

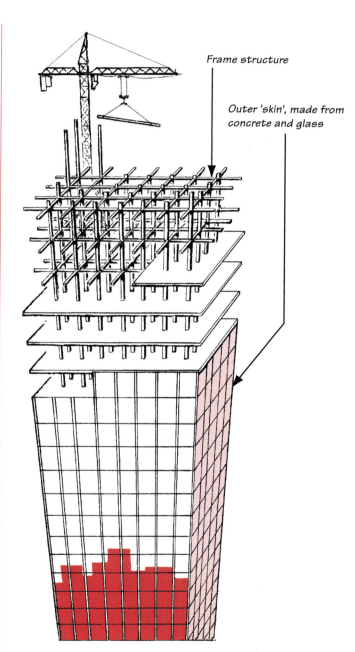

A man-made frame structure.

SHELL STRUCTURES

Shell structures rely on the shape they have been moulded into for their strength. They are usually lighter than frame structures. For example, a car body is a man-made shell structure, with sheet metal pressed into the shapes of the various panels

47

and welded together. Examples of natural shell structures are eggshells and the hollow stems of some plants.

The more curved or ridged a panel is, the stronger it will be. Curves or ridges may be put into a shell structure to strengthen it. For example, a plastic container for tomatoes or mushrooms would crumble easily without the ridges to strengthen it. An egg box is an excellent example of a shell structure. It relies upon the shape, i.e. the folds and curves, it has been moulded into to give it its strength. The egg box is made of thin, light and fairly weak material, yet is surprisingly strong.

The chair you are sitting on may combine both a frame structure and a shell structure – many chairs do. There may be a tubular steel frame structure that supports a polypropylene (plastic) shell structure that in turn supports you!

Shell structures: The egg box is a man-made shell structure and the eggshells are natural shell structures.

A man-made shell structure.

STRUCTURAL MEMBER

A structural member is a part of a structure. Every structural member is either in tension, compression or is redundant. (Tension and compression are explained later.)

REDUNDANT MEMBER

A redundant member is a part of a structure that is neither in tension nor compression. Redundant members can be removed from structures without the structure weakening. A good design has no redundant members.

WHAT IS FORCE?

A force is a push or a pull. Forces can make things move. Engines and motors make forces that cause machines to move. The force of gravity pulls everything downwards towards the earth.

Force is measured in newtons (N), after Sir Isaac Newton.

TYPES OF LOADS

Structures are built to support a load. Loads can be **static** (not moving) or **dynamic** (moving). Static loads do not produce as much force as dynamic loads. For example, someone standing on your toe would not be as painful as someone jumping on it! A chair is designed to support even the heaviest person sitting on it, i.e. ahere is dynamic force acting on it and the chair is more likely to break.

TYPES OF FORCE THAT ACT ON A STRUCTURE

There are five types of force that can act on all structures:

1. tension
2. compression / pressure
3. shear
4. torsion
5. bending.

All these forces must be catered for in designing structures. This can be difficult, and lack of correct designing has caused bridges and buildings to fall or structures to crumble, deform or distort. Think of the different changing combinations of force that an aeroplane must withstand when it takes off, flies through high winds and thunderstorms and lands. To be safe, most structures are designed to withstand greater force than would be expected.

TENSION

Tension is a stretching, straining, pulling, tensile force. If something in tension is cut, the two ends will pull apart. For example, a rope with a weight hanging on the end of it is in tension. If it is cut, it will pull apart. A coping saw always has its blade in tension. If the blade is cut, it will pull apart.

The rope is in tension. If it is cut, the weight will fall.

STRUCTURES

COMPRESSION / PRESSURE

Compression means being pressed into less space or being flattened by pressure. Something under a heavy load is in compression. Certain materials under compression will get smaller.

Get off me. I'm under too much pressure

An object is under pressure if there is a compression force acting on it.

pressure = force ÷ area

This means that the smaller the area the force is applied to, the greater the pressure. This explains why someone leaning on you with their hand is a lot less painful than the same person leaning on you with a compass point.

SHEAR

A shearing force is a tearing or ripping force that is trying to move one part of the material in the opposite direction to the other. For example, scissors cut through paper by applying a pair of forces on the paper, each force in the opposite direction. Cutting or clipping actions create a shear force in the material that they are cutting.

Shear force acts on the paper as the scissors try to cut through it.

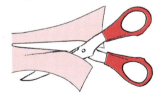

TORSION

Torsion is the act of twisting a structure. A torsion force causes something to twist or turn.

The ruler is in torsion, as it is being twisted.

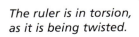

BENDING

Forces can bend a structure. For example, a bar bends due to the weight of a gymnast swinging on it, or a long narrow shelf may bend with books on it. In these situations, the upper surface is in compression and the lower surface is in tension.

The beam is being bent with the weight.

FRICTION

Friction is another type of force, but it does not act on all structures. Friction only occurs when two surfaces are in contact.

FRICTION

Friction is a force that tries to stop one surface from sliding against another. There is more friction between rough surfaces than between smooth surfaces. Yet no matter how smooth surfaces seem, they are actually quite rough when examined under a microscope.

Friction stops your feet from sliding on the ground as you walk. Friction stops things from slipping from your hand and stops car tyres from skidding when you brake. Brakes work by the brake blocks exerting a friction force on the wheel so that the wheel is forced to slow down and eventually stop.

Oil or grease reduces friction. It lets gear wheels turn more easily and makes bicycle chains more flexible. This makes movement easier and stops moving parts from wearing out. When oil is used in this way, it is called a lubricant. Oil also stops the metal parts from going rusty.

The girl falls, as there is less friction between her feet and the ground when it is icy or wet.

Advantages of friction:

✔ Friction allows us to walk, cycle and pick things up and allows cars to start and stop.

Disadvantage of friction:

✘ The friction between our car tyres and the road slows our cars down, so we have to use more petrol to keep going.

JUNIOR CERTIFICATE TECHNOLOGY

Sometimes we need to minimise friction and sometimes we need to maximise it. For example, on a bike it is important to minimise friction in the following places.

- Where the pedals are attached, as they are moving and need to move around smoothly.
- Where the wheels are attached, as they also have to move around smoothly.
- Between the chain and sprocket to help the bike travel faster and make it easier to change gears.

Yet it is important to maximise friction:

- Where the brake pads meet the wheels so that the bike will stop quickly when the brakes are applied.
- Where the wheels meet the ground so that the bike does not slip.

Lubrication is a common way of reducing friction, but you could also use bearings. Bearings are little metal balls that allow other devices, like bicycle wheels or pedals, to spin smoothly.

TYPES OF STRUCTURES/PARTS OF STRUCTURES

Basic structures like furniture, buildings and bridges often need structural modifications to make them stronger. They are often strengthened by extra beams, ties, struts or cantilevers.

BEAMS

A beam is a long rigid piece of wood or metal. It is the simplest way of supporting a load across a gap. It is the simplest structure, but it can also be part of a more complex structure.

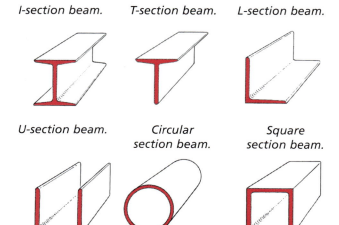

I-section beam.   *T-section beam.*   *L-section beam.*

U-section beam.   *Circular section beam.*   *Square section beam.*

In scaffolding, hollow tubes are used instead of solid ones as they are lighter, cheaper, safer and easier to construct the scaffolding with. Also, a hollow section is actually less likely to bend than a solid one. The way in which a beam is placed – i.e. its orientation – can affect its strength.

BRIDGES

A bridge is used to 'bridge' a gap, usually between the banks of a river. A bridge has supports at two ends. The first bridges were simple wooden beams, but nowadays they are often huge, complicated structures.

CANTILEVERS

Cantilevers are beams that are held and supported at one end only. They are brackets for supporting balconies, shelves, tree branches, outstretched arms, etc.

COLUMNS AND PILLARS

Columns and pillars are vertical beams, normally designed to support loads directly on top, e.g. table legs.

TIE

A tie is a part of a structure in tension for keeping two objects from spreading or separating. Ties are usually thin, e.g. the cross piece on a swing.

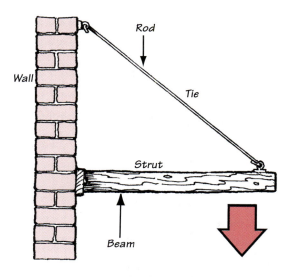

The beam is attached to the wall by a steel rod. The rod is in tension, and so, therefore, is the tie. The beam is in compression, and so, therefore, is the strut.

50

STRUCTURES

STRUT

A strut is a part of a structure in compression for keeping two objects from coming closer together. Struts are usually thick, e.g. a pillar supporting a roof.

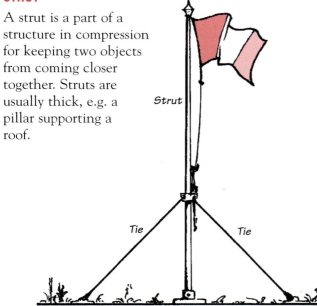

The wires on either side of the flagpole are being stretched, and so, therefore, are the ties. The pole is in compression due to gravity, and so, therefore, is the strut.

TRIANGULATION

Triangulation means using triangles arranged together to form a frame or part of a frame, with increased rigidity. Structures made from triangles are strong.

Many stepladders use the top platform to stop the two sides from separating. When the platform is fixed in position, the stepladder will not open or close. This is because the two sides and the platform form a triangle. The shape of a triangle cannot be changed or squashed. All other shapes can be squashed more easily. By adding to a structure and creating triangles, other shapes become stable. This is called triangulation.

Triangulation is used in structures such as bicycle frames, shelf brackets, house roofs, garden gates, pylons and much more.

The Eiffel Tower is an excellent example of triangulation being used to strengthen a structure.

STRUCTURES AND THE ENVIRONMENT

While many structures are needed in our world to house people and allow them easy transport, structures also impact on our environment. Structures can impact positively by being beautiful and enriching people's lives or structures can be ugly and damage the environment.

DAMAGE TO THE ENVIRONMENT

The environment can be damaged from structures being built in some or all of the following ways.

- Grassland is destroyed by the structure.
- There is pollution from the lorries and trucks used in the construction of the structure.
- The iron, stone and other raw materials have to be sourced in quarries and mines, which damage the landscape. There is further environmental damage in converting the raw materials into a form that can be used in the structure.
- Wildlife is disturbed and may no longer survive.

STRUCTURES ACTIVITIES

1. Fill in the blanks in these statements.
   (a) The two main kinds of structures are _____ and _____ structure.
   (b) If a frame structure has no 'skin' on it, it is called an _____-frame structure.
   (c) A structure that relies upon the shape it has been moulded into to give it its strength is called a _____ structure.
   (d) Loads can be _____ (non-moving) or _____ (moving).
   (e) Tension, compression, shear, torsion and bending are all types of _____.
   (f) All these forces must be catered for when _____ structures.
   (g) An object is in tension if it is being _____.

51

(h) An object is in compression if it is being _____.

(i) An everyday item that cuts using a shear force is a _____.

(j) Torsion is a _____ force.

(k) If a beam is bent, the top surface is in _____ and the bottom surface is in _____.

(l) _____ is a force that tries to stop one surface from sliding against another.

(m) When oil or grease is added to reduce friction, it is called a _____.

(n) A long, rigid piece of wood or metal used to support a load across a gap is called a _____.

(o) A beam supported at one end only is called a _____.

(p) A structural member in tension is called a _____.

(q) A structural member in compression is called a _____.

(r) The use of triangles to strengthen a frame is called _____.

(s) A common structure often found across water is a _____.

(t) Little metal balls that reduce friction and allow bicycle wheels and pedals to move smoothly are called _____.

2. Make the two types of frames below from cardboard.

Square frame.   *Triangular frame.*

Glue a piece of cardboard to the top and bottom of your frames to make them more rigid. Test the strength by putting weights on top of the cardboard. Match up the descriptions below with the frames.

(a) This frame is very strong when the pressure on it is straight down. If the pressure is from the side, it is weaker and may collapse.

(b) This frame is very strong. Many structures and buildings are made up of this type of shape.

3. As individuals or pairs, get the following materials:
   - 50 plastic straws
   - 50 straight pins or paperclips
   - 1 m of sticky tape
   - scissors for cutting straws
   - 10 weights, e.g. large washers or 35 mm film holders filled with sand
   - metre stick.

(a) What can you build with 50 straws and 50 pins? Explore your ideas.

(b) Build a bridge from one desk to another. How much weight will the bridge hold? What is the greatest distance you can span? What is the strongest bridge you can build between two desks? What is the longest bridge you can build between two desks?

(c) Build a cantilever, starting with one straw taped to the wall or tabletop with strong tape. Other straws may be pinned (or fastened with clips) to this straw and may rest against the wall or tabletop but may not be taped. How far out from the wall or tabletop can you build the cantilever? What is the strongest cantilever you can build 45 cm out from a wall or tabletop?

(d) Search for unnecessary straws. What happens if you cut them? What is the name given to these?

STRUCTURES

STRUCTURES CROSSWORD

Across
1. A piece of a structure that is in compression. (5)
3. Something that has supports at both ends. (6)
4. The simplest way of supporting a load across a gap. (4)
5. A force that tries to stop one surface from sliding along another. (8)
7. A moving load. (7)
8. Naturally occurring frame structure created by a spider. (3)
11. A non-moving load. (6)
14. A rope with a weight hanging on it is in this. (7)
15. The use of triangles in structures due to their strength. (13)

Down
1. The tendency of a force applied to cause a break parallel to the force. (5)
2. A type of structure, e.g. skeleton. (5)
4. If this force is acting on a bar, the upper surface is in compression and the lower surface is in tension. (7)
6. Something being squashed is in this. (11)
9. The act of twisting. (7)
10. A type of structure with no frame. (5)
12. A piece of a structure that is in tension. (3)
13. Supported at one end only. (10)

JUNIOR CERTIFICATE TECHNOLOGY

STRUCTURES WORD SEARCH

```
T  P  S  B  O  T  L  W  G  T  Z  L  V  S  C
E  H  L  C  E  I  T  A  U  T  T  P  N  H  I
C  Q  G  Y  A  W  I  R  R  I  R  O  D  H  M
R  O  W  I  E  F  N  L  G  U  T  F  J  R  A
O  L  Q  M  E  I  F  F  D  W  T  S  N  E  N
F  Q  A  V  N  W  R  O  E  C  G  A  U  D  Y
S  R  M  G  R  I  B  N  L  C  N  C  N  U  D
F  T  E  K  C  O  R  P  S  D  I  V  Z  N  S
D  K  E  T  E  D  I  A  F  U  I  V  S  D  T
F  U  I  E  C  I  T  A  T  S  R  N  T  A  R
D  O  N  K  L  S  H  E  L  L  M  F  G  N  U
N  C  F  T  M  T  L  R  G  B  Q  I  A  T  T
T  O  R  S  I  O  N  C  E  W  J  S  N  C  B
P  V  C  Z  F  R  Z  A  O  W  U  U  C  W  E
G  G  G  W  G  T  M  Q  G  T  K  B  M  V  B
```

1. The most common structural member. Lighter now than in the past, though just as strong or stronger, e.g. cantilever, 'I', 'T'. (4)
2. Deform. (7)
3. A moving load is this. (7)
4. The five basic types of this are compression, tension, bending, torsion and shear. (5)
5. A type of structure heavier than a shell structure. (5)
6. A force generated by two surfaces rubbing off each other. (8)
7. Trees, leaves, honeycombs and eggshells are examples of _____ shell structures. (7)
8. The unit of force, thanks to Sir Isaac. (6)
9. Members in a structure that are surplus to requirements and do no useful work. They can be removed without the structure failing. (9)
10. A frame structure erected to stand on when building, comprised of hollow metal tubes. (11)
11. Car bodies are this type of structure. Their moulded shape provides it with strength. (5)
12. There are two of these on a bike, one large, one small. A chain passes over them. (8)
13. A non-moving load. (6)
14. A type of metal used in the building of skyscraper frames. (5)
15. This resists compression. (5)
16. When a beam bends, the upper _____ is in compression. (7)
17. This resists tensile force. (3)
18. A twisting force. (7)
19. Torsion causes a structure to twist or _____. (4)
20. The force exerted on us due to gravity. (6)

54

STRUCTURES

PREVIOUS STRUCTURES EXAM QUESTIONS

TYPES OF FORCES THAT ACT ON A STRUCTURE

1. Label the sketch to indicate a member that is in tension and a member that is in compression.

   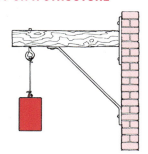

2. This saw blade is in tension/compression/shear. Circle the correct answer.

   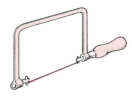

3. The rope marked X is in shear/compression/tension. Circle the correct answer.

   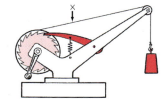

4. Name the force acting on the material shown.

   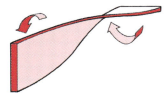

5. Name the force acting on the fabric.

   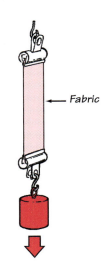

6. This rope is in tension/compression/torsion. Circle the correct answer.

   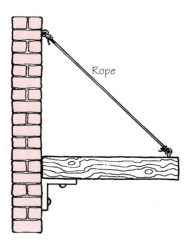

7. The pin shown is in tension/compression/shear. Circle the correct answer.

   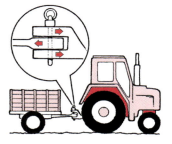

8. Identify the forces shown in the sketch.

   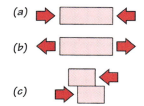

9. When bicycle brakes are pulled, the force between the brake blocks and the wheel is a bending force/friction force/shear force. Circle correct the answer.

10. The beam shown is bending under a load. Identify the parts X, Y or Z of the beam which are (a) in compression (b) in tension (c) neither in tension nor compression.

    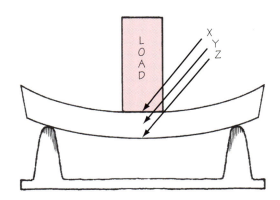

55

JUNIOR CERTIFICATE TECHNOLOGY

FRICTION

1. Name two areas on a bicycle where friction is of benefit to the cyclist.

2. Where on a bicycle is it important to minimise friction and maximise friction?

3. On the bicycle shown, clearly identify two areas where bearings are used.

4. State two reasons why oil is used on the chain of a bicycle.

TYPES OF STRUCTURES/PARTS OF STRUCTURES

1. The bridge shown will bend under the load. Sketch one structural improvement that will strengthen the bridge.

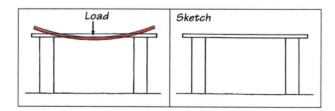

2. Which shelving unit is more rigid? Give a reason for your answer.

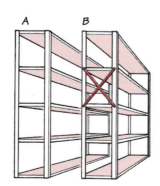

3. The bar labelled X is a cantilever/tie/strut. Circle the correct answer.

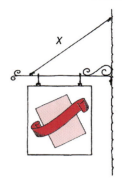

4. Solid beams are to be used for this bridge. Which one of the sections shown is most suitable?

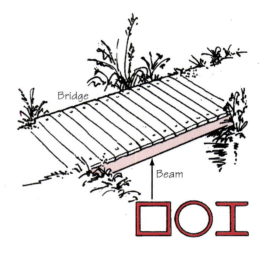

5. Name the structural feature of an electricity pylon which makes it stable and rigid.

6. State two reasons why hollow tubes are used in scaffolding in place of solid bars.

7. State the purpose of the ribs in the thin plastic packaging shown.

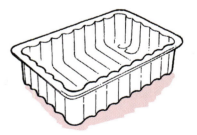

8. The chains on this sign act as struts/ties/beams. Correct the correct answer.

7 MECHANISMS

INTRODUCTION

This chapter is about how materials can be formed or combined in different ways to generate different kinds of useful movement. Mechanisms are mechanical devices like gears, screws, levers and pulleys that are found in machines. Mechanisms generally translate one kind of movement into another.

Our modern world contains mechanisms everywhere. In fact, there are so many of them around that we take them for granted.

Everyday items like scissors, wheelbarrows and taps are all based on a simple mechanism, while more complicated objects such as cars or the humans body contain thousands of mechanisms.

Mechanisms are concerned with motion and forces. Mechanisms often convert one type of force or motion into another type. For example, the pulling force you apply on the brake lever of your bike converts into another force that presses the brake blocks onto the wheel rim. Machines contain many mechanisms.

Mechanisms cannot help you by themselves. They need energy and someone or something to operate them. Energy required to get the mechanism to work is **effort**. Work done by the mechanism is **load**.

Mechanical devices have played a large part in human society. Devices such as gears, cams, screw threads and ratchets are used in many everyday products like cars, tin openers, vending machines, cranes, bulldozers, etc. The Industrial Revolution in the nineteenth century made good use of mechanisms to build trains, steam engines, weaving machines, etc.

Since then, the growth of newer technologies such as electric power, electronics, pneumatics and hydraulics has meant that the earlier dominance of mechanisms has declined. For example, early adding machines were mechanical, but now we use more powerful electronic calculators instead.

Advantages of using mechanisms:

✔ They are reasonably efficient if properly designed.

✔ They can be used for a wide variety of tasks, often being the only way to do something.

Disadvantages of using mechanisms:

✘ Sliding parts wear out unless lubricated.

✘ Moving parts may be dangerous.

✘ Manufactured parts must be very accurate, so can be expensive.

MECHANICS

Mechanics is the study of how things move.

MACHINES

Machines are things that make jobs easier and quicker to do. Some machines are very simple, like scissors, saws and wheelbarrows. People have used simple machines like these for thousands of years. Today, many machines are very complex.

ENGINES

Many powerful machines have engines that provide the power to make them work. For example, a car has an engine that makes its wheels turn. A ship has an engine that turns propellers in the water. A jet aircraft's engines push it through the air. All these engines need fuel to work. The engine turns the energy in the fuel into mechanical energy.

MOTION

Motion is another word for movement. Things cannot start to move on their own. They need a force (a push or a pull) to get them started. Once something has started to move, a force can make it move faster, slow it down or make it change direction. Speeding motion up is called acceleration. Slowing it down is called deceleration.

People used to try to make machines called perpetual motion machines that would keep moving forever. These machines never worked, as friction always made them stop.

The four principal types of motion are linear, reciprocating, rotary and oscillating.

- **Linear motion:** This is straight-line motion, e.g. a car drives past in a linear motion.

This arrow represents linear motion.

- **Reciprocating motion:** Reciprocating motion is backward and forward motion in a straight line, e.g. an engine crankshaft and piston move in a reciprocating motion.

  This arrow represents reciprocating motion.

- **Rotary motion:** This is motion in a circular direction, e.g. the chuck of a drill moves in a circular motion.

  This curve represents rotary motion.

- **Oscillating motion:** Oscillating motion is essentially reciprocating motion along an arc, like the swaying of a clock pendulum or a child's swing.

  This arc with an arrowhead at both ends represents oscillating motion.

LOAD, EFFORT AND MECHANICAL ADVANTAGE

LOAD
The load is the force applied by the mechanism.

EFFORT
The effort is the force applied by the user. It is the exertion of physical power.

MECHANICAL ADVANTAGE
The main reason for using mechanisms is to gain mechanical advantage. In other words, for the effort we put in, we want an increased load out.

TYPES OF MECHANISMS
The following are the main types of mechanisms:
- inclined planes
- levers
- linkages
- cam and follower
- cranks and crankshafts
- cranks and sliders
- ratchets and pawls
- springs
- gears
- pulleys.

INCLINED PLANES
An inclined plane is a tilted surface. Inclined planes, such as slopes and ramps, were used in ancient times to lift huge stone blocks when building large structures like the great pyramids. Mechanical advantage is gained because it is easier to pull a long way up a gentle slope than it is to lift a small vertical distance.

A screw is really a ramp wrapped around a rod. The wood screw, the nut and bolt and adjustable spanners are all based on the principle of an inclined plane. They convert rotary motion to linear and vice versa.

LEVERS
The lever was invented in the Stone Age, and was probably first used to move rocks and boulders. It is a rigid body or bar that can rotate around a fixed point, called a fulcrum. A lever provides mechanical advantages because by moving an easy force over a long distance it can move a very powerful force over a short distance. The closer the fulcrum is to an object and the longer the lever, the easier it is to lift or to apply force to the object. Archimedes once said, 'Give me a lever long enough and a place to attach it, and I will move the Earth.'

The fulcrum is the stone wheel. The man tries to gain mechanical advantage by holding the lever as far from the dinosaur as possible.

Levers do two things:
- They can move a large load with only a little effort.

MECHANISMS

- They can amplify (increase) movement. In other words, a small input movement can produce a large output movement.

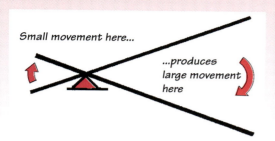

There are three classes of lever, depending on the position of the force, load and fulcrum.

- **Class 1:** Load at one end, effort at the other and fulcrum in the middle.
- **Class 2:** Load between effort and fulcrum.
- **Class 3:** Fulcrum at one end, load at the other and effort in the middle.

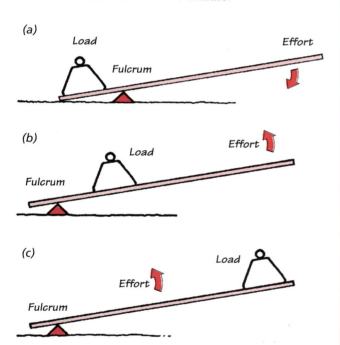

(a) Class 1 lever (b) class 2 lever (c) class 3 lever.

Moments

A moment is the force that moves or turns a lever.

A lever rotates or turns at its fulcrum. Imagine a simple lever, such as a see-saw, with the fulcrum in the middle. If the see-saw is not turning but remains level, then it is said to be balanced, or in a state of equilibrium.

Moments in levers take into account the force acting at right angles to the lever and the distance of this force from the fulcrum (pivot).

Principle of Moments/Law of the Lever

If a lever is balanced, then the total turning force, or moment, tending to turn it clockwise must equal the total moment of forces tending to turn it anticlockwise.

The moment is the force applied (F) multiplied by the distance (D) of the force from the fulcrum.

anticlockwise moments = clockwise moments (when balanced)

$F_1 \times D_1 = F_2 \times D_2$

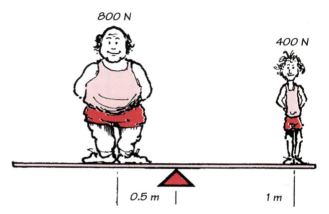

The heavy man applies 800 N force at a distance of 0.5 m. The small man applies 400 N force at a distance of 1 m.

LINKAGES

A linkage is a mechanism made by connecting levers together. Linkages can do many things, such as change the direction of a force or motion, make two things move at the same time or make objects move parallel to each other. Four common types of linkages are:

- reverse motion linkage
- push-pull linkage
- bell cranks linkage
- parallel motion linkage.

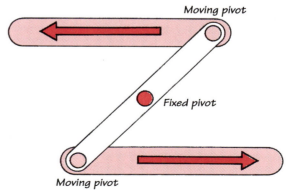

Reverse motion linkage: Makes things move in opposite directions.

59

JUNIOR CERTIFICATE TECHNOLOGY

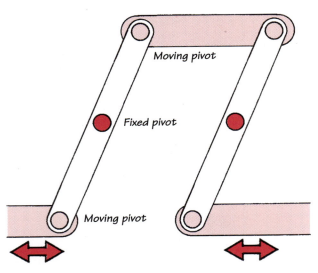

Push-pull linkage: The input and output motion are in the same direction.

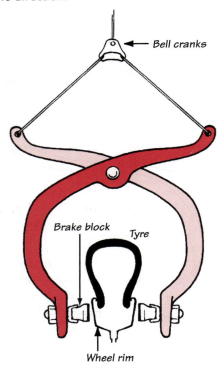

Bell cranks linkage: Changes the direction of movement through 90°, e.g. bike brakes.

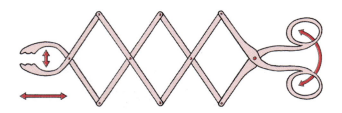

Parallel motion linkage: The parts of this lazy tongs are kept parallel to each other as it opens and closes.

CAM/CAM AND FOLLOWER

Cams are mechanisms that can be used to change one type of motion into another. Generally, cams change rotary (circular) motion into linear motion. Some cams can change the direction of a motion.

The **rotary cam** is a disc or cylinder with an irregular shape fitted to a rotary shaft. They are usually circular, pear shaped or heart shaped, with an off-centre hole for the shaft. A follower rests on the edge of the cam, and as the cam rotates, the follower moves up and down. Rotary motion (cam) is converted into reciprocating motion (follower). Different-shaped cams cause the follower to move in different ways. They are used in many reciprocating mechanisms. Most simple mechanical toys contain a rotary cam and follower.

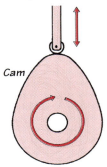

The follower moves up and down (reciprocates) as the pear-shaped cam rotates.

Cams and followers are used in car engines to control the movements of the inlet and exhaust valves.

Other types of cams include the **linear**, or **flat plate**, cam and the **cylindrical**, or **barrel**, cam.

CRANKS AND CRANKSHAFTS

A crank is a tool consisting of a rotating shaft with a parallel handle. A crank is like a bent rod. The handle allows the rod to be turned easily.

Cranks are found in some toys as parts of a mechanism or in machinery such as car engines. Some cranks are attached to mechanisms that are difficult to rotate. Old wind-up radios and record players used cranks to wind up the springs inside them. Old cars needed to be 'cranked up' to get them going (remember Chitty Chitty Bang Bang?).

The crank acts like a lever, increasing mechanical advantage (the distance between the

A crankshaft car. The wheels would be difficult to turn without the crankshaft.

60

MECHANISMS

handle and the central shaft is increased – this provides more of a lever and makes the handle easier to turn).

When a shaft has two or more cranks, it can be called a **crankshaft**. A typical example of a crankshaft can be found on small mechanical pedal cars made for young children. As the child pedals, the crankshaft rotates the wheels and the vehicle moves forward.

CRANKS AND SLIDERS

A crank and slider mechanism is composed of three important parts:

- The crank, which is the rotating disc.
- The slider, which slides inside the tube.
- The connecting rod that joins the parts together.

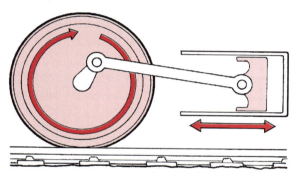

As the slider moves right and left, it forces the wheel to rotate. Steam trains work on this principle.

As the slider moves to the right, the connecting rod pushes the wheel around and the wheel starts to rotate. When the slider begins to move back into the tube, the connecting rod pulls the wheel around to complete the rotation. A steam train is an example of a crank and slider mechanism. Steam pressure powers the slider mechanism as the connecting rod moves in and out, and this causes the wheel to rotate.

RATCHETS AND PAWLS

Ratchets are used to allow a wheel to turn in one direction only and to prevent it from slipping back. A ratchet is a wheel with saw-like teeth cut out of it, as shown. The part that engages in the ratchet is called the pawl. The pawl follows as the wheel turns. The ratchet wheel turns and the pawl falls into the dip between the teeth. The ratchet cannot turn back the other way because it cannot lift the pawl out of the way.

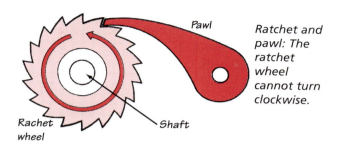

Ratchet and pawl: The ratchet wheel cannot turn clockwise.

Below is a picture of a water well with a ratchet mechanism that allows the person to rotate the handle anticlockwise. The full bucket is heavy, so the person can rest by taking their hands away from the handle. This is because the pawl has fallen into the dip between the teeth, preventing the bucket from falling back into the well.

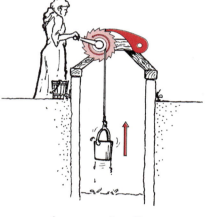

Ratchet mechanisms are useful devices. As well as being used in lifting systems, as shown in the illustration, they are used in mechanical clocks.

SPRINGS

Springs are available in a wide variety of shapes and sizes. Many people will have used a springboard at a swimming pool to dive into the water. The springboard may be made from laminated wood (layers of wood glued together) or be a more modern glass fibre-type material. The result is the same – the diver uses his/her weight to spring off the board into the air.

A diving board is also an example of a cantilever, as a diving board is supported at one end only.

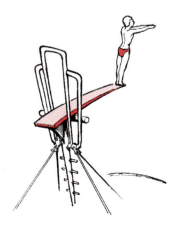

JUNIOR CERTIFICATE TECHNOLOGY

Springs have a wide range of uses and it is difficult to think of a mechanical device that does not have one or more of them. Springs are used in engines, motors, watches, clocks, door handles, locks, pens and much more.

GEARS

Gears can be found in many machines in the Technology Room, the factory and at home. They are an important part of mechanical devices. In a car, the gears help the driver to increase and decrease speed as he/she changes the gears with the gear stick.

Simple Gears

A gear is a wheel that has teeth cut in such a way that they mesh with teeth in another similar gear. The teeth are an equal distance apart. Gears are used to transmit rotary motion and forces. Gears that mesh together are called spur gears. Gears can be used to change speed and to change direction. Gears can transmit great loads. One reason for using gears is that they cannot slip like a belt drive can.

- **Driver and driven gears:** The input gear to any system is called the driver gear and the output gear is called the driven gear.

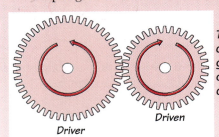

The driver gear drives the driven gear in the opposite direction.

Driver — Driven

- **Idler gears:** All gears fitted in between the driver gear and the driven gear are called idler gears. They change the direction of rotation. Idler gears only change direction – they never speed up or slow down gears.

The idler gear causes the driver gear and the driven gear to turn in the same direction as each other.

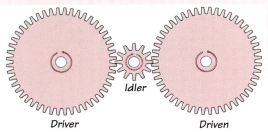

Driver — Idler — Driven

- **Changing speed of gears in gear trains:** A change in speed within a gear train is achieved by putting gears with different numbers of teeth together.
- **Gear ratio/gear velocity:** If a driver gear with 40 teeth is driving a driven gear with 20 teeth, the output speed will be double. For every turn of the driver gear, the driven gear will turn twice. This gear ratio is 1:2. If the driver has 30 teeth and the driven has 120 teeth, the gear chain will slow down. For every four turns of the driver, the driven will turn once. This gear ratio is 4:1.
- **Example:** Gear A has 30 teeth and gear B has 20 teeth. If gear A turns one complete revolution, how many times will gear B turn?

  Solution:

  $$\frac{\text{Gear A}}{\text{Gear B}} = \frac{30 \text{ teeth}}{20 \text{ teeth}} = \frac{30}{20} = 1.5$$

  In other words, when gear A completes one revolution, gear B turns 1.5 revolutions (1.5 times).

- **A basic rule of gears:** If a larger gear turns a smaller gear, the speed increases. If a smaller gear turns a larger gear, the speed decreases.

Chain and Sprocket

You have probably noticed that a bike is driven by a large driver gear wheel with pedals attached. There is also a smaller gear at the back being driven around, in turn driving the back wheel. These gear wheels are called sprockets, joined by a linked chain. They are particularly suited to bicycles, as they cannot slip and are strong.

In bikes, the pedal sprocket has twice as many teeth as the wheel sprocket. For every one rotation of the pedals, the wheel rotates twice, making it easier to pedal up a hill.

They are also used in machinery, motorcycles and car engines, and have many more applications.

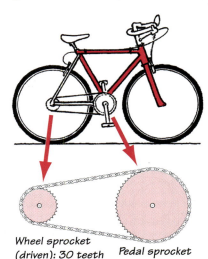

Wheel sprocket (driven): 30 teeth

Pedal sprocket (driver): 60 teeth

MECHANISMS

Toothed Belts

Toothed belts are sometimes used in computer printers and plotters instead of chains. The advantages are that:

- They are quieter.
- They are easier to replace and fit.
- Lubrication is not required.
- They have a lower cost.
- They are sometimes used instead of pulleys because they do not slip.

Compound Gears

Compound gears are two or more gears attached to and rotating around the same centre.

Compound gear, showing two gears attached to and rotating around the same centre.

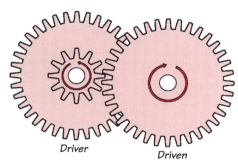

Driver   Driven

Worm and Worm Wheel Gears

This is another gear system to change the direction of rotation through 90°. A worm looks like a screw, but it is really a gear with only one long tooth. This single tooth is wrapped around a cylinder and is used to turn a gear. The gear ratio of worm drives is very low. They are often used to change the high speed of electric motors into more useful speeds.

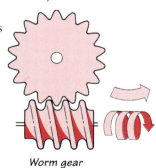

Worm (like a screw) and worm wheel (spur gear).

Worm gear

The worm drives the worm wheel. If the worm wheel tries to drive the worm, the system is designed to lock.

A worm gear reduces the speed of the spur gear many times, e.g. 60 times. If you need a gear system whereby the speed is reduced by a considerable amount, a worm and worm wheel are worth considering.

Advantages of worm and worn wheel:

✔ Reduces speed.
✔ Cannot slip.
✔ Small size.
✔ Power transfer – can translate many easy revolutions of the worm to a small turn/lift of a heavy weight on the worm wheel.

Bevel Gears

Bevel gears are used to change the angle of rotation in a gear system through 90°. A vertical shaft causes the centre gear to rotate, which in turn causes two horizontal shafts to rotate.

Hand drills use bevel gears as their main mechanism to both change the direction of rotation and to make the drill rotate faster than you could twist it by hand.

Rack and Pinion Gears

A rack and pinion system is composed of two gears. The pinion is the normal round gear and the rack is like a flattened-out gear wheel. The pinion rotates and moves the rack in a straight line, i.e. rotary motion is changed to linear motion.

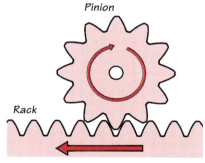

Rack and pinion gears are used in car steering systems where rotating the steering wheel causes a linear movement of a rack, which causes the car wheels to turn using a linkage. Another example is on trains that are designed to travel up steep hills. The wheels on a train are steel and they have no way of gripping the steel track. As the train approaches a steep hill, a gear is lowered to the track and it meshes with the rack. The train does not slip backwards but is pulled up the steep slope.

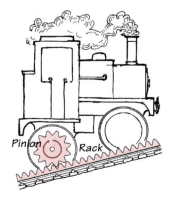

JUNIOR CERTIFICATE TECHNOLOGY

An example that you can see in your school Technology Room is on the table that moves up and down the central pillar of the pillar drill. The rack and pinion reduces the force needed to move the table and thus protects the user's back from strain.

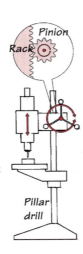

Pillar drill

Drawing Gears

It would be difficult to draw gears if you had to draw all the teeth every time you wanted to design a gear system. For this reason, a gear can be represented by drawing two circles. The outer circle represents the outside of the gear teeth. The inner circle represents the inside of the gear teeth.

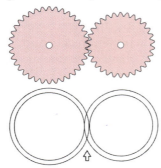

Clutch

The function of a car clutch is to facilitate safe meshing/unmeshing of gears when the gears are being changed, i.e. when a different-size gear is being chosen.

PULLEYS

A pulley is a machine that helps you to lift heavy objects. It usually consists of a rope that runs around one or more wheels. As you pull down on one end of the rope, the other end rises and lifts whatever is attached to it.

A pulley is a grooved wheel that turns on an axle. Pulleys can make lifting a load easier.

Pulley systems, using pulleys fixed on shafts, are used to transfer rotary motion from one place to another. They can also be used to change the speed of the motion. Pulleys must always fit tightly onto their drive shafts, otherwise they will slip and effort and energy will be lost. The speed of rotation is affected by the difference in size between the driver pulley and the driven pulley. If the driver is larger than the driven, the output speed will be greater than the input speed. If the driver is smaller than the driven, then the output speed will be slower than the input. Pulley systems are often used in warehouses and factories to help lift heavy weights, such as crates and machinery. A two-pulley system can have a mechanical advantage. This means that a load can be lifted using smaller effort, but the effort needs to travel further.

Pulley systems are used when there is a need to transmit rotary motion. The diagram below shows a simple system made up of two pulley wheels and a belt. It is a simple mechanical device to winch up and down a rope. When the motor is turned on, it revolves the driver pulley wheel. The belt causes the driven pulley wheel to rotate as well, winding out the rope.

Pulley wheels are grooved so that the belt cannot slip off. Also, the belt is pulled tight between the two pulley wheels (in tension). The friction caused by this means that when the driver rotates, the driven pulley follows.

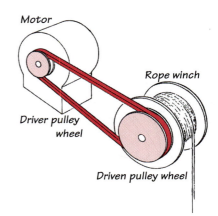

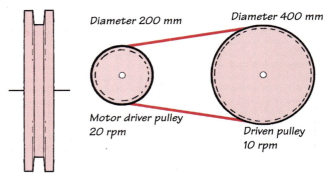

The diagram above shows a small driver pulley turning a larger driven pulley. The large pulley rotates more slowly than the smaller driver pulley wheel.

Sometimes it is necessary to reverse the rotation of the driven pulley wheel in relation to the driver pulley. If the driver is rotating in an anticlockwise direction, the driven pulley may be required to rotate in a clockwise direction.

This is achieved by crossing the belt, as shown in the following diagram. Care must be taken when this is done to not let the belt rub where it crosses. This may increase friction or damage it.

MECHANISMS

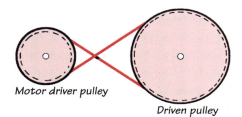
Motor driver pulley — Driven pulley

Pulley systems are an effective, safe method of lifting weights. In the diagram on the right, the rope is pulled on the left side – the effort – and the weight is lifting on the right side – the load. This pulley reduces the amount by which the operator bends his back, so is safe.

Formulas for Velocity Ratio

Velocity ratio (sometimes called movement ratio) is defined as the ratio of the distance moved by the effort to the distance moved by the load.

$$\text{Distance moved by load} = \frac{\text{Distance moved by effort}}{\text{Velocity ratio}}$$

$$\text{Velocity ratio} = \frac{\text{Distance moved by effort}}{\text{Distance moved by load}}$$

$$\text{Distance moved by effort} = \text{Distance moved by load} \times \text{Velocity ratio}$$

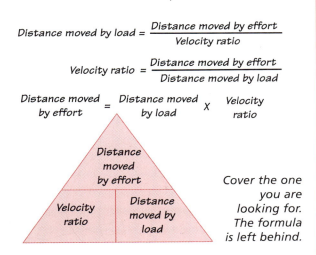

Cover the one you are looking for. The formula is left behind.

Example

A driver pulley is attached to a motor. When the motor is switched on, the driver pulley revolves at 20 rpm (revolutions per minute). The diameter of the driver pulley wheel is 200 mm and the driven pulley wheel is 400 mm. Calculate the velocity ratio.

Solution

$$\frac{\text{Distance moved by driven pulley}}{\text{Distance moved by driver pulley}} = \frac{400}{200} = 2 \text{ (or 1:2 driver:driven)}$$

This means that for every single revolution of the larger driven pulley wheel, the smaller driver pulley wheel rotates twice.

COMBINING MECHANISMS

In reality, most objects containing mechanisms actually combine a variety of mechanisms.

The mechanism seen below is a combination of a cam profile, a follower and a spring. As the cam rotates, the follower is held in position by the force of the spring. The spring resists stretching and so the follower is held onto the cam.

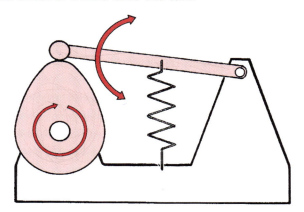

EFFICIENCY

Efficiency is the output energy as a percentage of the input energy.

$$\text{efficiency} = \frac{\text{energy out}}{\text{energy in}} \times 100\%$$

Nothing is 100 per cent efficient. Energy will always be lost somewhere in the machine. A good motor is 95 per cent efficient. To increase efficiency, lubricate moving parts.

Reasons for loss of efficiency (i.e. reasons why energy is lost in energy conversion):

- Cold parts heat up.
- Hot parts cool down.
- Energy is lost by parts rubbing against each other (friction).

PNEUMATICS: THE CONTROLLED USE OF COMPRESSED AIR

When air is compressed, it stores the energy that was used to compress it. Pneumatic systems use that energy to do work and to make things happen. Pneumatics means the controlled use of compressed air. Energy is stored in compressed air and converted into controlled motion by the use of valves and

65

cylinders. When used properly, compressed air is a safe form of stored (potential) energy. Pneumatic equipment is operated by the pressure or exhaustion of air.

The following use pneumatic power:

- pistons in a car engine
- doors on buses and trains
- brakes on lorries
- fairground rides
- pneumatic road drills (they use energy that is stored when the air is compressed)
- dentists' drills.

HYDRAULICS: THE CONTROLLED USE OF COMPRESSED FLUID

Hydraulics use fluids, usually compressed oil, to transfer energy, power and movement from one place to another. A car jack uses hydraulics to raise a car. As the handle moves up and down, oil is pumped into a large cylinder through a one-way valve, thus pushing up the piston and lifting the car. The large distance moved easily by the driver's hands is changed into the smaller but more difficult distance moved by the car.

The following use the power of hydraulics:

- car brake systems
- fire engines
- cranes
- tractors
- farm machinery
- aircraft wing flaps and wheels.

ROBOTICS: USING MACHINES TO DO HUMAN WORK

WHAT IS A ROBOT?

A robot is a machine that can do some human work. It therefore has up to six axes of movement (degrees of freedom) to allow it to move in many directions, making it as human-like as possible. Most robotic systems are anchored to fixed positions in factories where they perform a flexible, but restricted, number of operations in computer-aided manufacturing (CAM).

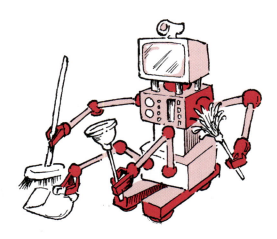

WHERE ARE ROBOTS USED?

Robots are used in assembly lines due to their accuracy and the fact that they can be pre-programmed and have non-stop production. Robots are also used where it is too dangerous for humans, e.g. in the exploration of planets and bomb disposal.

HOW DO THEY WORK?

Robotics is the extension of electronic and pneumatic systems, leading to controlled motion. Robots require a computer to control and coordinate the movement of all their parts. The controlling computers can be inside or outside the robot and are connected to the robot by a **computer interface**. Robots usually have some kind of visual and touch sensors so that the computer can 'see' and 'feel' where it is and how fast it is moving. This is called **sensor feedback**. Depending on its software program, the computer will move the robot parts in a certain way.

MECHANISMS ACTIVITIES

1. Fill in the blanks in these statements.

    (a) Everyday items like scissors, wheelbarrows and taps all work due to _____.

    (b) The force applied by the user getting the mechanism to work is _____. The force applied by the mechanism is the _____.

    (c) _____ is the study of how things move.

    (d) _____ are things that make jobs

MECHANISMS

easier and quicker to do. They usually contain one or more mechanisms.

(e) Cars, trains and aeroplanes all contain _____, which need fuel to work.

(f) _____ is another word for movement.

(g) Things need a _____, e.g. a push or a pull, to start them moving.

(h) The four principal types of motion are _____, _____, _____ and _____.

(i) Linear motion is motion in a _____ _____.

(j) _____ motion is represented by a double arrow.

(k) Motion in a circular direction is _____.

(l) Reciprocating motion along an _____ is called oscillating motion.

(m) The force applied by a mechanism is called the _____.

(n) The force applied by the user is called the _____.

(o) For the effort we put into a mechanism, we want an increased load out. This is called _____ advantage.

(p) The idea of moving something slowly along a long gentle slope instead of a small vertical distance is the principle of the _____ _____.

(q) A _____ is a rigid body that rotates around a fixed point called a fulcrum.

(r) A class _____ lever has the fulcrum in the middle.

(s) The force that turns or moves a lever is called a _____.

(t) On a balanced lever, the anticlockwise moments equal the _____ moments.

(u) Reverse motion, push-pull, bell cranks and parallel motion are all examples of _____.

(v) With a cam and _____ mechanism, the cam rotates and the follower _____.

(w) A hand tool made from a bent rod that allows it to turn easily is called a _____. When a shaft has two or more cranks it is called a _____ _____.

(x) A mechanism that is made up of a crank (rotating disc), the slider (slides inside a tube) and a connecting rod that joins the parts together is a _____ and _____.

(y) A mechanism that allows rotary motion in one direction only by a part falling into dips on a rotating gear-like wheel is called a _____ and _____.

(z) A _____ is a wheel that has cut teeth so that they mesh with teeth in another similar wheel.

2. Fill in the blanks in these statements.

(a) The input gear to a system is called the _____. The output gear is the _____. Gears between drivers and driven gears are called _____ gears.

(b) The mechanism used on a bike to make the wheels rotate is called a _____ and _____.

(c) Gears often used to change the high speeds of electric motors into more useful speeds are called _____ and _____.

(d) Gears used in hand drills to change the angle of rotation by 90° are _____ gears.

(e) A rod with teeth, like a flattened-out gear wheel, used with a pinion is called a _____.

(f) A mechanism used to transfer rotary motion, like a wheel with a groove in it, is called a _____.

(g) No mechanism is 100 per cent _____ due to parts heating or cooling or insufficient lubricant used.

(h) Using the energy in compressed air is called _____. Using the energy in compressed oil is called _____.

(i) Human-like machines, often used in factories with CAM, are called _____.

JUNIOR CERTIFICATE TECHNOLOGY

PREVIOUS MECHANISMS EXAM QUESTIONS

TYPES OF MECHANISMS

1. A sewing mechanism uses rotary motion/oscillating motion/reciprocating motion. Circle the correct answer.

2. Calculate the force applied to the lever microswitch at X in the sketch.

3. Point X is called the fulcrum/load/effort. Circle the correct answer.

4. Which lever requires the greatest effort to lift the load?

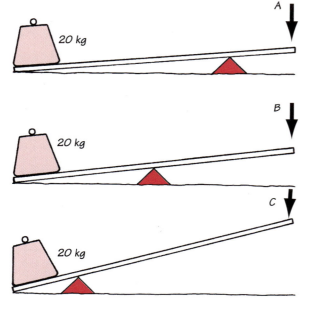

5. The fulcrum of this lever microswitch is at position A/ position B/ position C. Circle the correct answer.

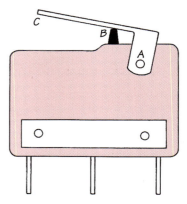

6. This mirror uses a parallel linkage/ crankshaft/ratchet. Circle the correct answer.

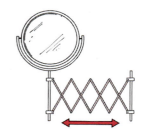

7. Name the mechanisms shown.

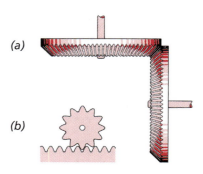

8. Gear X makes the driven go faster than the driver/makes the driven go slower than the driver/makes the driven and driver go in the same direction. Circle the correct answer.

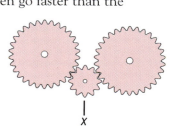

9. These gears are spur gears/bevel gears/worm gears. Circle the correct answer.

10. Calculate the number of turns of the handle required to rotate the drum three times. Circle the correct answer.

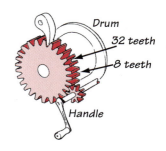

MECHANISMS

11. If the driven gear is turning at 120 rpm, calculate the speed of the driving gear.

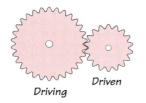

12. On the sketch, clearly indicate the direction of motion of the two gears X and Y shown.

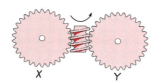

13. This gear mechanism is a rack and pinion/ratchet and pawl/worm and worm wheel. Circle the correct answer.

14. If gear X rotates at 400 rpm, gear Y will rotate at 200 rpm/400 rpm/100 rpm. Circle the correct answer.

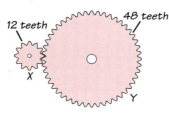

15. Name the gear mechanism used in a hand drill.

16. Which one of the shafts A, B or C cannot be the driver?

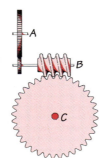

17. What is the function of a clutch in a car engine?

18. Name the gear system shown.

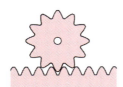

19. If an additional 18-tooth gear wheel is placed between the driving and driven gears, what effect will this have on (a) the speed of the driven gear (b) the direction of motion of the driven gear?

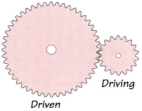

20. With an arrow, indicate the movement of part X in drawing (a) and drawing (b).

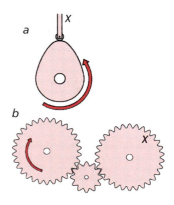

21. State one advantage of a chain drive over a belt drive.

22. Name this mechanism.

23. Why will the toy balance on the perch as shown?

24. With an arrow, indicate the directions of movement of part X in drawing (a) and drawing (b).

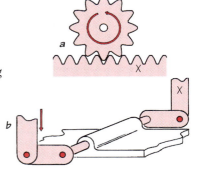

25. Clearly explain why a chain and sprocket mechanism and not a pulley and belt mechanism is used to raise the fork of a forklift truck.

26. This mechanism is a pulley drive/chain and sprocket/compound gear train. Circle the correct answer.

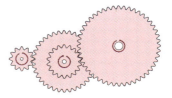

69

JUNIOR CERTIFICATE TECHNOLOGY

27. On the sketch, indicate the approximate location of the crane's centre of gravity.

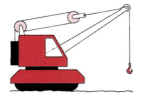

28. Which statement, (a), (b) or (c), describes the movement of the follower when the cam moves in the direction indicated?
    (a) The follower will rise slowly and fall slowly.
    (b) The follower will rise quickly and fall slowly.
    (c) The follower will rise slowly and fall quickly.

29. State two advantages of toothed belts over chains in computer printers and plotters.

30. State two advantages of using a pulley and belt.

31. Choose any two of the following mechanisms and briefly give an example of a use for each: bevel gears, rack and pinion, cam and follower, crank and slider.

EFFICIENCY

1. State two reasons why engines are not 100 per cent efficient.

2. The petrol engine of a motor bike is not 100 per cent efficient in converting chemical energy into kinetic energy. State two ways in which energy is lost in the energy conversion.

3. In the pulley system shown it was found that an effort of 50 N moving 2 m could lift a load of 80 N through a distance of 1 m. Using the formula shown, calculate the efficiency of the system.

   efficiency = work got out/work put in

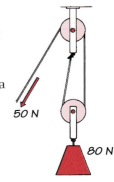

PNEUMATICS

1. Name two everyday applications of pneumatics.

2. If air enters the pneumatic cylinder at opening A, on the diagram, indicate the direction in which the piston will move. Explain the function of opening B.

8 COMPUTERS

INTRODUCTION

Computers have become an essential part of today's technology. You have probably been aware of computers all your life. You may have a PC (personal computer) at home, and you certainly have household appliances controlled by computers. Life has not always been like this for your parents, and certainly not for your grandparents!

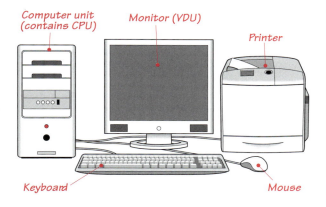

Computer unit (contains CPU)
Monitor (VDU)
Printer
Keyboard
Mouse

Life has changed dramatically due to these amazing machines.

Computers can do calculations, store and find information and communicate with other computers.

A computer cannot think for itself. A human being has to give the computer a set of instructions, called a program. These are usually stored on a disk inside the computer or on a CD.

- On a computer you can type documents, send e-mails and access the Internet.
- Robots controlled by computers put car parts together in a factory.
- Engineers use computers to design cars. The picture on the screen shows what the car will look like when it is built.
- Bar codes are patterns of black and white stripes. They contain information about the items they are printed on, like its price. A laser beam scans the bar code and sends the information to a computer. You can see an example of this in a supermarket.
- There is a type of complicated computer game called virtual reality. With a headset and special gloves, you can have the feeling of being in another world, e.g. among dinosaurs or in ancient Greece.

HARDWARE

Hardware refers to physical objects related to the computer, i.e. those that you can actually touch, like computer input, output and storage devices, and microprocessors.

MICROPROCESSOR/CENTRAL PROCESSING UNIT (CPU)

A microprocessor is at the heart of many computer-controlled systems. It is the part of the computer that does all the work, or the 'brain' of the computer.

A microprocessor is a tiny chip containing millions of electronic components.

At home micropocessors can be found in washing machines, microwaves and CD players. In industry they are used in robots and machine tools.

COMPUTER INPUT DEVICES

Computer input devices are hardware devices used to input information and instructions from the user to the computer. Input devices are needed to tell the computer to do something. For example, a keyboard is an input device. As you type information onto it, the information goes into the computer.

Computer input devices include:

- keyboard
- mouse
- trackball
- touch pad
- scanner
- joystick
- touch-screen monitor
- bar code reader
- microphone
- light pen
- modem (to connect your computer to your telephone line)
- fax

JUNIOR CERTIFICATE TECHNOLOGY

COMPUTER OUTPUT DEVICES

Computer output devices are hardware devices used to get information to the user from the computer. Once the computer has generated some information, it will do something with that information, e.g. put it on the screen or print it to paper. Output devices include:

- monitor (screen)
- printer
- speakers
- fax
- plotters
- modem.

Some devices, like **modems** and **faxes,** are both input and output devices.

Other purpose-built computers can control specific things, e.g. robots, railway tracks or sewing machines. These are more accurate than if they were controlled by hand. They have the advantage that they can be pre-programmed and are less likely to make a mistake.

COMPUTER STORAGE DEVICES

A computer storage device is a device onto which information can be stored from a computer. Some are portable but some are difficult to remove from the computer. Common storage devices include those shown in the table.

Storage Device	Portable	Capacity	Advantages	Disadvantages
Hard disk	No	Any size	All sizes available. Quite cheap.	Not portable.
Floppy disks	Yes	1.44 MB (very small)	Cheap.	Cannot store much.
CD-ROM (compact disc read-only memory)	Yes	About 700 MB (medium)	Quite cheap.	Not always big enough. Can only read it.
CD-RW (compact disc read-write)	Yes	About 700 MB (medium)	Can save data on them.	Not always big enough. Quite expensive.
DVDs (digital versatile discs) read only	Yes	417 GB (huge)	Can store a lot.	Expensive. Not all PCs can use them.
DVDs-RW (read and write)	Yes	417 GB (huge)	Can store a lot. Can save data on them.	Expensive. Not all PCs can use them.

When using floppy disks, you need to ensure you do not write over them by accident. There is a tab in the corner of the floppy disk that has two possible positions. In one position the disk is read only, and in the other position the disk is read-write.

Computer memory can be ROM (read-only memory) or RAM (random access memory).

SOFTWARE

Software means programs for directing the computer about what to do and how to work.

OPERATING SYSTEM

An operating system is the most important software that runs on your computer. Your computer must have an operating system to let it run other software. Operating systems do things like reading text, i.e. letters and numbers, that you type on the keyboard, and sending those letters to the monitor. For example, Windows 98, Windows 2000 and Windows XP are operating systems for PCs.

WORD PROCESSOR

Software designed for writing reports, letters and documents is called a word processor, e.g. Microsoft Word, Microsoft Works Word Processor and MacWord.

SPREADSHEET

A spreadsheet is software suitable for putting information in table format. Spreadsheets are handy for drawing tables and doing calculations on the information in the tables, e.g. adding up columns.

DATABASE

A database is a computerised filing system. It is a collection of data stored in computer memory and designed for easy access. Databases store lots of information related to people or objects, e.g. storing school information related to pupils, storing insurance and tax information related to car registrations. Examples of database software are Microsoft Access and Oracle.

CAD (COMPUTER-AIDED DESIGN)

CAD is software that assists in designing, e.g. it helps architects design buildings, engineers design machines, electronics and roadways and materials specialists design fabrics. CAD software will draw to a plotter if the user wants a paper copy. (A plotter is a special printer for drawing. Drawings are done by a pen moved around by an arm.)

The advantages of using CAD instead of hand drawing are:

- It has more accurate measurements.
- The drawings look neater.
- It is easier to fix mistakes.
- It is easier to reuse some or all of the drawing.
- The drawings can be e-mailed to other users or stored for future use.

CAM (COMPUTER-AIDED MANUFACTURE)

Computers can be used in many different areas when products are being manufactured in a factory. They can be used for the technical and market research data, for the data required to control machinery and robots and for the data to print on the packaging. This data can be used by many departments in the same company.

GRAPHICS/PAINT SOFTWARE

Graphics paint software is used for visual and artistic design of images, usually with colours. It is often used for doing logos. (A logo is a name, symbol or trademark designed for easy and definite recognition.)

A variety of symbols ued in paint software

COMMUNICATIONS SOFTWARE

Communications software refers to software for personal communication, like e-mail and browser software for accessing the Internet. Microsoft Outlook is e-mail software and Microsoft Internet Explorer is browser software.

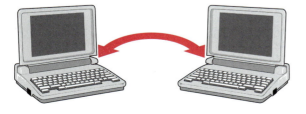

OTHER COMPUTER TERMS

INTERNET/WORLD WIDE WEB (WWW)

The Internet is a network of computers that communicate with each other. Millions of websites are on this network of computers.

WEBSITE

A website is information in words and pictures provided on electronic pages that are accessible over the Internet. A website can provide entertainment, education or enjoyment. It may contain art, music, politics, religion and culture.

E-MAIL

E-mail is a common way of passing information (text and images) from one computer to another via the Internet. Users on different computers (and even in different parts of the world) can get an e-mail address, which is similar to a phone number. Other e-mail users can then send letters, pictures and documents to that e-mail address, similar to the way we can phone people on a telephone line. Microsoft Outlook is an e-mail software application that can be installed on your computer.

Nowadays, many people have web mail accounts. This is an e-mail service that can be accessed via a website. These are usually free and can be accessed from any PC in the world with an Internet connection.

FILE

A file is a collection of information that a computer uses. For example, if you create a Microsoft Word document, the information is saved in a file so that Microsoft Word can read it and open it. Often files are not readable by humans, but rather are simply data files the computer understands.

BITS AND BYTES

The smallest piece of computer data to be stored in memory is called a bit, which can have two values, on (1) or off (0). Bits are stored together in groups of eight, which are called bytes.

- **Kilobyte (KB):** One thousand bytes.
- **Megabytes (MB):** One million bytes.
- **Gigabytes (GB):** One thousand million bytes.

JUNIOR CERTIFICATE TECHNOLOGY

PIXELS

The letters and pictures that appear on a computer screen are made up of tiny dots of coloured light called pixels.

BASIC OPERATION OF A PC

CORRECT START-UP AND SHUT-DOWN PROCEDURE

To start up your computer, simply switch on the power button, usually located on the front. Wait until the computer has run through its start-up sequence and then open the software program you want.

To shut down your computer, follow the recommended shut-down procedure given in the operating system manual. As most of you will be using some version of a Windows operating system, the procedure to shut down the computer is to left click on 'Start' and then left click on 'Turn off Computer'.

Never power the computer off using the power button.

BACKING UP

You should always back up, i.e. save a spare copy of, important files and programs, e.g. on CD or DVD.

COPYING A FILE

To copy a file to a new location, simply highlight the file, then right click on it and choose 'Copy'. Go to the location you wish to copy it into, right click again and choose 'Paste'. This makes a duplicate copy of the file.

DELETING A FILE

If you want to delete a file, most computer systems have some kind of dustbin that unwanted files can be put in. Files that are deleted by the user are moved here. They are effectively removed from the file storage system, though they may sometimes be restored from the bins.

MOVING OR COPYING DATA IN A FILE

Text is the letters and numbers in your files; images are the pictures. If you wish to move text or an image from one place to another, cut the text, i.e. remove it from its current position, and then paste it, i.e. put it in its new position. If you want the text or image to be copied and put somewhere else, i.e. you want two copies of it, copy it from its current position and then paste it to its new position.

COMPUTERS ACTIVITIES

1. Fill in the blanks in these statements.
   (a) The physical parts of a computer you can actually touch are called _____.
   (b) At the heart of computers and computer-controlled household appliances like washing machines are _____.
   (c) A _____ is a device that enables one computer to communicate with another via a phone line.
   (d) Keyboards, mice, scanners and joysticks are examples of _____ devices.
   (e) Monitors, speakers and printers are examples of _____ devices.
   (f) Floppy disks and CD-ROMs are examples of _____ devices.
   (g) Programs for processing data and instructing the computer what to do are called _____.
   (h) Windows 98, Windows 2000 and Windows XP are examples of _____ systems.
   (i) _____ is software that assists in drawing pictures on the computer.
   (j) The _____ or _____ is a network of computers that communicate with each other via telephone lines. Anyone can access it.

PREVIOUS COMPUTERS EXAM QUESTIONS

TERMS

1. State the meaning of the following abbreviations: (a) CD (b) ROM.

INPUT AND OUTPUT DEVICES

1. Which one of the following is an input device to a microcomputer (i.e. PC)? (a) Printer (b) Keyboard (c) Monitor

2. A monitor/scanner/printer is a computer input device. Circle the correct answer.

COMPUTERS

3. A joystick is a computer output device/input device/storage device. Circle the correct answer.

4. Name one computer input device and one computer output device.

5. Name two devices that can be controlled from a computer.

STORAGE DEVICES

1. The diagram shows the tab on a floppy disk. State the function of this tab.

2. Which one of these computer disks can store the largest amount of data? (a) 3.5 inch floppy disk (b) 5.25 inch floppy disk (c) CD-ROM

3. Floppy disks are used to store electronic data. Name two other methods of storing electronic data.

SOFTWARE

1. Which one of the following programs should be used to prepare a written report? (a) Word processor (b) Database (c) Spreadsheet

2. Motor car registration numbers and information about the owner can be stored in a computer file. Which one of the following programs should be used to create this file? (a) Word processor (b) Database (c) Spreadsheet

3. Which one of the following programs would require the use of a plotter? (a) Word processor (b) CAD (c) Spreadsheet

4. Accurately dimensioned drawings are produced using (a) CAD software (b) paint software (c) communications software. Circle the correct answer.

5. State two advantages of using CAD instead of traditional drawing to produce drawings.

6. Fancy logos are produced using (a) a word processing program (b) a database program (c) a paint program. Circle the correct answer.

7. What are these computer desktop icons used for?

8. Explain the meanings of the symbols labelled X and Y, which can be found in a software painting application.

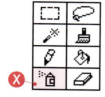 

9. Computer users talk about using e-mail. Briefly explain the meaning of e-mail.

10. Which one of the following is software? (a) Computer keyboard (b) Floppy disk (c) Windows 98

BASIC OPERATION OF A PC

1. Explain the terms 'cut' and 'paste' when used in computer-aided drawings.

GENERAL

1. State two advantages of a microprocessor-controlled sewing machine.

2. List two uses of computers in school. Select one of these uses and state how the introduction of computers has helped.

75

9 ELECTRICITY AND ELECTRONICS

INTRODUCTION

Electricity and electronics have completely changed the world we live in. It is hard to imagine life without electric light, CD players, television, mobile phones and washing machines, but none of these things existed 100 years ago. Nowadays, most businesses could not work without computers and aeroplanes could not fly without electronics. Hospitals save our lives using electronic machines.

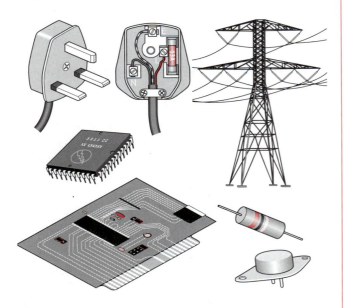

At the heart of all these fantastic inventions lies a small set of simple components. Most electronic machines are made by combining this same set of components in new, different and complex ways. This chapter introduces you to the electronic components that make up our electronic world.

Each electronic component has a special symbol associated with it. These symbols are recognised throughout the world.

Electronics is about controlling the flow of electricity around a circuit using electronic components. A **circuit** is a connection of components joined together so that some electric current can flow. When electric current flows it can cause interesting things to happen, like lighting a bulb or switching on a motor.

Electronic circuits have become smaller over the years. A computer from the 1940s would not fit in your Technology Room! Now, most electronic circuits are built using **integrated circuits**, or chips. One chip looks like a single component, but actually contains hundreds, or even millions, of components wired inside it. Microelectronics refers to miniature electronic components.

Before we can understand electronic components, we need to understand electricity, current and voltage.

ELECTRICITY, CURRENT AND VOLTAGE

Electricity is electrical energy which is caused by the movement of electrons through a material. (An electron is the tiniest part of an atom. All material is made up of atoms.) Electricity flows along like a water current in a stream, so we call it **electric current (I)**.

The higher the **voltage** in a circuit, the more power there is to drive the electrons around. It is the driving force that causes them to flow. Voltage is like the steepness of a river – the bigger the difference in height between the start and end of the river, the faster the water current will flow. Voltage is also called potential difference and is measured in volts (V).

Electricity can only flow through wires and other components if they are joined together in a complete loop called a **circuit**. In a torch, a circuit joins one end of a battery to the other through a bulb and a switch. The bulb will only light if there are no breaks in the circuit and the electricity can flow from one end of the battery to the other through the bulb.

Electric current is measured in amperes (amps, A) for large amounts or in milliamperes (milliamps, mA) for small amounts. There are 1,000 milliamps in one amp.

Current can be DC (direct current) or AC (alternating current). Current from batteries is DC. Charge flows in one direction only when a DC power source is used. Current from mains electricity is AC. Alternating current constantly changes direction.

ELECTRICITY AND ELECTRONICS

ELECTRIC CURRENT FLOW THROUGH MATERIALS

Some materials allow electric current to flow through easily, some materials block electric current and others allow a small amount through. Materials are said to be either conductors, insulators or semiconductors.

- **Conductor:** A material that allows an electric current to pass through easily. Conductors are usually made from metal.
- **Insulator:** A material that does not allow electricity to pass through easily. Insulators are usually made from plastic or rubber.
- **Semiconductors:** Materials whose ability to conduct electricity is somewhere between a conductor and an insulator. Many electronic components like resistors, transistors and chips are made from semiconductors.

POWER SOURCES

In order to work, electronic components and circuits must have a source of electrical energy, i.e. a source of electrons, called a power source. Examples of power sources are batteries, mains and power supplies.

CELL

A cell is a single 1.5 V battery. It has a positive and a negative side, or 'pole'. Current flows from positive to negative.

The symbol for a cell.

BATTERIES

Batteries are a source of DC electricity and come in all shapes and sizes. Those used in school projects usually range from 1.5 V to 9 V. Batteries are made up of one or more cells, and so come in multiples of 1.5 V, e.g. 1.5 V, 6 V, 9 V.

Chemical energy is stored in a battery. It is converted to electrical energy in an electrical circuit. When you turn on a torch, electric current flows along a wire from one end of the battery through a bulb and back to the battery to make the torch glow.

When the chemicals in the battery are used up, the battery can no longer produce electricity. Then we say that the battery is flat. Because batteries contain chemicals, they should be disposed of carefully and in an environmentally friendly way.

Batteries have two terminals, a positive and a negative. They are connected to circuits by battery snaps.

A selection of common batteries.

Symbols for a battery.

Low battery voltages are safe for us to handle. Most electronic equipment runs on low DC voltages between 1.5 V and 12 V. (The input mains voltage is 'stepped down', i.e. reduced, to the required DC voltage.)

- **Batteries connected in series:** Add up their voltage, e.g. two 1.5 V batteries in series give a total voltage of 3 V.
- **Batteries connected in parallel:** Their voltage does not add up, e.g. two 1.5 V batteries in parallel still give a total voltage of 1.5 V, but will last twice as long.

MAINS ELECTRICITY

Most of the electricity in our homes is made in generating stations and travels to our homes along thick cables. We call this mains electricity. Mains electricity is supplied into our homes at 220 volts and is highly dangerous. Touching the mains supply can kill you. The only reason we can use mains electricity safely in our homes is because we are shielded by strong insulators around the wires that contain mains electricity.

Devices powered by mains electricity also contain an **earth** wire. The earth wire is provided so that if there is a fault which causes a leak of current, the current will choose to go down the earth wire rather than into you.

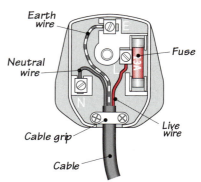

The wiring inside a plug. The live and neutral wires carry the electricity.

77

JUNIOR CERTIFICATE TECHNOLOGY

We are also protected by **fuses**. A fuse is a thin wire inside a glass or ceramic case fitted with metal ends. Fuses detect if too much current is flowing and break the circuit if it does. Most of our mains plugs contain a 13 amp fuse. This means that if more than 13 A flows in the wire, the fuse will blow (it actually melts) and cut off the power. A cartridge fuse is a common type of fuse.

TRANSFORMER

A transformer is an electrical device that takes electricity of one voltage and changes it into another voltage. You can see transformers at the top of electricity poles outside your house, converting a very high voltage to a lower voltage for use in your house.

COMPONENTS

Components are electronic devices that control the flow of electricity around a circuit. The most common electronic components are wires, resistors, diodes, light-emitting diodes (LEDs), transistors, sensors, capacitors and integrated circuits. Some components have 'polarity', which means that, in order to work, they must be connected in a certain way in a circuit.

WIRE

Wire is used to connect up the separate components in a circuit. Wire is made from metal and so is an excellent conductor of electricity between the components. Connections to wires are usually made by soldering (see p. 40). Wires usually have copper centres and a plastic, e.g. PVC, covering.

Question: Why do you think wires have a plastic outer coating?

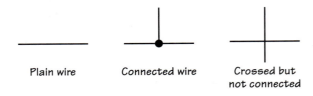

Plain wire   Connected wire   Crossed but not connected

RESISTORS

Resistors are components for reducing and directing the flow of current in a circuit.

The **resistance** of a resistor is the amount that it restricts the flow of current. A resistor with a large value resists a lot of current. A small-value resistor just restricts a small amount of current. Resistors can have a fixed or variable resistance.

Flow of current before   Flow of current after

Symbol for a fixed resistor.

A fixed resistor is one whose resistance cannot be changed.

Remember:
- If the resistance (R) is high, the current (I) will be low.
- If the resistance (R) is low, the current (I) will be high.

Resistance is measured in ohms, after George Ohm. The symbol for an ohm is Ω.

The amount of current that will flow through a resistor can be figured out using **Ohm's Law**. Ohm's Law is the most important law in electronics.

Here is Ohm's Law:
current = voltage ÷ resistance
resistance = voltage ÷ current
voltage = current x resistance

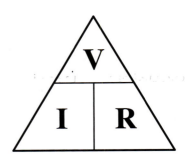

Cover the one you're looking for. The formula is left behind.

Question: If I connect a 10Ω resistor across a 6 V battery, what current flows through the resistor?

Answer: current = voltage ÷ resistance
= 6 V ÷ 10 Ω
= 0.6 A or 600 mA

Question: A 9 V battery is connected to an unknown resistor. 1 A is measured flowing through the resistor. What is the value of the resistor?

Answer: resistance = voltage ÷ current
= 9 V ÷ 1 A
= 9 Ω

ELECTRICITY AND ELECTRONICS

Reading Resistor Values

The resistance of resistors is indicated using colour-coded bands on the body of the resistor.

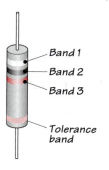

Colour	Value
Black	0
Brown	1
Red	2
Orange	3
Yellow	4
Green	5
Blue	6
Violet	7
Grey	8
White	9

The coloured bands make it easy to read the resistor value from any angle.

The first three coloured bands indicate the value of the resistor in ohms. The first band tells us the first digit, the second band tells us the second digit and the third band tells us the number of zeros.

For example, if the first band is green (5), the second digit is blue (6) and the third band is orange (3), then the value of the resistor is 56,000 ohms. When writing resistor values, 'R' represents 0, 'K' represents 1,000 and 'M' represents 1,000,000. These letters are used instead of decimal points. For example, 560 Ω = 560 R; 4,700 Ω = 4K7; 6,800,000 = 6M8.

Tolerance

The fourth coloured band on the resistor indicates how accurate the resistor value is. Red means its value is within 2 per cent of the stated value. Gold means its value is within 5 per cent. Silver means it is within 10 per cent. If there is no fourth band, the value is within 20 per cent of the stated value.

YELLOW 4	VIOLET 7	RED 00	RED +/- 2%	4K7 +/- 2%
GREEN 5	BLUE 6	BLACK None	GOLD +/- 5%	56R +/- 5%
BROWN 1	GREY 8	GREEN 00000	SILVER +/- 10%	1M8 +/- 10%
ORANGE 3	ORANGE 3	ORANGE 000	NONE +/- 20%	33K +/- 20%

Examples of fixed resistors.

Question: The first three bands on a resistor indicate that the value of the resistor is 330 Ω. The fourth band is gold. What could its true value be?

Answer: The gold band means 5 per cent tolerance. This means the real resistance will be within 5 per cent of 330 Ω.

5 per cent of 330 Ω = 17.5 Ω

The true resistance will be between (330 Ω − 17.5 Ω) and (330 Ω + 17.5 Ω), i.e. between 312.5 Ω and 347.5 Ω.

Variable Resistor/Potentiometer

This is a resistor whose resistance can be adjusted from 0 Ω up to the value given on the base of the component, e.g. 10K Ω. The resistance is usually adjusted by twisting a knob. Variable resistors are used to dim lights, slow down motors and turn up the radio.

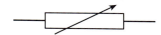

Symbol for a variable resistor.

Two Resistors in Series

When two resistors are placed one after the other, current must go through the first and then through the second. Their resistance adds up.
$R_{total} = R_1 + R_2$

Question: A 1K Ω resistor and a 10K Ω resistor are in series in a circuit. What is the total resistance from them?

Answer:
$$R_{total} = R_1 + R_2 = 1K\,\Omega + 10K\,\Omega = 11K\,\Omega$$

Two Resistors in Parallel

When two resistors are parallel to each other, current can flow through both resistors at the same time. The total resistance is found by:

$$\frac{1}{R_{total}} = \frac{1}{R_1} + \frac{1}{R_2}$$

Question: Two 10K Ω resistors are placed in a circuit in parallel. What is the total resistance from them?

Answer:
$$\frac{1}{R_{total}} = \frac{1}{R_1} + \frac{1}{R_2} = \frac{1}{10K\,\Omega} + \frac{1}{10K\,\Omega} = \frac{2}{10K\,\Omega} = \frac{1}{5K\,\Omega}, \text{ so } R_{total} = 5K\,\Omega$$

Using Resistors as Potential Dividers

Resistors connected in series between points at different potentials act as a potential divider.
They cause a splitting of the potential difference (or voltage).

JUNIOR CERTIFICATE TECHNOLOGY

The fraction of the total voltage across each resistor is exactly equal to the fraction of the total resistance it represents. For example, if a 9V source is split across a 10K Ω resistor and a 20K Ω resistor, there will be 3V across the 10K Ω resistor and 6V across the 20K Ω resistor.

DIODES

Diodes are semiconductor devices that allow current to flow in one direction only. This can be very useful in circuits.

Diodes have two legs, the anode (positive) and the cathode (negative). The diode will conduct electricity when the anode of the diode is connected to the positive end of the battery and the cathode of the diode is connected to the negative end of the battery. This is called forward-biased. The arrow of the diode symbol must point in the direction of the current flow. The diode will not conduct electricity when it is connected the other way round. Try it!

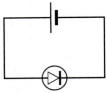
Diode conducts.

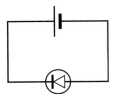
Diode does not conduct.

LED (LIGHT-EMITTING DIODES)

LEDs are electronic components with coloured tops, i.e. blue, green, yellow or red. LEDs give off light when current flows through them. Many electronic appliances use LEDs to indicate that the power is on.

Calculators and digital clocks use LEDs for their display, using seven diodes to make each digit.

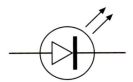
The symbol for an LED.

LEDs light like a bulb, but they only use a fraction of the power. Batteries will last longer if LEDs are used instead of bulbs, which is one of the reasons they are so popular. LEDs are damaged by voltage sources higher than 3 V. LEDs must always be connected in series with a resistor in order to limit the current flowing through the LED and avoid burning it out.

Unlike bulbs, LEDs are diodes and so will only work one way around in a circuit. A LED has an anode (positive) and a cathode (negative). The long leg of the LED (the anode/positive) should be connected to the positive end of the battery, and the short end (the cathode/negative) should be connected to the negative end of the battery.

Also, beside the short leg is a flat part on the LED, which helps identify it when it is in a circuit (as the legs may be cut or not visible).

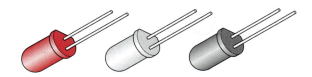
LEDs come in different colours. Red, yellow and green are popular.

TRANSISTORS

Transistors are sensitive electronic switches and are the main components in most electronic devices and all chips.

Transistors have three connections or legs: emitter, base and collector. The three legs must be connected the right way around for the transistor to work correctly. The collector and base must be connected (usually with a resistor) to the positive side, and the emitter must be connected to the negative or 0 V side.

The base is really what causes the transistor to turn on and off. A small voltage of about 0.6 V between the base and the emitter will cause the transistor to switch on.

When the transistor switches on, it allows a large current to flow between the collector and the emitter. If you remove the voltage from the base, the transistor will switch off and no current will flow from the collector to the emitter.

As well as being a switch, a transistor is also called an amplifier. This is because a small amount of current flowing into the base will cause a much larger (i.e. amplified) current to flow from the collector to the emitter.

Like diodes and most electronic components, resistors must be used with transistors in order to limit the current and stop them from burning out. A resistor should be connected to the base and to the collector.

ELECTRICITY AND ELECTRONICS

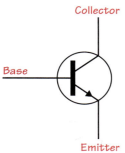
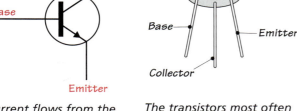

Current flows from the collector to the emitter when the transistor is switched on.

The transistors most often used in your Technology Room are BC108s.

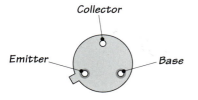

Turn your transistor upside down. The pin layout is shown here.

When the transistor is switched on, the current flowing from the emitter is the sum of the currents to the base and the collector: $I_e = I_b + I_c$.

Darlington Pair

A darlington pair is two transistors connected together to give a very high current gain. The emitter of the first is connected into the base of the second.

SENSORS

Sensors are devices that convert a physical signal, e.g. heat, light, movement, sound, into an electrical signal, i.e. the flow of current. Examples are heat sensors (called thermistors), light sensors (LDRs), moisture/dryness sensors, movement sensors, humidity sensors and sound sensors, i.e. microphones.

Heat Sensor

Thermistors (also called thermal resistors or temperature-dependent resistors) are components whose resistance is high in the cold and low in the heat. They are very useful in temperature detection circuits, e.g. fire alarms.

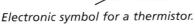

Electronic symbol for a thermistor.

Light Sensor

LDRs (light-dependent resistors) are components whose resistance is high in the dark and low in the light. They are used in circuits to switch on street lighting in the evening and off again in the morning. These are also used in meters which measure light intensity, for example in a camera.

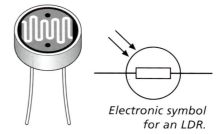

Electronic symbol for an LDR.

Moisture Sensor

Moisture sensors are simply made using metal strips or a small printed circuit board. They have a high resistance when dry and a low resistance when wet. These are used to detect when a water tank is full, in a flood warning system or when soil is dry.

CAPACITORS

Capacitors are used for storing electrical charge (electrons). A capacitor fills with charge similar to the way a toilet cistern fills up with water. And a capacitor loses its charge (i.e. discharges), like when you flush the toilet and the water flows out.

A capacitor is made up of two metal plates that are separated by an insulator. When a voltage is applied across a capacitor, it charges up. This means electrons are forced onto one plate and stripped off the other. Current does not pass across the plates due to the insulator. When the capacitor is fully charged, the voltage across it is the same as that of the battery. Capacitance, i.e. how much charge the capacitor can hold, is measured in farads (F).

The capacitor will hold onto the charge when the battery is disconnected from the capacitor. If a resistor is connected across the capacitor, the electrons (current) will flow out of one side of the capacitor and into the other side, so that eventually there is no voltage (charge) left across the capacitor. The amount of time that the capacitor takes to charge up and discharge again is used in timing circuits.

The following are different types of capacitors.

- **Fixed/non-electrolytic:** This type of capacitor is non-polarised, i.e. it can be connected any way around in a circuit. There are no positive and negative sides.
- **Electrolytic:** This type of capacitor is polarised, i.e. has a positive and negative leg. The positive terminal connects to the positive of the supply, and the negative

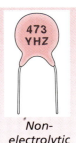

Non-electrolytic capacitor.

81

JUNIOR CERTIFICATE TECHNOLOGY

terminal to the negative of the supply. Electrolytic capacitors can hold much more charge than non-electrolytic capacitors. Electrolytic capacitors are often used with resistors to create a time delay.

Electrolytic capacitor.

- **Variable:** Capacitors whose capacitance can be varied, usually by twisting a knob or screw.

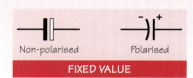

| FIXED VALUE | VARIABLE |

Integrated Circuit (IC)

An IC is a chip which contains many components, e.g. resistors, transistors, diodes, in a tiny electronic circuit. ICs usually have eight or more metal legs to connect them into a larger circuit. Each leg or pin has a number. The numbers of the pins are not written on the component, but you can figure it out using the diagram below.

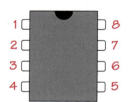

Integrated circuits (ICs): Pin 1 is the top left. Read anticlockwise.

OTHER COMMON ELECTRONIC DEVICES

Bulb

A bulb gives off light when current flows through it. A bulb can be connected either way around, i.e. it has no polarity.

Electronic symbol for a light bulb.

Buzzer

A buzzer gives a continuous sound when current flows through it. Buzzers are often used in alarm systems. They have polarity – their red wire must connect to the positive of the battery and their black wire to the negative.

Electronic symbol for a buzzer.

Speaker

A speaker translates electric current signals into sound. Speakers are the opposite of microphones (which convert sound into electric current). Speakers can be used to create continuous noises, musical notes or speech.

Electronic symbol for a speaker.

Motor

A motor translates electric current into circular motion. DC motors can be connected either way around, causing them to turn clockwise or anticlockwise. Motors are used in numerous electrical devices, e.g. washing machines, tape recorders, refrigerators, food processors and central heating pumps.

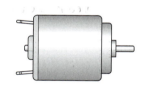

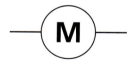

Electronic symbol for a motor.

Timers

Timers can be used to do several things, such as:

- Create a time delay before something happens.
- Switch something on or off for a specified period.
- Control the rate of the flashing of a bulb.

ELECTRICITY AND ELECTRONICS

The charging and discharging of capacitors can be used to create time delays in a circuit for times of up to approximately five minutes.

555 Timer Integrated Circuit
For times greater than five minutes, a 555 timer integrated circuit is better than a capacitor circuit. It is very flexible and can give long time delays. It can be used to control flashing lights and sounds. It has eight legs. The 555 is one of the most useful electronic devices.

Solenoid
A solenoid is an electrical device that converts electric current into movement in a straight line. A coil of wire wound around a soft iron core has a current passed through it. This causes a magnetic force that pulls a metal bar into the centre of the wire coil. When the current is switched off, a spring returns the bar to its original position. This straight line motion can be used to lock doors and operate switches.

Relay
A relay is a mechanical switch that is electrically activated on and off. A relay has a solenoid inside it. When a current is passed through the solenoid, the iron core becomes magnetised and attracts a small metal plate which operates the switch. When the current is removed from the solenoid, a spring returns the switch to its normal position. Relays are widely used in the automatic control of devices such as motors.

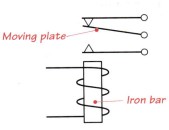

Relay: The moving plate is attracted to the iron bar when current flows.

TEST INSTRUMENTS

AMMETER
An ammeter is a test instrument that measures electrical current flow in amps or milliamps. Place it in series with the current to be measured.

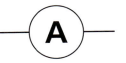

VOLTMETER
A voltmeter is a test instrument that measures voltage difference between two points in volts or millivolts. Place it in parallel with the voltage to be measured.

MULTIMETER
A multimeter is a test instrument that measures electrical current flow, voltage difference and resistance, and occasionally other electrical values.

ANALOGUE AND DIGITAL
Older test instruments are analogue, and are easily identifiable by the needle that points to the correct value. Modern test instruments are digital, which are easily identifiable by the digital display.

Digital multimeters like this one accurately measure voltage, current and resistance.

OPERATION
Set your test instrument to the reading you want to take, e.g. current. Connect the probes across your circuit as needed for that reading. Always choose the largest setting and work down.

UNITS

Value Being Measured	Unit	Symbol
Resistance	Ohms, kiloohms	Ω, kΩ
Current	Amps, milliamps	A, mA
Voltage/potential difference	Volts, millivolts	V, mV
Capacitance	Farads, microfarads	F, μF
Energy	Joules	J
Power	Watts, kilowatts, megawatts	W, kW, MW
Electricity used (ESB use this: 1 kWHr is the amount of electricity used when 1 kW is being used constantly for one hour)	Kilowatt hour	kWHr

JUNIOR CERTIFICATE TECHNOLOGY

MANUAL SWITCHES

We have seen how relays and transistors can act as electronic switches. You can also have manual switches, which are activated by a user. Using a manual switch is a safe way for a person to interrupt the electron flow in a circuit without touching the wire.

Switches allow you to turn current flow on and off in circuits. Switches are used in all electronic appliances, e.g. lights, computers, electric tools, televisions.

MECHANICAL SWITCHES

Types of mechanical switches, each activated differently include:

- rocker switches
- push switches
- toggle switches
- slide switches
- limit switch/microswitch
- reed switch
- tilt switch.

Rocker Switch

An ordinary light switch is a rocker switch. It has two positions – on or off.

Push Switch

This is a switch you push to activate.

Toggle Switch

In a toggle switch the toggle (handle) moves or swings to make or break the circuit.

Slide Switch

In a slide switch a slider moves linearly (slides) from position to position.

Limit Switch/Microswitch

A microswitch is used to limit something. It has a lever coming out of it that is easily pressed, e.g. by a gate opening or by a closed lid touching it.

The three legs on a microswitch are:

- NC – normally closed
- NO – normally open
- COM – common

Reed Switch

A switch operated by a magnet. They are often used on doors and windows in burglar alarm systems.

Tilt Switch

A switch activated by a mercury ball that is free to roll. When the mercury ball rolls away from a contact, it is an open switch. When it touches the contact, it is a closed switch.

ELECTRICAL SWITCHES

Inside each of these mechanical switches is one or more electrical switch. Each electrical switch is made up of a pole and one or more throws.

- **Pole:** A moving wire in a switch that can move to a fixed wire to make a closed circuit or away from the fixed wire to make an open circuit.
- **Throw:** A fixed wire stopping point inside a switch.

When you close a switch, you are moving a pole to touch a throw. Electricity can flow through the metal which joins the pole to the throw, as metal conducts electricity. When you open a switch, electricity cannot travel across the air, as air is an insulator.

TYPES OF ELECTRICAL SWITCHES

The number of poles and throws a switch has and how the poles move to touch the throws determines what type of switch it is.

Types of switches include:

- push to break
- push to make
- SPST
- SPDT
- DPST
- DPDT
- DPDTCO.

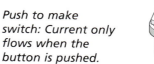

Push to break switch: Current flows normally, but not when the button is pushed.

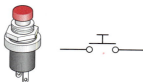

Push to make switch: Current only flows when the button is pushed.

ELECTRICITY AND ELECTRONICS

SPST Switch

SPST (single pole single throw) switches are used for on/off operations and have only one switch and one way to make a connection, e.g. a light in a bedroom.

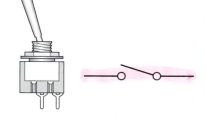

SPST switch: One pole and one throw.

SPDT Switch

SPDT (single pole double throw) switches are used for on/off operations but have two switches and two ways to make a connection, e.g. a light in a hall that can be switched on and off from the hall or the landing.

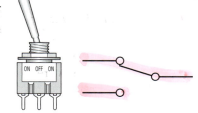

SPDT switch: One pole with two throws.

DPST Switch

A DPST (double pole single throw) switch is a pair of SPST switches that operate together. Both are open or closed at the same time.

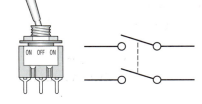

DPST switch: Two poles, each with a single throw.

DPDT Switch

A DPDT (double pole double throw) switch is a pair of SPDT switches that operate together. Switching the DPDT switch controls two circuits. It is usually used to change the speed or direction of a motor. For example, when you switch on a hairdryer (with one mechanical switch), two electrical switches are activated inside – one to turn on the fan and one to turn on the heat.

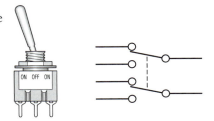

DPDT switch: Two poles, each with two throws.

DPDTCO Switch

A DPDTCO (double pole double throw centre off) switch is a slight variation of the DPDT with a centre off position.

METHODS OF JOINING COMPONENTS

Electronic components can be joined together to make a circuit. Some common methods of joining components include breadboards (temporarily joined), copper stripboards and PCBs (both permanently joined).

BREADBOARD

The advantages of using a breadboard instead of a method of permanently attaching components are:

✔ You can easily take out some or all of the components and start again if you make a mistake.

✔ You can spread the components out more or put them closer together to make the circuit fit better.

✔ You can reuse the breadboard at a later date if you do not need your circuit any more.

✔ You do not need to solder it. You do not even have to know how to solder.

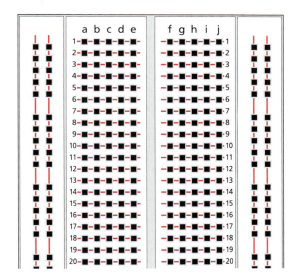

The red lines indicate internal connections. Current can flow along these lines.

COPPER STRIPBOARD

Copper stripboard is made from an insulating material. The underside of stripboard has strips of copper running in one direction. Through the stripboard and the copper strips are lines of holes.

85

A circuit is built on copper stripboard using the copper strips to connect the components. The legs of the components are pushed through the insulated side of the board and soldered onto the copper strips at the back. Breaks in the strips can be made with a small drill or a strip cutter turned by hand.

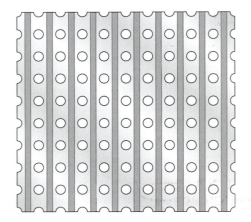

Copper stripboard.

Advantages of using copper stripboard instead of breadboard are:

✔ The components will not fall out if shaken or disturbed.
✔ It is a permanent way of holding a circuit together.

Before you start inserting components or soldering, transfer your circuit diagram onto copper stripboard layout paper first. You can photocopy the copper stripboard layout on p. 147 to help you.

PRINTED CIRCUIT BOARD (PCB)

Modern electronics usually involves the use of PCBs. The boards are made from glass-reinforced plastic (an insulator) with copper tracks in the place of wires (a conductor). Components are fitted to the boards by drilling holes through the board. The copper tracks link the components together, forming a circuit.

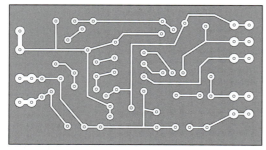

Printed circuit board (PCB).

The advantages of PCBs are:

✔ PCBs are much more suitable for mass production, as it is less time consuming and cheaper to produce many of them.
✔ You are not restricted to working in straight lines.

The disadvantage of PCBs are:

✘ Special equipment is needed to make them.

UNDERSTANDING AND DESIGNING CIRCUITS

Circuits are explained using a **circuit diagram**, i.e. a picture, using internationally agreed symbols that are always used to represent the components in a circuit.

INPUT, CONTROL AND OUTPUT

Circuits are usually composed of an input part, a control part and an output part.

- **Input:** The input in an electronic system is a section, usually made up of a sensor that detects changes in the environment. Depending on what happens to the input device, it may send an electrical signal to the process system.

- **Process:** The process section in an electronic system responds to the electrical signal received from the input. Depending on what happens to the process section, it may send an electrical signal to the output system.

- **Output:** The output section in an electronic system responds to the electrical signal received from the process. It converts the electrical signal it receives into other forms of energy, like heat, sound, light or movement.

A successful circuit has three main blocks: an input, a process and an output.

For example, in a circuit in which a bulb lights when a toggle switch is pressed:

- **Input:** Mechanical switch, i.e. the handle of the toggle switch that the user pushes.

ELECTRICITY AND ELECTRONICS

- **Process**: Electronic switch, i.e. the closed circuit that the toggle switch makes as a result.
- **Output**: Bulb.

Another example is a circuit in which an LED lights and buzzer sounds when a certain temperature is reached:

- **Input**: Thermistor.
- **Process**: Transistor.
- **Output**: LED and buzzer.

COMMONLY USED ELECTRONIC CIRCUITS

WET SENSOR

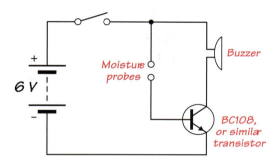

Remember, a moisture sensor has its resistance high in the dry and lower in the wet.

1. The SPST switch is a master on-off switch. When it is open, no voltage is connected to the circuit so nothing can happen.
2. When the SPST switch is closed and the moisture sensor is dry, current cannot pass through the moisture sensor (as it is an open circuit) or through the transistor (as it is not switched on due to no voltage at the base). Nothing happens.
3. When the moisture sensor gets wet, the water on the moisture sensor conducts electricity, allowing current to flow into the base of the transistor.
4. The transistor switches on.
5. When the transistor is on, it pulls a current down from the collector to the emitter.
6. This current flows through the buzzer. The buzzer buzzes.

DARK SENSOR

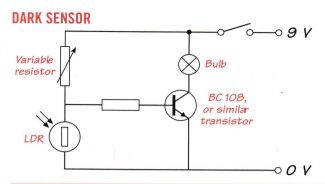

Remember, an LDR has its resistance high in the dark (approximately 1M Ω) and low in the bright (approximately 400 Ω).

1. The SPST switch is a master on-off switch. When it is open, no voltage is connected to the circuit so nothing can happen.
2. When it is bright, the resistance of the LDR is very low. The two resistors on the left-hand side act as a potential divider, so the voltage at the base of the transistor is close to 0 V. The transistor will not switch on.
3. As it gets darker, the resistance of the LDR increases. The voltage at the base increases as a result.
4. When it is dark enough, the voltage at the base reaches the trigger voltage for the transistor and the transistor switches on. This pulls a current from the collector to the emitter. The bulb lights.
5. When it becomes bright again, the resistance of the LDR and the voltage at the base of the transistor become small and the transistor and bulb turn off.

HEAT SENSOR

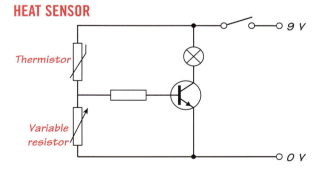

Remember, a thermistor has its resistance high in the cold and low in the heat.

1. The SPST switch is a master on-off switch. When it is open, no voltage is connected to the circuit so nothing can happen.
2. When it is cold, the resistance of the thermistor is very high. The voltage at the

87

base of the transistor is close to 0 V. The transistor will not switch on.

3. As it gets warmer, the resistance of the thermistor decreases. The voltage at the base increases as a result.
4. When it is warm enough, the voltage at the base reaches the trigger voltage for the transistor and the transistor switches on. This pulls a current from the collector to the emitter. The bulb lights.
5. When it becomes cold again, the resistance of the thermistor and the voltage at the base of the transistor become small, and the transistor and bulb turn off.

ELECTRONIC EGG TIMER/TIME DELAY CIRCUIT

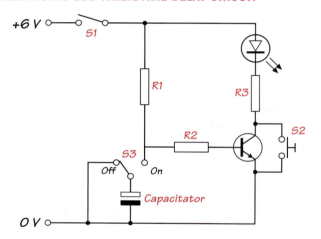

1. The SPST switch, S1, is a master on-off switch. When it is open, no voltage is connected to the circuit so nothing can happen.
2. S2 is a test switch to test if the LED and power supply are working. If they are, pressing S2 will allow current to flow from the collector to the emitter and the LED should light if the power supply and LED are good.
3. With S3 on, the capacitor begins to charge. As it charges, the voltage across the capacitor rises from 0 V. When it reaches the trigger voltage for the transistor, the transistor switches on. A small current flows from the base to the emitter, allowing a larger current to flow from the collector to the emitter. The LED lights.
4. With S3 off, the capacitor discharges. The voltage drops at the base of the transistor, turning off the transistor and LED. The circuit is ready for use again.

Notes:
- The capacitor is an electrolytic, i.e. polarised, capacitor. It has a positive and a negative, and has to be connected in the right way in the circuit.
- The maximum time delay this circuit could achieve is about five and a half minutes.
- If longer time delays are needed, you could:
  ▲ Replace the capacitor with a larger capacitor, but larger capacitors become unpredictable.
  ▲ Replace the capacitor with a 555 timer integrated circuit, which allows time delays of up to 20 minutes.
- If variable time delays are needed, you could:
  ▲ Replace Relay 1 with a 1M Ω variable resistor.
  ▲ Replace the capacitor with a variable capacitor.
  ▲ Replace the capacitor with a 555 timer integrated circuit.

TWO-STATE MOTOR CONTROL: TURNING A MOTOR IN EITHER DIRECTION

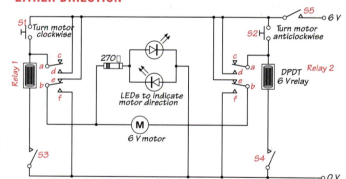

1. The SPST switch, S5, is a master on-off switch. When it is open, no voltage is connected to the circuit so nothing can happen.
2. S1 and S2 are push to make switches. S3 and S4 are lever microswitches acting as limit switches.
3. With S5 closed, S1 open and S2 open, both sides of the motor are connected to the 6 V line. There is no drop in voltage across the motor, so no current flows through it. It does not rotate.
4. With S1 and S3 closed, Relay 1 contacts switch: a → d, b → f. The left side of the motor is connected directly to the 0 V line and the right side of the motor is connected to the 6 V line, so current flows through the motor and it rotates (assume clockwise).
5. When S3 opens, there is no current through Relay 1. Relay 1 contacts switch back: a → c,

ELECTRICITY AND ELECTRONICS

b → e. Both sides of the motor are connected to the 6 V line. No current flows through the motor. It stops rotating.

6. With S2 and S4 closed, Relay 2 contacts switch: a → d, b → f. The right side of the motor is now connected to the 0 V line and the left side of the motor is still connected to the 6 V line, so current flows through the motor and it rotates. This time it goes anticlockwise.

7. When S4 opens there is no current through Relay 2. Relay 2 contacts switch back: a → c, b → e. Both sides of the motor are back at 6 V. It stops rotating.

Uses:
- As part of an automatic gate circuit.
- To open and close curtains automatically.
- To raise and lower a lift.

DIGITAL COMPONENTS

The electronic components we have seen so far have all been analogue components. This means they work with analogue signals. An analogue signal rises and falls in a continuous manner and can have all possible values in between, like the reading on a mercury thermometer, the petrol gauge in a car or the waves on the ocean.

Digital components work with digital signals. Digital signals can have only two values – on or off. These two values are also referred to as 1 and 0. A light switch in your house is an example of a digital component. The light is either on (1) or off (0) depending on the switch position.

Most modern electronic products like computers and mobile phones are built using digital components.

Digital circuits called logic gates are at the heart of **digital electronics**.

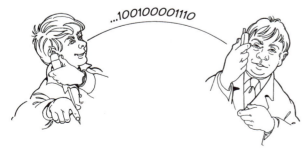

Modern mobile phones transmit a digital series of 1s and 0s rather than actually transmitting voices.

LOGIC GATES

The simplest type of digital component is a logic gate. Logic gates have one or two inputs and one output. Because logic gates are digital components, all the inputs and outputs must have a value of either 1 or 0. Logic gates are useful for turning things on or off when a certain combination of inputs is present. A 'truth table' is used to show what the output will be for all the possible inputs.

The main types of logic gate are described below.

INVERTER OR NOT GATE

An inverter or NOT gate reverses the input value it gets. It has one input and one output. If the input is 0, the output will be 1. If the input is 1, the output will be 0.

Input	Output
0	1
1	0

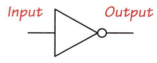

NOT gate: (a) truth gate (b) symbol.

AND GATE

An AND logic gate has two inputs and one output. The output will only be 1 if both inputs are 1. Otherwise the output will be 0. Can you see why it is called an AND gate?

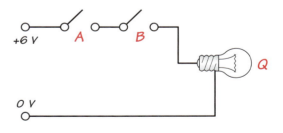

This simple circuit works like an AND gate: When A and B are closed, the bulb will light. For all other conditions, the bulb will not light.

A	B	Q
0	0	0
0	1	0
1	0	0
1	1	1

AND gate: (a) truth table (b) symbol.

89

JUNIOR CERTIFICATE TECHNOLOGY

OR GATE

An OR gate gate has two inputs and one output. The output will be 1 if either (or both) of the inputs are 1. The output will be 0 if both inputs are 0. Can you see why it is called an OR gate?

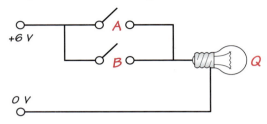

This circuit works like an OR gate. If either A or B are closed, the bulb will light. The bulb will not light if both switches are open.

A	B	Q
0	0	0
0	1	1
1	0	1
1	1	1

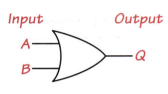

OR gate: (a) truth table (b) symbol.

NAND GATE

A NAND gate is the same as an AND gate followed by a NOT gate. This means the output of a NAND gate is the opposite of an AND gate.

A	B	Q
0	0	1
0	1	1
1	0	1
1	1	0

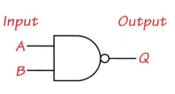

NAND gate: (a) truth table (b) symbol.

LATCH

With logic gates, each time the input values change, the output value may change depending on the new inputs.

A latch is like a logic gate, but once the output becomes 1, it will stay there, even if the input values that caused it changes.

Latches are useful when you want the output to stay on when the input that triggered the output has gone away. For example, if a burglar triggers a house alarm by opening a window, the house alarm should keep sounding even if the window is closed again. This is achieved using a latch.

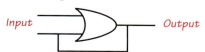

DIGITAL CIRCUITS/LOGIC CONTROL SYSTEMS

A digital system is one that contains digital components. In digital systems, logic gates are combined to perform more complex and useful tasks. Digital systems can be used in control systems. For example:

- heating and refrigeration systems
- washing machines
- dispensing machines
- machines for controlling water levels in tanks (e.g. in a factory).

The simplest digital system is made by connecting the output of one logic gate to the input of another.

For example, if a NAND gate was needed for a particular digital circuit, but was not available, how could you make it from other logic gates?

Answer: The output of an AND gate could be connected to the input of a NOT gate. Together, the AND gate and the NOT gate perform the same task as a NAND gate.

Truth tables can be used to find out the output of a combination of logic gates.

DIGITAL SYSTEM 1: COMBINING LOGIC GATES

Use a truth table to find the values of the output Q, for every possible combination of values for inputs A and B.

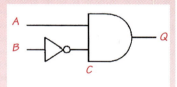

Answer
First calculate C from B. Then calculate Q from A and C.

Inputs		Intermediate Value	Output
A	B	C	Q
0	0	1	0
0	1	0	0
1	0	1	1
1	1	0	0

DIGITAL SYSTEM 2: COMBINING LOGIC GATES

Use a truth table to find the values of the output Q, for every combination of values for input A, B and C.

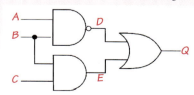

ELECTRICITY AND ELECTRONICS

Answer
First calculate D from A and B. Then calculate E from B and C. Finally calculate Q from D and E.

Inputs			Intermediate Values		Output
A	B	C	D	E	Q
0	0	0	1	0	1
0	0	1	1	0	1
0	1	0	1	0	1
0	1	1	1	1	1
1	0	0	1	0	1
1	0	1	1	0	1
1	1	0	0	0	0
1	1	1	0	1	1

DIGITAL SYSTEM 3: HEATING CONTROL SYSTEM

Question
A student's design for a system to control a heater is shown as a block diagram below.

The heating system must operate if the temperature is low and the timer is on. The timer produces a logic state of 1 when active. The heat sensor produces a logic state of 0 when it is cold. The system can be turned on at any stage with a master switch.

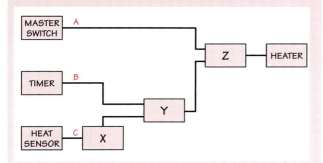

(a) Identify the logic gates which should be used at X, Y and Z in this system.

Answer
X must be a NOT gate, as it is the only logic gate with only one input and one output.

Master switch off: 0
Master switch on: 1
Timer off: 0
Timer on: 1
Heat sensor cold: 0, Output of X: 1
Heat sensor hot: 1, Output of X: 0

Output of Z has to be 1 when the master switch is on, or when the timer is on and the heat sensor is cold. In all other cases, the output of Z is 0, i.e. output of Z is 1 when master switch is 1, or when the timer is 1, heat sensor is 0 and output of X is 1.

If A is 1 **OR** B **AND** C are 1, then the output of Z is 1. So Z must be an **OR** gate and Y must be an **AND** gate.

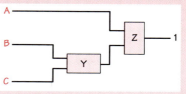

(b) Include a modification that will automatically turn off the system if there is insufficient oil in the heating tank or low water levels are detected in the feeder tank.

Answer
We need two new sensors, as follows:
Oil sensor (sufficient oil):   0
Oil sensor (insufficient oil):   1
Water detector (high water):   0
Water detector (low water):   1

The modification that will satisfy these conditions is shown below.

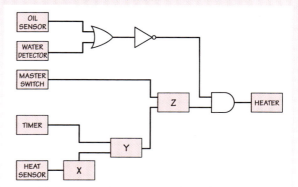

Put the oil sensor and water detector through an OR gate, then a NOT gate. The output of the OR is gate 1, if there is insufficient oil or low water. The output of the NOT gate is 0, if there is insufficient oil or low water. The heater cannot switch on in these cases as the output of the AND gate is 0.

DIGITAL SYSTEM 4: FORKLIFT TRUCK CONTROL SYSTEM

Question
The logic gates shown are to be used as part of a safety system in a forklift truck. Copy and complete the output from the truth table for the system shown and hence state the conditions under which the forklift truck will function.

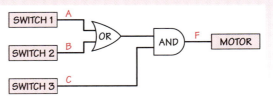

JUNIOR CERTIFICATE TECHNOLOGY

Inputs			Output
A	B	C	F
0	0	0	
0	0	1	
0	1	0	
0	1	1	
1	0	0	
1	0	1	
1	1	0	
1	1	1	

Answer

Inputs			Intermediate values	Output
A	B	C	(output of OR)	F
0	0	0	(0)	0
0	0	1	(0)	0
0	1	0	(1)	0
0	1	1	(1)	1
1	0	0	(1)	0
1	0	1	(1)	1
1	1	0	(1)	0
1	1	1	(1)	1

The forklift will function when:
- B and C are high and A is low.
- A and C are high and B is low.
- A, B and C are high.

In other words, the forklift will function when:
- Switches 2 and 3 only are pressed.
- Switches 1 and 3 only are pressed.
- All switches are pressed.

ELECTRICITY AND ELECTRONICS ACTIVITIES

1. Fill in the blanks in these statements.
   (a) Every circuit must have a _____ source to provide it with electricity. Usually batteries or mains are used.
   (b) An electric _____ is a flow of charge, usually along a wire or through an electronic component.
   (c) The higher the _____ in a circuit, the more power there is to drive the current.
   (d) A material that allows electric current to pass easily through it is called an electrical _____. The opposite of this is an _____.
   (e) A component that resists current flow through it is called a _____.
   (f) Components that allow current flow in one direction only are called _____.
   (g) Three-legged components that act like a switch are called _____.
   (h) Components that can store electrical charge are called _____.
   (i) _____ circuits are tiny chips that contain a tiny electronic circuit.
   (j) The moving part of a switch is the _____. The fixed part is the _____.
   (k) A switch operated by a magnet is a _____ switch.
   (l) _____ is measured in watts.
   (m) Resistance is measure in _____.
   (n) _____ is measured in amps.
   (o) Voltage is measure in _____.
   (p) Ammeters, voltmeters and multimeters are all test _____.
   (q) Every circuit has three building blocks: _____, _____ and _____.
   (r) _____ law states that V = I x R, i.e. voltage = current x resistance.
   (s) _____ signals rise and fall in a continuous manner. _____ signals rise and fall in a non-continuous manner.
   (t) AND, OR and NOT are all examples of _____ gates.

ELECTRICITY AND ELECTRONICS

2. Circle the bulbs or LEDs that light in the following circuits.

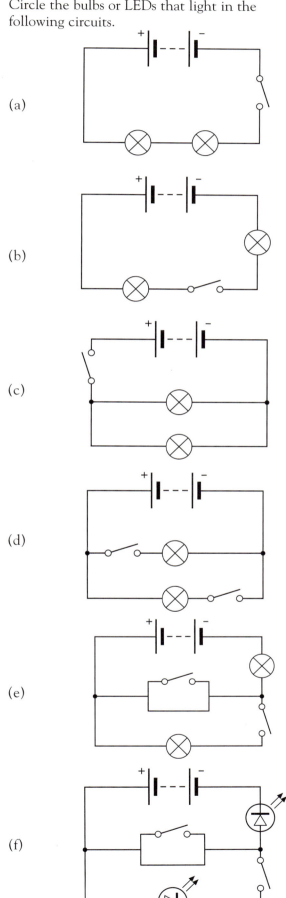

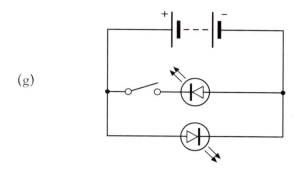

(g)

3. Design and make a simple tester to check cartridge fuses.

4. Using a light bulb, switch, battery and battery snap (holder) and some wire, make the bulb light when the switch is in one position and turn off when the switch is in the other position.

5. Design a circuit that will switch on a fan motor when it gets too hot in a room.

6. Design a circuit that will wake you up when it gets light in the morning.

7. Design a circuit that will sound an alarm when the temperature falls below freezing point.

8. Design a circuit that will sound an alarm when the soil in a plant gets too dry.

9. Design a circuit that will sound an alarm when the temperature in a greenhouse gets too hot.

10. Build the following circuit in your Technology Room.

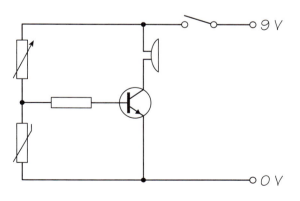

93

JUNIOR CERTIFICATE TECHNOLOGY

ELECTRICITY AND ELECTRONICS WORD SEARCH 1

S	C	R	E	T	T	I	M	E	J	N	P	F	U	U
T	M	O	F	C	N	T	S	Y	E	G	A	S	V	P
Y	N	H	L	O	N	R	H	G	Q	M	R	E	V	K
O	R	E	O	L	E	A	A	R	U	J	A	R	K	Z
B	J	O	R	D	E	T	T	L	O	L	L	E	T	D
L	J	F	L	R	I	C	A	S	Q	W	L	P	N	K
U	D	O	H	V	U	I	T	O	I	N	E	M	E	A
B	S	Q	E	R	T	C	E	O	S	S	L	A	D	N
D	G	F	E	N	B	R	O	T	R	B	E	X	N	O
U	S	F	E	C	A	P	A	C	I	T	O	R	E	D
R	O	T	S	I	S	N	A	R	T	D	C	G	P	E
K	O	E	L	O	P	B	V	U	E	E	W	S	E	C
P	S	B	G	F	G	B	X	R	L	T	M	Z	D	M
F	U	S	W	I	T	C	H	L	H	Y	U	I	F	Z
O	R	L	V	T	A	A	P	H	H	R	J	T	T	F

1. Long version of amps. (7)
2. This is one end of a diode. (The cathode is the other.) (5)
3. A device that emits light when current passes through it. (4)
4. A device that stores charge and is used in time delay circuits. (9)
5. An example is a push to break and single pole single throw. (6)
6. DC energy source. (4)
7. A leg of a transistor. (9)
8. The flow of charge is an electric _____. (7)
9. Light _____ resistor. (9)
10. The pin nearest the tag on a BC108 transistor. (7)
11. The sign of the charge on an electron. (8)
12. Whose law states that voltage = current x resistance? (4)
13. Components can be connected in series or _____. (8)
14. The negative or positive side of a battery. (4)
15. Voltage is also called _____ difference. (9)
16. The band on a colour code on a resistor corresponding to the number 2. (3)
17. Increasing this decreases the current. (10)
18. An alloy with a core of lead that melts readily when heated. (6)
19. What the T stands for in DPST. (5)
20. This type of component forms the basis of most electronic circuits that involve electronic switching. (10)

ELECTRICITY AND ELECTRONICS WORD SEARCH 2

```
A  S  J  N  D  E  E  U  K  P  L  B  L  O  A
F  A  N  W  C  I  B  G  N  H  U  P  O  V  M
N  Y  E  R  M  R  A  M  R  I  T  R  B  R  M
Q  O  U  R  E  K  E  G  R  A  T  T  M  W  E
F  O  I  A  I  A  L  E  R  T  H  S  Y  V  T
S  K  K  T  S  W  T  B  S  A  Y  C  S  K  E
P  R  I  U  C  H  R  P  V  R  M  B  I  O  R
S  R  R  A  G  E  S  A  T  E  S  R  S  P  H
K  E  C  I  S  N  R  H  Z  T  L  O  M  G  V
Z  W  R  G  E  D  O  I  D  E  M  W  J  X  E
U  B  E  M  J  O  V  B  D  M  B  N  B  O  S
F  L  A  S  H  I  N  G  M  T  O  X  J  B  I
V  F  R  I  D  G  E  W  A  L  S  M  H  O  R
B  H  K  Q  J  O  I  U  K  O  F  L  V  Q  R
S  X  Q  B  S  Z  T  D  L  V  L  D  R  A  W
```

1. Current will only flow through a diode in one _____. (9)
2. A type of meter used to measure current. (7)
3. Push to _____. (5)
4. If a bulb gets more current, it shines _____. (8)
5. The band on a colour code on a resistor corresponding to the number 1. (5)
6. Current is the flow of this. (6)
7. We represent electronic circuits by drawing a circuit _____. (7)
8. An electronic component that will allow current to flow through it if it is forward biased, but not if it is revere biased. (5)
9. A household appliance that could use a push to break switch to turn off the light when the door is closed or turn on the light when the door is opened. (6)
10. Its resistance is high in the dark and low in the light. (3)
11. A multimeter can _____ voltage, current and resistance. (8)
12. What states that V = I x R? (4, 3)
13. In the cold, the resistance of a thermistor will _____. (4)
14. A battery is an electrical energy _____. (6)
15. A type of LED that goes on and off when current is flowing through it. (8)
16. A type of switch with one pole and one throw. (4)
17. A simple picture to convey information. (6)
18. Watts, ohms, amps and volts are examples of these. (5)
19. A meter for measuring voltage. (9)
20. Used to join up separate components. (4)

JUNIOR CERTIFICATE TECHNOLOGY

PREVIOUS ELECTRICITY AND ELECTRONICS EXAM QUESTIONS

ELECTRICITY/ELECTRIC CURRENT FLOW THROUGH MATERIALS

1. Name two electrical conductors and two insulators.
2. Name (a) one good conductor of electric current and (b) one poor conductor of electric current.

POWER SOURCES

1. State the function of a transformer in an electric circuit.

COMPONENTS

1. Explain the following abbreviations: (a) LED (b) LDR.
2. Name an electronic component that allows current to flow in one direction only. Draw the symbol.
3. Which of these is the function of a fuse in an electric circuit? (a) Acts as a safety device (b) Used to amplify current (c) Backs up power supply
4. Name the two electronic components represented by the symbols shown.

   (a) (b)

5. This electronic component is a(n) capacitor/transistor/integrated circuit. Circle the correct answer.

   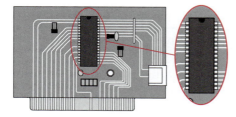

6. Clearly identify the location of pin 4 on this chip.

   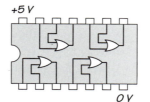

7. Sketch the electronic symbol for the capacitor shown.

8. Name the electronic components that are represented by the symbols shown.

   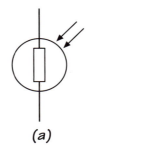 

   (a) (b)

9. Name two household items that use an electric motor.

10. This electronic component is a(n) resistor/transistor/integrated circuit. Circle the correct answer.

    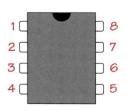

11. LEDs have one leg longer than the other to indicate that the long leg should be connected to the positive end of a battery/should be connected to the negative end of a battery/should not be connected to a battery. Circle the correct answer.

12. Why are resistors marked with coloured bands?

13. This electronic device is a resistor/transistor/light-emitting diode. Circle the correct answer.

14. The resistance of an LDR increases when it is light/dark/hot. Circle the correct answer.

ELECTRICITY AND ELECTRONICS

15. State the colour codes for a 2k2 resistor.

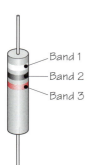

Colour	Value
Black	0
Brown	1
Red	2
Orange	3
Yellow	4
Green	5
Blue	6
Violet	7
Grey	8

16. State the value of the resistor shown in the diagram.

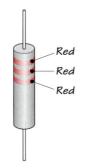

Colour	Value
Black	0
Brown	1
Red	2
Orange	3
Yellow	4
Green	5
Blue	6
Violet	7
Grey	8
White	9

17. The resistor shown has a value of 330 Ω. What information is given about this resistor by the fourth band (gold)?

18. Clearly indicate the location of the emitter on the sketch of the transistor shown.

Pin view

SWITCHES

1. Draw the electronic symbol for the components shown: (a) microswitch SPDT (single pole double throw) (b) diode.

2. This switch is a push switch/toggle switch/slide switch. Circle the correct answer.

3. This switch is a toggle switch/rocker switch/slide switch. Circle the correct answer.

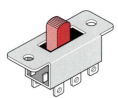

METHODS OF JOINING COMPONENTS

1. State one advantage of using breadboard instead of copper stripboard.

UNITS

1. Name the units used to measure (a) current (b) power (c) capacitance.
2. The bands on a resistor indicate its value in volts/amps/ohms. Circle the correct answer.

UNDERSTANDING CIRCUITS

1. An ammeter is to be used to measure the current flowing in a circuit. The meter has three settings – 2 A, 200 mA, 2 mA. Which setting should be used when measuring the current for the first time?

2. What would happen to this circuit if you covered the LDR?

97

JUNIOR CERTIFICATE TECHNOLOGY

3. Calculate the value of the voltage (V) as measured across the 200 Ω resistor shown.

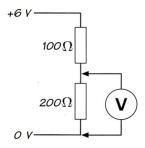

4. In which circuit (A, B, C) will the LED light?

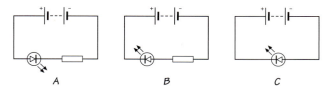

5. One of the components shown has been incorrectly wired on the copper stripboard. Indicate this component with an X.

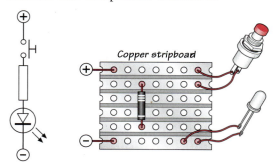

6. These bulbs are connected in parallel/series/parallel and series. Circle the correct answer.

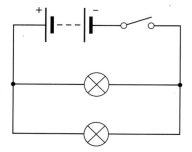

7. Clearly indicate how this circuit can be arranged on the copper stripboard.

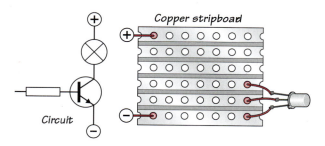

8. Complete the wiring diagram for this double pole double throw (DPDT) switch to allow the motor to turn clockwise and anticlockwise.

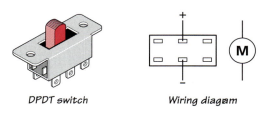

DPDT switch   Wiring diagram

9. Clearly indicate how the circuit below should be arranged on the copper stripboard shown.

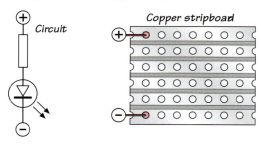

10. Calculate the current flowing through a 100 Ω resistor if a potential difference of 12 V is applied across it.

11. As part of a toy, an LED can be turned on and off using a switch. Draw the electrical circuit diagram for this toy.

DIGITAL COMPONENTS

1. A computer is a device that uses digital electronics. List two others.

LOGIC GATES

1. This logic circuit symbol is a(n) AND gate/OR gate/NOT gate. Circle the correct answer.

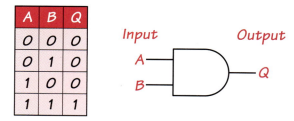

A	B	Q
0	0	0
0	1	0
1	0	0
1	1	1

2. State the meaning of any two of the abbreviations: COM, NC or NO (often found on the lever microswitch).

98

3. Complete the truth table for the logic gate shown.

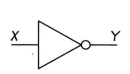

4. State the term for the arrangement of the OR gate in diagram 1 which keeps the output at 1 after the input changes from 1 to 0.

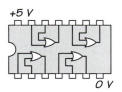 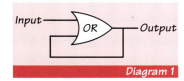

Diagram 1

5. This truth table is for a(n) AND gate/OR gate/NOT gate. Circle the correct answer. Sketch the symbol.

Input	Output
0	1
1	0

6. Complete the truth table for the logic gate shown.

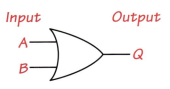

A	B	C
1	1	
1	0	
0	1	
0	0	

7. Which combination of logic gates, (A), (B) or (C), will produce this truth table? (a) OR + NOT (b) OR + AND (c) AND + NOT

A	B	C
1	1	0
1	0	1
0	1	1
0	0	1

SOME EXTRA ELECTRONICS QUESTIONS

1. Complete the table below using Ohm's Law.

Voltage	Current	Resistance
9	0.2	
12		4
9		18
6	0.05	
240	3	

2. A resistor has colour codes orange, orange and brown and is connected to a 6 V battery. An ammeter is placed in the circuit to measure the current flowing. Draw a circuit diagram and find the reading on the ammeter.

3. Describe how the resistance of an unmarked resistor might be found using a multimeter.

4. Draw a circuit diagram to show a diode connected in series with a bulb and a 6 V battery so that (a) the bulb lights and (b) the bulb does not light.

5. The current through a particular LED is limited to 20 mA by placing a resistor in series with the LED.
   (a) Draw a circuit diagram.
   (b) Calculate the value of the resistor which must be placed in series with the LED if it is to be used with a 6 V supply.
   (c) What value of resistor would you use in this circuit? Give the colour code of this resistor.

6. Name two household electrical appliances which use LEDs.

7. Draw a diagram of a buzzer connected in series with a light-dependent resistor (LDR). State what happens when they are connected to a battery. If a bright light is brought close to the LDR, what happens then?

8. In a fridge, the light comes on when the door is opened and switches off again once the door is closed. What kind of switch would you use to achieve this? Give a suitable circuit diagram of a circuit which behaves in this way.

9. Complete the truth table for an AND gate, with inputs A and B, followed by a NOT gate.

A	B	OUT

10. Complete the truth table for an OR gate, with inputs A and B, followed by a NOT gate.

A	B	OUT

10 TECHNICAL GRAPHICS

INTRODUCTION

The shape and relationships of objects can be difficult to describe using words, but a diagram can make this very easy. According to an old saying, 'A picture is worth a thousand words'. Most people find pictures and diagrams much easier to understand than words.

Drawings are particularly important in technical subjects because they are used to provide accurate dimensions for building or manufacturing the objects. Technical drawings are usually composed of straight lines, precise angles and shapes like circles and ellipses.

These days, computers also provide valuable help in producing high-quality drawings.

In industry, a product is usually built by a different set of people than the people who designed it. It is important to have a common language between the designer and the builder that shows ways of displaying information on different types of drawings. These are called **conventions** and are understood all over the world.

Graphical designs vary from simple sketches of basic ideas to complete working drawings. Graphics are used to show what something will look like when made, both in shape and size, and also to explain how to manufacture the item.

Outlines: thick and continuous

Projection lines: thinner than outlines

Centre lines: chain lines

Hidden outside and short dashes

Dimension lines: lighter than outlines and with arrows

First-angle orthographic projection

Graphical communication is an international language of communication. Like other languages, it has rules and conventions for its use.

At Junior Certificate level, freehand and ruled drawing is acceptable for most purposes, but it is even better if you can also use some CAD packages to introduce you to using computer graphics.

DRAWING EQUIPMENT

- **Drawing paper/sketch pad:** The most common type of drawing paper is white cartridge paper, which is available in various sizes and thicknesses. The sizes of paper most useful to designers are A4 and A3.
- **Pencils:** Pencils range from very hard to very soft. Hard pencils produce a grey line, while soft pencils produce a black line. You will need two pencils to begin with: a 2H to give you a fine, light line and a HB to give a softer, darker line. Soft pencils like 3B, 4B and 5B are useful to produce varying degrees of tone to represent shadow, but will make your drawing smudge, so use them with care.
- **Eraser:** Plastic erasers are more efficient and cleaner to use than old-fashioned rubber erasers. Use an eraser to produce highlights by removing areas of tone.
- **Sharpener:** You will always need to keep your pencil sharp, but take care not to get the graphite dust onto your drawing.
- **Compass:** Needed to draw accurate, neat circles. School compasses are fine, but to draw small, accurate circles, draughtsman's compasses are better.
- **Stencils/templates:** Using templates for circles and ellipses, etc. is recommended.
- **Underlay:** An underlay is useful if you want to rub on texturing.
- **Set square:** Set squares are used to draw a line at 90°, 60°, 45° or 30° to a straight edge on a piece of paper.
- **Protractor:** To draw angles other than 90°, 60°, 45° or 30°.

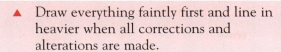

- **T square/tee square:** In the shape of a T, for drawing parallel and perpendicular lines.
- **Drawing board and parallel motion:** To aid your drawing you can use drawing boards with a parallel motion fitted, i.e. a wide ruler that can slide up and down over the paper. You can also use a drawing board and T square with the square pressed firmly up to the edge of the board so that your lines will be horizontal and parallel.
- **Masking tape:** Can be used to stick your paper to the drawing board, with the edges of the paper parallel to the edges of the drawing board.
- **Colours:** Coloured pencils are perfect for most colouring or highlighting tasks, though watercolours, markers, etc. may also be used.

GENERAL DRAWING TERMS

- **CAD:** Computer-aided design.
- **2-D:** Two-dimensional. A two-dimensional shape has only two dimensions of measurement: height and length.
- **3-D:** Three-dimensional. To draw properly, we need to use three dimensions that show objects as solid rather than flat shapes. A three-dimensional shape has three dimensions of measurement: height, length and width.
- **Freehand sketching:** Freehand sketching is an important skill. Practice is the best way to gain confidence. Everyone can learn to sketch:
  ▲ Use a soft pencil, e.g. HB or softer.
  ▲ Hold the pencil lightly. Move your whole arm, not just your wrist. Move your hand freely, using your little finger as a guide and support.
  ▲ Rotate the sheet so that the work is comfortable to your hand.
  ▲ When drawing freehand circles, first sketch the square into which the circle will fit exactly. Mark off the mid-point of each side, and sketch the circle through the four points. For ovals, start with a rectangle.

  ▲ Draw everything faintly first and line in heavier when all corrections and alterations are made.
- **Lettering:** Lettering on sketches can be done using a neat handwriting style.
- **Symbols:** Symbols are simple pictures to convey instructions or information without the need for lots of words. For example, maps contain symbols to represent bridges, railways, seas, etc. and electronic components have standard symbols for different components.

DRAWING TECHNIQUES

RENDERING

Rendering is the use of techniques such as colour, tone and texture to make your drawings more realistic. Rendering can create an impression of shape and form by shading with a pencil. Texture is the way something feels when you touch it. Artists create the illusion of texture in artworks such as paintings, drawings and prints.

Some common rendering techniques are:

- Soft pencils will give dense black areas of tone, which are good for creating contrast.
- Using the soft pencil to produce varying degrees of tone represents shadow or light. This is known as **tone shading**. When light falls on an object, the part closest to the light will be the most lit. The part furthest away will be the darkest.
- You can get a similar effect by using lines, dots and crosshatching. The closer the lines or the more dots there are, the darker the tone.
- Use an eraser to produce highlights by removing areas of tone.
- Use an underlay to rub on texturing.

COLOUR RENDERING

The use of colour (usually using coloured pencils) makes a sketch much more attractive. Colour rendering can give a feeling of solidity and reality to an object. Colour can produce emphasis and draw attention to certain features. The simplest techniques can prove highly effective. For example, using a coloured background to highlight a sketch is effective and simply done. Coloured pencils, watercolours or markers may also be used.

JUNIOR CERTIFICATE TECHNOLOGY

HATCHING, WOOD GRAIN AND SHADING

Hatching means to draw closely set parallel lines, as for shading and filling in drawings.

To represent materials using rendering – such as shading and wood grain effect – look at the following illustrations.

For example, to copy grain patterns on wood, take a piece of wood and copy the grain.

For shiny surfaces, e.g. metal, plastic, glass, a soft panel can reqpresent a shadow and a shine.

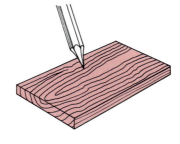

DIMENSIONS AND SCALE

Dimensions are measurements. Dimension lines are lines that are not part of the object itself but instead show a measurement from one point to another.

Dimensions are added to orthographic or working drawings, as this is usually the last drawing before manufacture, so dimensions must be clearly shown. Drawings are done to convey information, so measurements are an essential part of the drawings. Dimensions can also be added to simple sketches and designs, as they help the observer to understand the overall size.

Dimensions are usually drawn following a certain set of instructions:

- When drawings are not to scale, the dimensions given are the measurements of the object.
- Give dimensions in millimetres. Remember, 1 cm = 10 mm.
- Measurements should be upright when the page is upright, or when the page is turned 90° clockwise.
- Draw arrowheads small, sharp and neat.
- Keep dimensions a bit away from the drawing so they do not confuse or overcrowd the drawing. Where possible, put them outside the drawing.

- Draw dimension and extension lines lighter than the drawing outline.
- The extension lines should not touch the drawing outline and should extend just beyond the dimension line.
- Place smaller measurements closer to the drawing.
- When a dimension is shown in an elevation, it is not necessary to show it again in the plan.
- Ø is the diameter symbol. For example, if you are drawing a circle with a diameter of 100 mm, write Ø100 beside it to show this.

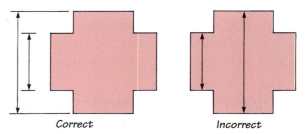

Correct and incorrect dimension lines.

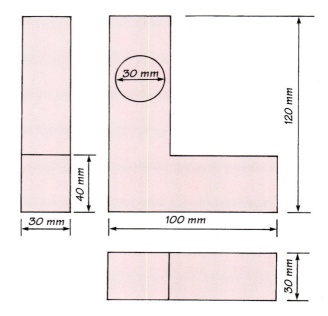

The dimension lines are correctly drawn in this first-angle orthographic projection drawing.

(There is more about orthographic projection on pages 105 and 106).

SCALE

It is not always possible to draw your design to full size, or scale, on the page. Sometimes the drawing would be too large to fit onto the page or it would be too small to read the sizes. Choose a suitable scale and write it on the drawing.

TECHNICAL GRAPHICS

Examples of scales are:
- A full-size drawing is 1:1.
- A half-size drawing is 1:2.
- Drawing shown at twice the size is 2:1.

HIDDEN DETAIL AND CENTRE LINES
Hidden detail is shown by dotted lines and centre lines are shown by dashed lines.

CONSTRUCTION LINES
Construction lines, i.e. lines you used to help you draw your object, are best left in the drawing. Do not rub them out.

BEND LINES
Bend lines show where material is to be bent or folded.

DEVELOPMENT
Take a look at any cardboard packaged item, like a cereal box. That package started life as a flat piece of cardboard. The shape was drawn on a piece of card, cut out, folded and glued to make the package. The flat, two-dimensional shape is the *development* of the package.

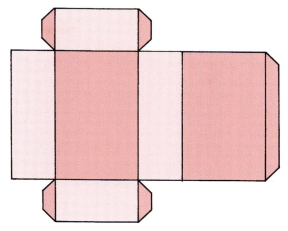

Development of a cuboid (2-D).

Cuboid (3-D).

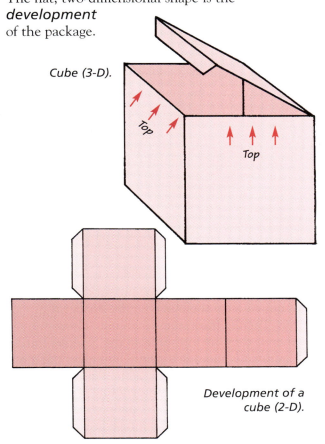

Cube (3-D).

Development of a cube (2-D).

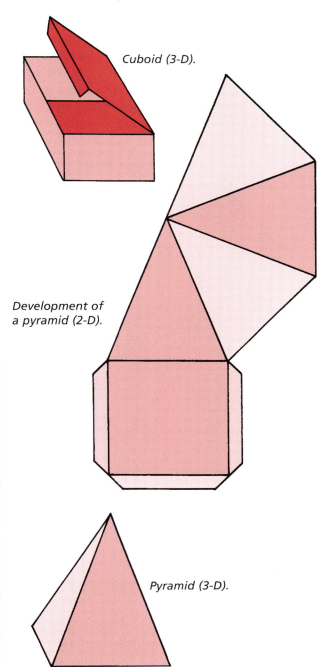

Development of a pyramid (2-D).

Pyramid (3-D).

103

JUNIOR CERTIFICATE TECHNOLOGY

PICTORIAL DRAWINGS

Pictorial drawings represent an object in picture form and are used to give an idea of the overall appearance of an object.

As our eyes are used to seeing in 3-D, we find it difficult to understand 2-D drawings. A pictorial drawing is much easier to read. There are three main methods of doing pictorial drawings:

- oblique projection
- isometric projection
- perspective.

OBLIQUE PROJECTION

All vertical lines on the object remain vertical in the drawing. Horizontal lines to the front remain horizontal, but horizontal lines on the top and side are at a 45° angle. The front surface is drawn in its true shape. The other two visible surfaces, the top and one side, are drawn back at a 45° angle.

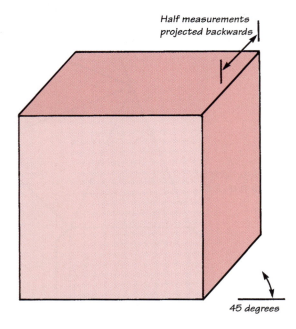

Oblique drawing of a cube.

To draw a cube in oblique projection:
1. Draw the front of the object with the original measurement.
2. Draw all lines backwards at a 45° angle.
3. All measurements drawn backwards are half the original measurement.

To help you draw oblique drawings, photocopying the oblique paper at the back of this book (see p. 146) may help you.

ISOMETRIC PROJECTION

All vertical lines on the object remain vertical in the drawing, but the horizontal edges of the object are drawn back at a 30° angle.

To draw a cube in isometric projection, follow five main rules:

1. Draw a vertical line for the edge that is nearest to you using the original measurement.
2. Draw all lines backwards from the top and bottom of this vertical line at a 30° angle.
3. All measurements drawn backwards are the original measurement.
4. Draw the two verticals for the far edges of the two sides.
5. To complete the top, draw lines at 30° (to the horizon) that meet.

Isometric grid paper, like that given at the back of this book (see p. 145), can assist in 3-D drawing. If you sketch carefully along the lines, it will help you to visualise an object in good proportion. Or you can go over the grid lines with black marker and use it as a backing sheet to be placed underneath your drawing paper.

Isometric projection gives a much more realistic pictorial view than oblique projection.

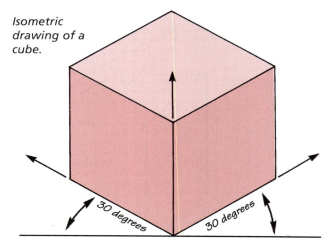

Isometric drawing of a cube.

PERSPECTIVE

Perspective drawing represents objects as you would actually see them. That is, the further away something is from the observer, the smaller it appears. Parallel lines seem to become closer together as they are further from the observer until they eventually meet at a point. This gives the most realistic pictorial drawings possible. Perspective drawing tries to capture the way a row of houses appears to get smaller in the distance, and the way a long straight road appears to vanish at a point on the horizon.

TECHNICAL GRAPHICS

When using perspective, the scene tends to converge to one or two points called the vanishing points (VP). There are two types of perspective drawing: single-point perspective and two-point perspective.

Single-Point Perspective

Single-point perspective is a little like oblique drawing in that you can begin your sketch by drawing a straight-on view of one face of the object. Next, position a line to represent the horizon (which is also your height relative to the object). The vanishing point is on the horizon line. Its position depends on where you are viewing the object from. Join the corner points of the front face to the VP. Complete the drawing.

Two-Point Perspective

Two-point perspective is more similar to isometric projection, as no face is straight on towards you. The horizontal lines will recede in two different directions towards two different vanishing points. The vanishing points are on the horizon line and also represent the observer's eye level.

Draw a horizon line and position two VPs. Position the front corner of the object and join to the VPs. Mark the lengths of each side of the object. Complete the sketch.

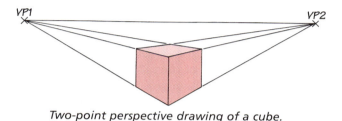

Two-point perspective drawing of a cube.

While pictorial drawings are excellent for giving an overall impression of the appearance of an object, they are less suited to representing all the constructional details necessary to allow an item to be manufactured.

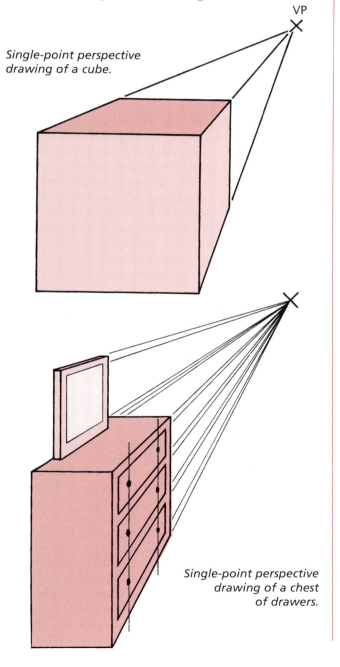

Single-point perspective drawing of a cube.

Single-point perspective drawing of a chest of drawers.

ORTHOGRAPHIC PROJECTION

An **elevation** is a view of an object taken straight on from a particular direction. There are six possible elevations of a house.

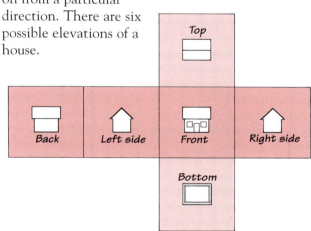

- **The front elevation:** The view looking straight on at the front of the object. This view normally carries most of the dimensions.
- **The end/side elevation:** The side view of the object.

105

JUNIOR CERTIFICATE TECHNOLOGY

- **Plan:** This is the view looking directly down on top of an object from above.
- **Orthographic projection:** A collection of different views of an object. Each of the views in orthographic projection is an elevation. Usually a front, side and top view are drawn, as these have the most useful information. Orthographic drawings are done when a design is at the point of being almost ready to manufacture. It is harder to visualise the object than with pictorial drawings, but is ideal for giving sizes and measurements, so is often used. There are two ways of doing orthographic drawings – first angle and third angle. They differ only in the position of the plan, front and side elevations on the page.
  - ▲ **First-angle projection:** This is most commonly used in Europe.

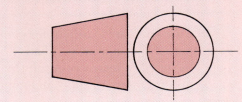

Symbol for first angle projection.

Front elevation	Side elevation
Plan	Layout of elevations on page for first-angle projection.

  - ▲ **Third-angle projection:** This is more commonly used in the US.

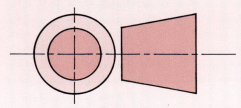

Symbol for third-angle projection.

Layout of elevations on page for third-angle projection.	Plan
	Side elevation	Front Elevation

SHADOW

To find the shadow of an object, draw an outline of the elevation of the object from the direction of the light source. Colour the elevation black or grey.

WORKING DRAWINGS

These are precise drawings that show details of the working drawings construction of an item, such as centre lines, dimensions, bend lines, hidden detail lines, materials, construction details and assembly instructions. This will help in the manufacture of the item that was designed.

Ideally, working drawings contain:

- cutting lists
- component lists
- tools required
- processes required
- skills to be acquired
- sequential plan of execution
- procedural sketches.

Most working drawings are in the form of first-angle orthographic projections, with pictorials to aid understanding.

INFORMATION BLOCK

Create a border around your drawing, and in the information block at the bottom display your name, date and the title 'First-Angle Orthographic Projection'. The symbol for first – or third – angle orthographic drawing must be shown on the drawing, not in the information block. Write titles carefully between faintly ruled lines. Stencils or transfers can be used, as shown below.

PROPER NEAT HANDWRITING FOR TITLES

Or using stencils

Or transfers

Use a 2H pencil or a fine black pen for the final outline. This will allow the drawing to stand out. The dimensions are usually quite faint, apart from the arrowheads and the measurement.

TECHNICAL GRAPHICS ACTIVITIES

1. Fill in the blanks in these statements.
   (a) Pencils, sketch pads, masking tape and T squares are all essential _____ _____.
   (b) Technical graphics done without any special tools or computers is called _____ drawing.
   (c) Technical graphics done on a computer is done using _____.
   (d) The use of techniques such as colour, tone and texture to make your drawings more realistic is called _____.
   (e) Hidden details on a drawing are shown by _____ _____.
   (f) Drawing closely set parallel lines as for shading in drawing is called _____.
   (g) The word for 'measurements' used in technical drawings is _____.
   (h) Dimensions in a drawing are usually given in _____.
   (i) The symbol beside Ø shows the dimension of the _____.
   (j) The _____ on a half-size drawing is 1:2.
   (k) A flat 2-D shape that can fold into a 3-D shape is called a _____.
   (l) _____ drawings represent an object in picture form and are used to give an idea of the overall appearance of an object.
   (m) _____ drawings are pictorial drawings that have horizontal drawings on the top and side faces drawn at 45°.
   (n) A type of pictorial drawing where vertical lines remain vertical and horizontal lines are drawn at 30° is _____.
   (o) _____ drawings can be single point or two point. They give a very realistic pictorial view.
   (p) A single-point drawing has one _____ _____ and a two-point drawing has two _____ _____.
   (q) A view of an object looking straight on from a particular direction is called an _____.
   (r) A collection of different elevations of an object is called _____ _____.
   (s) The most common type of orthographic projection used in Europe is _____ _____.
   (t) The block at the bottom of your working drawing page that contains your name, the date and the title is called the _____ _____.

2. Using freehand, draw a number of dots down the left and right side of a page spaced approximately 1 cm apart, as shown below. Join the dots horizontally.

3. Using freehand, draw a number of dots across the top and bottom of a page spaced approximately 1 cm apart, as shown below. Join the dots vertically.

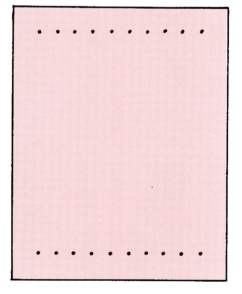

JUNIOR CERTIFICATE TECHNOLOGY

4. Draw the dot pattern as shown with dots spaced approximately 1 cm apart. Join the dots to produce a series of rectangles of decreasing size.

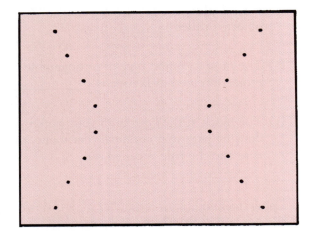

5. Draw a number of freehand circles of different sizes.

6. Apply tone shading to each of the objects below to show how they are lit from a light source positioned as shown. Use a soft pencil.

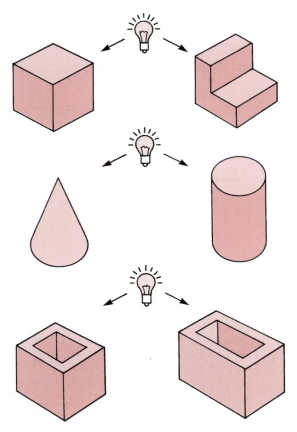

7. Choose a simple everyday item, e.g. a pencil box, CD, tissue box, a speaker, video or cassette box, and make a freehand oblique drawing of it.

8. Match up the flat package (development) with its corresponding first-angle orthographic projection.

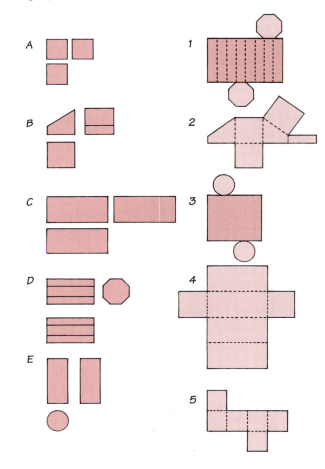

9. Draw the development of an open cylinder.

10. Draw the development of a closed cylinder.

11. Draw five 3-D cubes and make them look like (a) wood (b) leather (c) plastic (d) metal (e) concrete.

12. Draw four cylinders of different sizes. Make them look like they have light sources placed (a) above and to the right (b) above and to the left (c) below and to the right (d) below and to the left.

13. Have a look at a map. What is the scale? What does that mean?

14. Figure out which elevation matches which isometric projection when looked at in the direction shown.

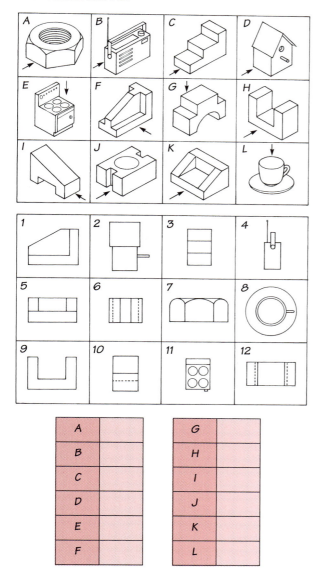

15. Figure out which elevation matches which oblique projection when looked at in the direction shown.

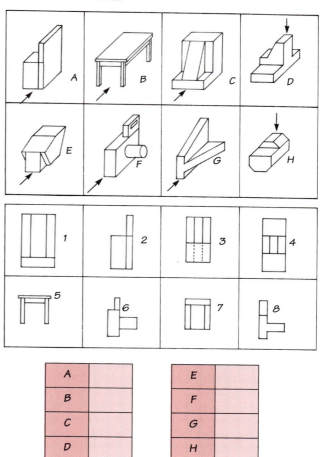

JUNIOR CERTIFICATE TECHNOLOGY

TECHNICAL GRAPHICS CROSSWORD

Across
2. The view looking down on top of an object from above. (4)
3. The elevation drawn on the top right of your page in first-angle projection. (4)
4. This type of drawing can be single point or two point. (11)
6. Computer-aided design. (3)
8. A type of drawing that represents an object as it really looks to the eye, like a picture. (9)
10. Applying colour, lines, dots, etc. to make your drawing more realistic. (9)
12. First- or third- _____ projection. (5)

Down
1. The point at which lines on perspective drawings seem to converge. (9)
5. Tells you what size your drawing is compared with the original. (5)
7. Measurements. (10)
9. Drawing without the aid of instruments. (8)
11. A 2-D shape that can be cut out and folded into a 3-D object. (11)

TECHNICAL GRAPHICS

PREVIOUS TECHNICAL GRAPHICS EXAM QUESTIONS

GENERAL DRAWING TERMS

1. Explain the meaning of the drawing terms (i) CAD (b) 3-D.

DRAWING TECHNIQUES

1. Explain the meaning of the hatched lines on the sketch.

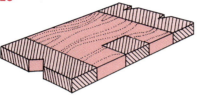

2. Shade the hand torch shown to suggest (a) part A is made from glass and (b) a light is shining on the torch from above, as shown.

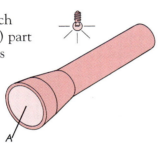

3. (a) Apply shading to the object shown to suggest a light source from the bulb position shown.

   (b) State two types of rendering that might be used to enhance this sketch.

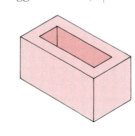

4. Which position (A, B, C, D or E) must the light source be in to produce the shadow shown?

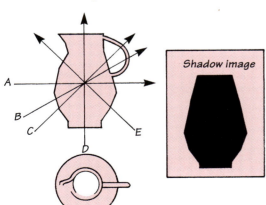

5. Use shading to indicate the materials shown on the sketch.

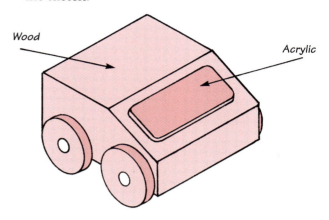

DIMENSIONS AND SCALE

1. On the drawing, clearly indicate any four dimensions needed to manufacture this template. Label the dimensions A, B, C and D and include the dimension lines.

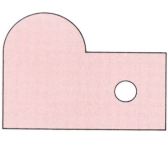

2. What are the values of the dimensions X and Y on the diagram shown?

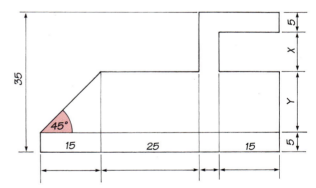

3. The length X in this development is 140 mm/70 mm/ 120 mm. Circle the correct answer.

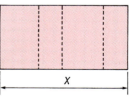

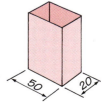

111

JUNIOR CERTIFICATE TECHNOLOGY

4. Clearly show four dimension lines on this sketch.

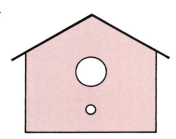

5. The length X in the development is 120/220/160. Circle the correct answer.

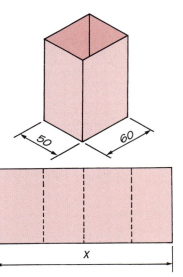

6. A working drawing is required of a cabinet with the following dimensions: width = 200 mm, height = 300 mm, depth = 100 mm. A drawing space measuring 30 mm x 20 mm is available. Which one of the following scales would best suit the drawing? (a) 2:1 (b) 20:1 (c) 200:1

7. Calculate the missing dimensions A and B in the drawing shown.

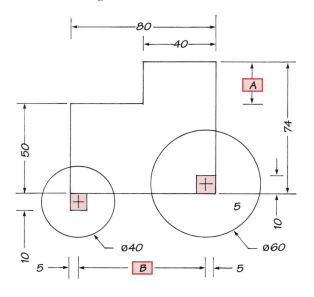

DEVELOPMENT

1. A development of a closed container is shown. Complete the isometric sketch of this container.

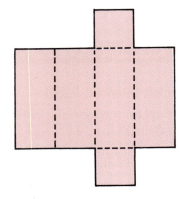

2. Complete the development of the closed cardboard box shown.

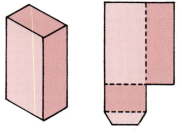

3. Draw the development of the dustpan shown.

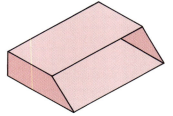

4. A development of a carton is shown. Make a 3-D sketch of the carton when the sides are folded into position.

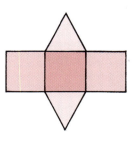

5. Which one of the developments, A, B, C, or D, will fold to make the dice shown?

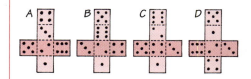

TECHNICAL GRAPHICS

6. The development of a cradle is shown. Complete the isometric view on the grid.

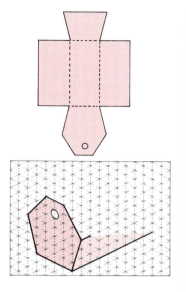

PICTORIAL DRAWINGS

1. What type of drawing is done at a 30° angle?

2. Complete the isometric view of the acrylic shape shown.

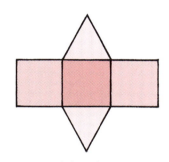

3. Complete the isometric view of the object shown in orthographic projection below.

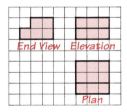 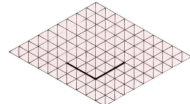

4. Show how to locate the two vanishing points used to draw the sketch shown.

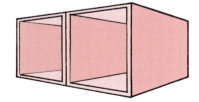

5. Complete this perspective drawing by locating both vanishing points.

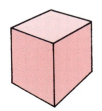

6. Locate the two vanishing points on this sketch.

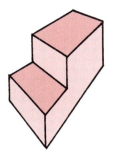

7. Locate the second vanishing point, VP2, in the sketch shown. Complete the perspective view of object X identical to object Y.

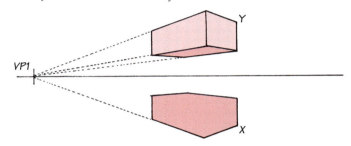

8. Complete the two-point perspective of the object shown.

ORTHOGRAPHIC PROJECTIONS

1. The sketch shows the plan, elevation and end view of a ladder resting against a wall. On the plan view (C), clearly indicate the location of the support ties T1 and T2.

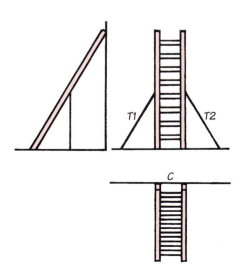

113

JUNIOR CERTIFICATE TECHNOLOGY

2. Which drawing, A, B or C, is the correct elevation when viewed from X?

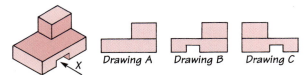

3. This radio is shown in elevation/plan view/pictorial view. Circle the correct answer.

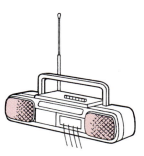

4. Which drawing, A, B or C, is the correct elevation when viewed from X?

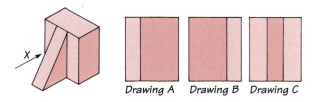

5. This railway track is shown in plan/ elevation/ perspective. Circle the correct answer.

6. What does this drawing show?

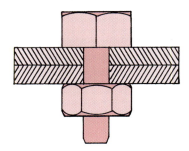

7. Which one of the shapes labelled A, B, C or D will fit correctly into the socket shown?

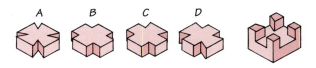

8. Sketch the plan view X on the grid provided.

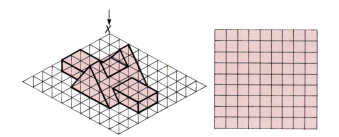

114

11 PROJECT

INTRODUCTION

You will probably do many projects over the course of your three years studying Junior Certificate Technology. These projects put into practice much of the theory that you learn in class, as well as teach you new skills.

You will work on your Junior Certificate project from the start of November until the start of May in your Junior Cert year. You should aim to finish it by the middle of April. It is worth 50 per cent of your marks if you do higher level and 60 per cent of your marks if you do ordinary level.

Each project is made up of a design folder and a product. This section deals mostly with the design folder. Chapter 10 is also a very important section for the design folder, as working drawings must be included. Making the product is covered throughout the rest of the book.

The design folder is worth 40 per cent of the project marks. The product is worth 60 per cent. You must do both well to get a good overall mark.

Projects you do in the first two years of your Technology course will not be as long or as difficult as your Junior Cert project. However, copy the style of the Junior Cert project each time.

A project is an undertaking that:

- Involves designing an artefact or a solution to a problem.
- Draws on your knowledge and skills.
- Results in a completed work.

The knowledge and skills that are drawn on include an understanding of:

- materials
- equipment and processes
- technical graphics
- computers
- possibly technology and society, electronics, structures and mechanisms.

When doing your project, remember:

- Presentation of the design folder and the product are important.
- The project must be your own work.
- All important operating features must be clearly seen without dismantling the product.
- For projects containing electronics, power sources must not exceed 12 V DC.
- Any switches must be clearly labelled. The voltage at which the task operates should be clearly indicated.

THE DESIGN FOLDER

For your Junior Cert project, the design folder should be:

- typed
- A4 size
- bound in a simple manila folder or better.

Below is a list of project stages that must be carried out and shown in your design folder. (This list is set out by the Junior Certificate examination board.)

- Brief (this is given to you by the Department of Education).
- Analysis of chosen task.
- Research – investigation of existing solutions.
- Generation of ideas.
- Selection and justification of solution.
- Drawings for manufacture.
- Mock model/prototype.
- Materials list, cost of materials, plan of manufacture.
- Testing and evaluation.

You may choose to add to this list or alter it slightly. For example, you may add a 'Developments and Improvements' or 'Summary' section at the end. You may decide to have a 'Materials List and Cost of Materials' as one section and 'Plan of Manufacture' as another section. You may add a 'Design Development' section after 'Selection and Justification', which would contain more information than the design idea.

However, you must ensure that all the project stages listed are carried out and are in your design folder.

JUNIOR CERTIFICATE TECHNOLOGY

You should also build a mock model before manufacturing your real product. Information on this can be added to your design folder.

Presentation is important in the design folder. Add photographs, overhead projector slides, video or audio recording as supplements.

BRIEF

A brief is the starting point for a Technology project. It will be given to you by your teacher or by the examination board.

It is usually in the form of a simple sentence or short paragraph. In the design brief, the designer describes, as accurately as possible, a problem to be solved, what the finished product should be like or what it should be able to do. Take the brief exactly as it is given. Do not add or change anything. The following are two examples of a brief:

- Using the materials supplied, design and make a CLOCK. A three-dimensional element must be incorporated into your design.
- Design the back of a cereal box. The design must include some kind of cut-out toy or puzzle suitable for children age 6–8. The cereal box will be cardboard and A4 size.

You will often have a choice of briefs. When choosing between them, consider the following:

- Are the necessary tools and materials available?
- Do you have time to make the product?
- Do you have the skills, and if not, would it be a good time to learn them?

ANALYSIS OF CHOSEN TASK

Break down/analyse how you could do the chosen task. The easiest way to do this is to list all the questions you can think of relating to the task, answering each as you go along. This takes the form of question, answer, question, answer, etc.

The analysis is a list of questions (about 20 often suits) to help understand exactly what is required. There may be some questions that come to mind easily, while others may arise later in the project. It is okay to go back and forward through the project to clarify your work. The questions asked should cover as many aspects of the project as possible.

Most questions should be answered, but it is okay to leave some blank if you do not know the answer at this stage. When answering the questions, do not be too specific. Do not say things like 'It will be a blue bear holding a yellow bucket', as you may change your mind as the project develops.

There may not be one set of key factors appropriate to any one problem or brief, but the following are worth considering:

- appearance
- colour
- cost
- environment
- finish
- function, i.e. what it will do
- maintenance
- manufacture
- materials
- operation, i.e. how it will work
- reliability
- safety
- shape
- size
- storage
- strength
- who it is aimed at.

Examples of questions that could be asked in analysis:

- Where will the product be used?
- Who will use the product or system?
- When will the product be used?
- What materials will the product be made from?
- How much money will it cost to create the product?
- Where will I get the resources from?
- How long will it take me to make the product?
- Will the product need much maintenance?
- How can I ensure that the product will be safe to use?
- When will I have the time to make the product?
- How will the product be protected from the weather or the abuse of the user?

PROJECT

Example of analysis for a project to design a child's lamp:

1. *How can I ensure that the lamp is totally safe?*
   I will ensure that the lamp is safe by:

   - Using materials in the lamp that are electrical insulators so that electricity cannot go through them.
   - Using non-toxic materials so that a child could not poison himself/herself.
   - Having no sharp edges or loose components that a child could cut themselves on.

2. *How can the lamp be easy for a child to switch on and off?*
   I could put the on-off switch along the wire so that the child would not have to put his/her hand near the bulb. The on-off switch could be large and brightly coloured so it is easy for him/her to see.

3. *How can I make this lamp appealing to small children?*
   I could use bright colours. I could use cartoon characters. I may even put the child's name on it.

Example of analysis for a project to design a safety helmet:

1. *How can the helmet be made strong enough to protect the wearer?*
   I will research materials until I find a suitable material that will not shatter on impact. I will also research what other safety helmets are made from and how they are strong enough to protect the wearer.

2. *What kind of foam or padding will I use against the head to absorb shock?*
   I will use some kind of strong foam or padding. I will research foams to find one that is suitable and that is good for absorbing shock. I will research what padding is in other safety helmets.

3. *What kind of safety straps will I use to prevent the helmet from falling off?*
   I will need safety straps that can tie tightly without hurting the wearer's neck or chin. It is important that they will not loosen over time. I will research what kind of straps are on other safety helmets to give me ideas.

Example of analysis for a project to design a weighing scale:

1. *What is the weight range that the scales will have to measure?*
   The scales will have to read from 200 g to 3 kg. Mostly it will be measuring around 1 kg.

2. *How accurate does it need to be?*
   Not too accurate. Within 5 or 10 per cent accuracy is fine.

3. *Should it be in pounds, stones, kilograms or all of them?*
   It should be in metric measurements only, e.g. grams and kilograms.

The priority of these factors will vary with the brief. For example, environment will be a high priority to meet a brief to design recycling bins for a classroom, and safety will be a high priority to meet a brief to design a child's toy.

RESEARCH – INVESTIGATION OF EXISTING SOLUTIONS

Find out things you do not know about the area/topic of the design. This may include answers to some of the questions you asked in your analysis.

Investigation leads to a clearer understanding of the limits of the design problem. First of all, you should read and understand the key words in the brief.

Having analysed the brief, you then need to research the problems. For example:

- Visit shops or exhibitions to view current products.
- Draw up a questionnaire to discover further information.
- Interview people about the problem.
- Visit libraries and read magazines and books to find further information.
- Write to and/or visit the relevant industry to discover more information.
- Take a similar existing product or system and analyse it carefully.
- Search catalogues, magazines and books; write letters; ask in shops/schools/playschools; ask at home and school; search the Internet; give questionnaires.

There should be a reason for each thing that you include in your project folder. To help with this:

- **Record what you find**, e.g. pictures, diagrams, charts, information.
- **Record where you find it**, e.g. website address, name of company or catalogue.
- **Record what use you think it has**, e.g. similar product, mechanism or appearance.

Do not just put in lots of pictures with simple explanations. For example, do not write 'This is a picture of a clock I got from an Argos catalogue.' Instead, write something like 'I saw this picture in an Argos catalogue and I liked the way it solves the problem of…using a…'. Draw and/or include pictures and write notes.

As well as researching the product you intend to make, research the materials you are going to use, e.g. research hardwood, softwood, manufactured wood.

Use sketches, charts, graphs and notes to record the results of your research.

Part of your research could include marketing. Marketing is working out who your customers are and finding out what they want.

GENERATION OF IDEAS

Design ideas should be neat, large, labelled, detailed, include notes, be in colour and be different. Ideally, the design ideas should be drawn in two-point perspective.

You should provide a minimum of three to five ideas. With complex problems, ideas may be created for parts of the problem rather than the whole solution. Use the following guidelines:

- **Look and adapt:** Look at existing solutions to similar problems. From these you can often develop ideas of your own.
- **Start drawing:** Start sketching ideas. Once you start to visualise possible solutions, many more ideas should come to you.
- **Brainstorming:** This is where a group of people get together to share ideas. It will usually trigger more new ideas for everyone.
- **Show your ideas to family and friends:** This will help you to see if they are good and whether you have explained them properly. You may even get some advice that will help you.

- **Choose a material to use:** First, know what each part of the solution will do. Then you can begin to identify an appropriate material for each part, considering the properties and cost of various materials.
- **Sketch ideas** freehand pictorially and in orthographic projection. Insert explanatory notes, possible dimensions, etc. Use a highlighting pen to pick out favoured solutions.

SELECTION AND JUSTIFICATION OF SOLUTION

First, the ideas must be evaluated. This is where the design ideas are looked at carefully. These questions may be useful for you to ask:

- Is it possible?
- Does the idea meet the brief?
- Is it achievable with the resources of time, materials, equipment and knowledge available? (Do not forget to check with your teacher and order materials if necessary.)
- Is it good value for money?

One of the ideas generated must be selected as the final solution. This solution must be justified. There are different ways of doing this, and the way you do it may depend on the complexity of the project.

For example, for a simple project you may decide that it is okay to state which design idea you are choosing and give three clear reasons for that decision.

For a more complex project, you may decide that it is necessary to go through each of the design ideas and list the good points and bad points of each. For each bad point, think through and possibly write about how you are going to fix it. It may not be possible to solve it, e.g. if a tool was required that you do not have access to. Writing out the good and bad points of each generated idea helps to make and justify the selection. Following the listing of the good and bad points, state which you have decided to do and why.

Make it clear exactly which design idea you are choosing. For a complex project, you may choose a combination of design ideas, e.g. 'For my toy, I chose to make design idea 1. For the circuit to make the eyes light, I chose to use design idea 5.'

PROJECT

DRAWINGS FOR MANUFACTURE

Prepare first-angle orthographic projection drawings showing all details of construction, all dimensions and finishes.

Prepare pictorial presentation drawings to show the finished product.

MOCK MODEL/PROTOTYPE

A key part of designing a product is modelling the proposed solution. The reasons for having a mock model are:

- You can see what your final product will look like.
- You can check your measurements.
- You can check if things will work.
- You can see if the size will be right.
- You can check proposed colours.
- It can help to find faults in the construction and operation of the design.
- You can see if the mechanics of the final product will work.
- It can help to stimulate new ideas.
- It can help you to choose suitable ways of constructing the final design.

Mock models can be made from a range of materials, but usually cheap, light materials are used, such as:

- art straws
- balsa wood
- cardboard
- fabric
- Lego
- lollipop sticks
- mechano
- paper
- papier mâché
- plasticine
- specialised kits.

You can also 'model' your electronic circuits. This can be done physically or by using software.

- **Physically:** On a breadboard or piece of wood with screws and wires.
- **With software:** By using special software on a computer, e.g. Crocodile Clips, you can test if your circuit will work. You can see motors turning, bulbs lighting and components blowing up on your screen!

MATERIALS LIST, COST OF MATERIALS, PLAN OF MANUFACTURE

MATERIALS LIST

List the materials you will use for each part of your project, e.g. 'I will use softwood (pine) for the base. I will use plastic (acrylic) for the frame. I will use 4 mm self-tapping screws, etc.'

List the tools and machines you will use, e.g. 'I will use the band saw and the coping saw for cutting the pine. I will drill with a power drill, etc.'

COST OF MATERIALS

Use price catalogues and the Internet to help you price the materials for the project. Ask your teacher to help you. See the sample cost of materials table below.

Part Number	Number of Parts	Description	Material	Dimensions	Finish	Cost
1	1	Clock (face)	MDF	Circle: radius 100 mm	Red paint	€0.30
2	1	Clock (back)	Black perspex	Circle: radius 100 mm	None	€0.30
3	1	Clock (mechanism)			None	€1.50
4	1	Clock (front)	Glass	Circle: radius 100 mm	Polish	€0.80
5	2	Hands	MDF	Long hand: 40 mm x 10 mm Short hand: 30 mm x 10 mm	Blue paint	€1.60
6	15	Numbers	Pine		White paint	€1.50
					Total	€6.00

PLAN OF MANUFACTURE

The plan of manufacture describes the processes you will use in order to make your design. (You can also list the tools and the machines here if you have not done it in your materials list.) A plan of manufacture is like a recipe for baking. It lets you know what you need to gather together for making the project. It gives you a step-by-step guide for working, i.e. what you need to do first, second, etc.

Your plan of manufacture can be done in the future tense ('I will cut the wood') or the instructional tense ('Cut the wood'). It can be adjusted once manufacture starts if you realise that something is not working out as you expected.

It is often a good idea to split the plan of manufacture into a few areas, like you would a recipe.

Example of the plan of manufacture to make a stage with curtains and lights:

For the stage
I will measure and mark the MDF wood. I will use the try square to get accurate angles. I will cut the MDF using the band saw…

For the circuit
I will cut my copper stripboard to size using a Stanley knife. I will collect my components and clean them using sandpaper…

For the curtains
I will draw my sizes on my fabric and cut them using sharp scissors…

For the people
I will draw my people on cardboard and cut them out using scissors…

TESTING AND EVALUATION

TESTING

The testing is where you discover whether your solution works, and if so, how well. It is done by placing the solution in its intended environment, e.g. in the dark, outdoors, with small children, and observing how well it works. Do so using sketches and notes to record it.

- Describe how you tested your made design.
- Talk about changes you made.
- Were there any problems?
- Did it turn out as you planned?
- Was it age/gender appropriate?
- Did it operate as specified?

EVALUATION

In the evaluation you assess the whole process, from deciding upon the task and the creation of ideas through to the manufacture and testing of a solution. The evaluation should identify faults in the process and lessons you have learned. Questions you may want to ask include:

- Did my solution meet the requirements of the brief?
- Does it work?
- Was my solution safe?
- Does it solve the problem it was supposed to solve?
- What are the good and bad points in my design?
- Did I manage my time well?
- Were the planning and working drawings adequate?
- What are the views of others about the solutions?
- Was it good value for money?
- Should I have chosen different materials?
- Is it pleasant to look at?
- Is it easy to handle?
- If this was in a shop, would I buy it?

For example, for a school bag you could ask:

- Is it big enough to hold the schoolbooks?
- Are the straps strong enough?
- Are the straps comfortable for the user?
- Are there pockets for lunch, pencil cases, calculators, mobile phones, etc.?
- Is it made from a hard-wearing material?
- Is there a strap/buckle on it to keep it closed?

DEVELOPMENTS AND IMPROVEMENTS

Now that the project is complete, if you had to go back to the beginning again, would you have done anything differently?

- How could you improve on your design?
- Is it worth improving?
- What would you do differently if you were to do this again?
- What could have made it nicer/better/stronger/more interesting/more suitable?

SAMPLE DESIGN FOLDER LAYOUT

Some sample pages of a design folder are shown below.

Page 1

Flood Warning System Project

Gráinne Enright

April 2006

Page 2

Contents	
Brief	3
Analysis	4
Research	5
Background information from books	6
Information from the Internet	7
Letter sent to companies requesting information	8
Response received	9
Generation of Ideas	
Design idea 1	10
Design idea 2	11
Design idea 3	12
Design idea 4	13
Selection and Justification	14
Working Drawings	
First-angle orthographic projection	16
Pictorial of finished product	17
Prototype	
Photos of prototype	18
Information	20
Materials List/Cost of Materials	21
Plan of Manufacture	22
Testing and Evaluation	
Testing	24
Evaluation	25
Photos of finished product	26
Developments and improvements	27

Page 8

Lovely Secondary School,
Co. Dublin.

Wet-Socks Ltd,
25 Flood Lane,
Dublin 6.

To whom it may concern,

I am a Technology student at Lovely Secondary School, Co. Dublin.

I am currently doing a project, the brief of which reads:

'Design and manufacture a flood warning system. The system should contain an external sensor and an internal warning device. The warning device should alarm when the external sensor is wet by rising water levels.'

I saw your advertisement in the Golden Pages. I would greatly appreciate if you could send me some information on the flood warning systems that your company manufactures.

Also, if you could answer either of the questions below, I would be grateful:
- How do you ensure that rising water levels trigger the alarm but rainwater does not?
- How do you ensure the safety of children and animals, as you have an electronic component held outdoors?

I enclose a large, stamped, self-addressed envelope for your convenience.

Yours sincerely,

Gráinne Enright

Gráinne Enright

Page 20

Prototype: Information

The materials I used for the prototype of my product were as follows:

- House: Cardboard (painted).
- Case for internal alarm system: Vacuum-formed box covered in fabric.
- Case for external alarm system: Cardboard.
- Electronic circuit: Breadboard.

Good things about my prototype were as follows:

- It worked.
- I liked the case for the external circuit.

Problems I found with my prototype were as follows:

- I do not like the colour brown I painted the house. I will change this to reddish-brown and paint in a brickwork pattern for my final product.
- The internal alarm system is too big and noticeable. There is no need for it to be so big, as the copper stripboard inside it will be very small. I will use a smaller vacuum-formed box instead.

Page 22

Plan of Manufacture

Electronic circuit

- I will draw out the circuit on the copper stripboard layout paper.
- I will cut my copper stripboard carefully to size using a sharp Stanley knife.
- I will put the components in place and follow the proper soldering procedures to attach them to the stripboard.
- I will test my circuit and fix it if it is not working.

Case for external sensor

- I will mark out my box onto pine, with the measurements as shown in the working drawings. I will use a try square to get accurate angles.
- I will cut the wood using the band saw. I will cut it approximately 2 mm from the marked line on the waste side.
- I will cut the joints as shown in my working drawings, i.e. two butt joints and the rest lap joints.
- I will plane, file and sand my wood until it is at the marked line.
- On the bench drill, I will drill pilot holes where I want to screw my joints.
- I will glue the joints together using PVA.

Case for internal alarm system
Etc.

House
Etc.

PROJECT ACTIVITIES

1. Fill in the blanks in these statements.
   (a) For most of your Junior Cert year, you will be working on a _____.
   (b) The starting point for this is given to you by the Department of Education. _____
   (c) The next stage, in which you will question the brief, is known as _____.
   (d) Next, using magazines, catalogues, books and the Internet, you will do some _____.
   (e) It is now time to generate some of your own _____.
   (f) In the selection and justification you must _____ one idea to do, giving reasons and information.
   (g) You could give more details in the _____ _____.
   (h) You must do detailed _____ drawings for your project folder.
   (i) These would often be done in first-angle _____ projection.
   (j) Using some kind of light material, like cardboard, fabric, lollipop sticks or balsa wood, make a _____ _____.
   (k) The _____ _____ gives a full list of the materials you will use and their cost.
   (l) The plan of _____ outlines the steps you will carry out when making your design.
   (m) After manufacture, you must _____ and _____ your product.
   (n) Finish with the _____ and _____ section, which gives you the chance to say what you would have done differently if you had the chance to start again.
   (o) When working on this kind of project, it is very important that you manage your _____ well and do not let deadlines slip.

2. Design a cut-out, fold-up toy suitable for including on the back of a cereal box.

3. Design and make a package to hold six table tennis balls. It should be colourful, attractive and strong enough to protect the balls from damage.

4. Design a DVD case for your favourite film.

5. Design and make a birthday card to send to your friends. It should have either a pop-up surprise or moving part inside, made from card.

6. Design and make a simple action toy made from card. It should be operated by moving a lever or linkage. Possible ideas include moving train wheels, animated toys, funny faces, etc.

7. Design and make a 'steady hand' game that will buzz if a wire is touched by a wire loop passing over it.

8. Design and make a rubber band-powered vehicle that will climb as far as possible up a sloping track.

9. Design and make a rocket (out of an empty mineral bottle) and a launch pad from which to launch it.

10. Design and make a wind-powered vehicle that moves freely in the wind.

11. Design and make a device to fire a table tennis ball as far as possible.

12. Design and make an artefact that will display three photographs. The artefact should be robust and be able to stand on a shelf.

13. Children's slippers can clutter up floor space in a bedroom. Design and make an artefact to hold four pairs of children's slippers. It should be wall mounted.

14. Given the following problem, write a design brief only for the situation. Problem: Your desk at home is untidy. There are pens, pencils, colouring pencils, markers, a stapler, paper punch, sticky tape and paperclips thrown everywhere. It is difficult to find things.

JUNIOR CERTIFICATE TECHNOLOGY

PREVIOUS PROJECT EXAM QUESTIONS

1. State two reasons for making a model as part of the design process.

2. State two questions which should be asked when evaluating a design task.

3. A bracelet was produced as a solution to a design task. State two questions which should be asked when evaluating the bracelet.

4. Identify two features which should be present in a bedside lamp suitable for small children.

5. If you were designing a safety helmet for cyclists, name two important points which should be included in the design.

6. Name two features which should be researched before designing a bathroom scales.

7. State two features that should be included in the design of a schoolbag.

8. A design task folder should describe a number of stages, including one on investigation. Name two other stages and briefly state what should be contained in each.

9. List four important questions that you should ask when carrying out your investigation.

10. List two important design features of a wooden swing structure.

11. List two safety features to be incorporated into a design for a desk tidy.

12. A design folder for a technology task should contain information about the investigation and the evaluation. Write a brief note about what should be included in each of these sections.

12 THE JUNIOR CERTIFICATE EXAM

INTRODUCTION

Your Junior Certificate exam is worth 50 per cent of your overall Junior Cert result if you do higher level and 40 per cent of your result if you do ordinary level. The higher level paper is split into three sections, A, B and C. The ordinary level paper is split into two sections, A and B. You have two hours to do the exam.

TOP EXAM TIPS

- Always read the question fully and answer everything that is asked.
- Follow the instructions exactly.
- Make sure your handwriting is legible.
- When sketching is required, make it neat, clear and well drawn. It must clearly illustrate the point asked for.
- Always do all the questions you can in section A. If you do not know the answer to a multiple choice question, then make your best guess. Never leave a blank.
- At the end of the exam, check over all your work, improving if you can, and tidy up drawings.
- If you have enough time, you should do extra questions from sections B or C. The examiner will take the questions with the highest mark.
- Do not use Tippex. Put a line through mistakes.

HIGHER LEVEL

HIGHER LEVEL: SECTION A

- **Summary:** Section A is a mixed, short-answer section, covering the entire course.
- **Marks:** 100 marks = 50 per cent.
- **Time:** Spend about 50 minutes on this section.
- **Instructions:** You will get marked for your best 25 questions in this section. There are 32 questions in total. It is best if you try to do all of them.

HIGHER LEVEL: SECTION B

- **Summary:** You must do one of two technical graphics questions. You must also do either a question on electronics or a question on mechanics.
- **Marks:** 50 marks = 25 per cent.
- **Time:** Spend about 25 minutes on this section.

HIGHER LEVEL: SECTION C

- **Summary:** You must answer one question out of four on one of the following: 'Technology and Society', 'Design and Manufacture' or 'Control Systems'.
- **Marks:** 50 marks = 25 per cent.
- **Time:** Spend about 25 minutes on this section.

ORDINARY LEVEL

ORDINARY LEVEL: SECTION A

- **Summary:** Section A is a mixed, short-answer section, covering the entire course.
- **Marks:** 80 marks = 50 per cent.
- **Time:** Spend about 50 minutes on this section.
- **Instructions:** You will get marked for your best 16 questions in this section. There are 20 questions in total. It is best if you try to do all of them.

ORDINARY LEVEL: SECTION B

- **Summary:** Section B is a mixed, long-answer section, covering the entire course.
- **Marks:** 80 marks = 50 per cent.
- **Time:** Spend about 50 minutes on this section.
- **Instructions:** You must do any two out of four questions.

STUDY GUIDE

When you are approaching the exam, do a final revision of each section, reading the theory and previous exam questions. If there are questions you do not know how to do, look back through this textbook. All the past questions are covered in the text.

Keep revising the symbols and glossary until they are fresh in your mind. If there are any that you do not fully understand, look them up for a more thorough explanation. You may want to employ a helpful brother, sister, friend, parent or other relative to ask you what the terms mean. Often saying things aloud for others helps to clarify it in your mind.

Read over the short questions. If there are any questions that you are unsure about, look them up in the index and find out how to answer them. But **do not waste time**. You are nearly out of time, and this is not the time to be learning new material!

Cover all topics. Junior Certificate Technology has a large amount of overlap between different sections, so all sections need to be covered.

Finally, **relax**. You will do better if you have slept well and are clear and confident going into your exam.

13 REVISION

QUESTIONS/QUIZZES

Do these questions when you have finished all the questions for the given section or get your teacher to do them as class quizzes. These questions are also a handy way of revising and testing yourself as exams approach.

HEALTH AND SAFETY

1. Always follow your _____ instructions.
2. If there are strong fumes or dust, wear a _____.
3. Untidy work areas are a safety _____.
4. Report injuries to your _____.
5. Know where the _____ _____ kit is.
6. If someone is getting an electric shock, turn off the _____ immediately.
7. Store your work in the _____ _____ assigned to you.
8. Never force a _____ blade.
9. Use a centre punch where you want to _____ a hole.
10. Remove the _____ _____ before drilling.
11. Use a timber support when drilling through acrylic so that the acrylic does not _____.
12. Do not use a mallet to _____ in nails.
13. _____ clothing should be worn when using adhesives.
14. When soldering, keep the sponge _____, but not wet.
15. When lots of students are soldering, _____ is needed to clear the fumes.
16. For a child's sit-on toy, the _____ of _____ should be low.
17. There should be no toxic _____ used in the construction of the children's item.
18. You can use gloves or _____ _____ on your hands if using adhesives.
19. Never remove _____ from the mouth of the plane with a chisel.
20. Switch off the _____ before inserting or removing a plug.

TECHNOLOGY IN SOCIETY

1. The Wright brothers invented the _____.
2. George Stevenson invented the first _____ _____ engines.
3. _____ _____ invented the submarine.
4. James Spangler invented the _____.
5. _____ _____ discovered radiation.
6. Vaccinations are available, which help prevent the spread of _____.
7. Waves that pass through flesh but not bones are _____.
8. Some _____ _____ have been linked to cancer, food allergies and hyperactivity in children.
9. In _____ _____ crops scientists extract a gene from a living thing and place it into a different food.
10. _____ have been used for thousands of years. Early ones were log rafts.
11. Aeroplanes have very high fuel needs, which cause _____ _____ _____.
12. A fax machine plugs into a _____ line.
13. A satellite is an object in space that travels around another object, such as a _____.
14. Photography is now regularly done with _____ cameras, which can be checked

JUNIOR CERTIFICATE TECHNOLOGY

directly from the camera as soon as the photos are taken.

15. _____ _____ are placed on supermarket items so that the price is scanned in.

16. _____ are used at ATMs.

17. Reduce, _____, recycle.

18. Cancer, asthma and global warming are all caused by air _____.

19. Plastic bottles may never _____.

20. Most of the environmental problems in the world are caused by the _____ World.

ENERGY

1. Energy is important – never _____ it.

2. _____ is what allows work to be done.

3. Nearly all the energy we use _____ came from the sun.

4. The energy you use in your body comes from your _____.

5. The type of energy we use to light our houses and cook our food is _____.

6. Mechanical, chemical, electrical, heat, light and sound are all _____ of energy.

7. There are two types of _____ energy – potential and kinetic.

8. Renewable energy means the _____ of the energy is still there after energy is taken from it.

9. Fossil fuel energy is _____-_____.

10. For solar energy, lots of solar _____ are required.

11. Solar energy is _____.

12. Water power is stored in a _____.

13. With hydroelectric energy, a water wheel, called a _____, is turned by water.

14. _____ _____ is released by using atoms of the metal uranium.

15. _____ _____ provides the majority of our energy in Ireland.

16. The principle or law of _____ of energy states that energy can change from one type to another, but it cannot be created or destroyed.

17. An electric pump converts electrical energy into _____ energy.

18. A battery radio converts _____ energy to _____ energy and then to _____ energy.

19. A TV converts electrical energy to _____ and _____ energy.

20. The most important room to insulate in your house is the _____.

MATERIALS

1. The most common materials are paper, _____, metal, _____, plastic and _____.

2. Appearance, feel, texture and colour are all _____ of materials.

3. Paper is made from _____ and from recycled _____.

4. Another word for fabric is _____.

5. Silk, mohair and angora are _____ fabrics.

6. Nylon, polyester and acrylic are _____ fabrics.

7. Tents are usually made from _____.

8. _____ are made from ore.

9. _____ _____ (or _____) is used in packaging to protect electrical goods when being delivered.

10. A substance made up of two or more metals is called an _____.

11. _____ comes from trees.

12. Wood contains natural _____ like knots, rot, resin and cracks.

13. Oak, elm, beech and ash are _____ hardwoods.

14. Mahogany, teak and ebony are _____ _____ hardwoods.

15. Plywood, blockboard, chipboard and hardboard are all _____ woods.

16. Manufactured boards may irritate the _____ and _____ when they are being cut.

17. Most plastics are made from _____.

18. _____ is a type of plastic used when making bottles.

REVISION

19. Saucepan handles are often made from _____ plastics.
20. Tiles are examples of _____.

EQUIPMENT AND PROCESSES

1. Before you can make anything, you must know what each _____ does.
2. Before using the tools, reread your _____ and _____ notes.
3. Tools operated by hand are called _____ _____.
4. _____ and _____ your material accurately is the key to a successful finished product.
5. The stiff metal back on a Tenon saw is usually made from _____.
6. The blade on a coping saw is too _____ to sharpen.
7. A _____ uses a shearing action to cut heavy sheet material.
8. To make a recess or cut into an awkward corner, use a _____.
9. Jack, smoothing and try are all types of _____.
10. A _____ has two smooth metal jaws brought together by a screw thread.
11. A tool used to hold hot material is a _____.
12. Panel pins are very small _____.
13. Files, rasps, surforms and abrafiles all cut using _____ action.
14. Screws that cut their own thread as they go in are called _____ _____ _____.
15. Doors, gates and lids usually use _____.
16. A machine that holds and cuts cylindrical material is a _____.
17. Changing the shape of a material is called _____.
18. _____ means attaching two or more pieces of material together.
19. A type of wood joint called after a white bird's tail is a _____ _____.
20. _____ is a type of colourless paint which provides a hard waterproof finish for wood.

STRUCTURES

1. Structures are designed not to _____ under a force.
2. A tie withstands _____ force.
3. Anything that causes acceleration, e.g. a push or a pull, is a _____.
4. A member opposing compression in a frame is a _____.
5. This member withstands tension in a frame structure: _____.
6. The unit of force is the _____.
7. The force acting on a tie is _____.
8. The force acting on a strut is _____.
9. A distorting force due to twisting is _____.
10. A load that is not moving is said to be _____.
11. Pressure = force ÷ _____.
12. It is important to _____ between the chain and sprocket.
13. Friction is a _____ that tries to stop one surface from sliding against another.
14. Certain materials under compression will get _____.
15. The _____ of a beam is increased by reinforcing it or changing the orientation.
16. A moving load is _____.
17. When a beam bends, one surface is in _____ and the other is in _____.
18. The _____ layer of the beam (in Q17 above) is neither in tension nor compression.
19. In a frame structure, members that are not in compression or tension and are not supporting anything are said to be _____.
20. The name of the principle by which many bridges, towers and masts are strengthened is _____.

MECHANISMS

1. Two pulleys with the belt crossed between them turn in _____ directions.
2. When oil is used to reduce _____, it is referred to as a lubricant.
3. _____ and follower.

129

JUNIOR CERTIFICATE TECHNOLOGY

4. A _____ is a mechanism made by connecting levers together.
5. _____ gears turn in opposite directions.
6. Another word for 'rotate' is _____.
7. The system will _____ if the wheel tries to turn the worm.
8. You calculate the _____ of a lever by multiplying force by the distance from the _____.
9. Gear 1 rotates at 50 rpm. It is meshed with Gear 2, which has twice as many teeth. Gear 2 rotates at _____ rpm.
10. A rack and _____ change rotary motion to _____ motion.
11. A _____ is a tool consisting of a rotating shaft with a parallel handle. A crank is like a _____ rod. The _____ allows the rod to be turned easily.
12. A _____ is a rigid body, free to rotate around one fixed point.
13. A system that changes linear to rotary motion or vice versa is a _____ and _____.
14. A gear is a wheel with _____.
15. A worm and worm wheel gives a big _____ in speed.
16. Ratchets are used to allow a wheel to turn in one direction only and to prevent it from _____ back.
17. When a shaft has two or more cranks, it is called a _____ _____.
18. One of the main tools of the _____ Revolution was the steam engine.
19. A round wheel with a _____ that a belt rides in is a pulley.
20. The main reason to use mechanisms is to gain _____ advantage.

COMPUTERS

1. PC stands for _____ _____.
2. A computer cannot _____ for itself.
3. Parts of a computer you can actually touch are called _____.
4. The microprocessor is the _____ of the computer.
5. Bar code readers, scanners and keyboards are all computer _____ devices.
6. Printers, plotters and speakers are all computer _____ devices.
7. Modems and faxes are input and _____ devices.
8. All CDs can read, but only some can be _____ on.
9. _____ look like CDs, but store much more data.
10. The _____ system is the program that lets all other programs run.
11. All big companies now have their own _____, which helps customers identify the company's products.
12. One megabyte is one _____ bytes.
13. One gigabyte is one _____ million bytes.
14. The tiny dots of coloured light on your computer screen are _____.
15. 'Backing up' means _____ spare copies of important files.
16. Another word for an image is a _____.
17. Another word for the letters and numbers you type on your keyboard is _____.
18. To shut down your computer, follow the recommended shutdown procedure given by _____ _____ _____.
19. CAM is short for _____-_____ _____.
20. CAD is short for _____-_____ _____.

ELECTRICITY AND ELECTRONICS

1. The flow of charge is an electric _____.
2. A number of cells connected in a series. _____
3. The band on a colour code on a resistor corresponding to the number 1. _____
4. Computer memory (also a male sheep). _____

REVISION

5. The band on a colour code on a resistor corresponding to the number eight. _____

6. Darkness causes the resistance of an LDR to _____.

7. The units of potential difference. _____

8. Short for light-emitting diode. _____

9. Often used to join up separate components. _____

10. This alloy is used to attach electronic components onto circuit boards. _____

11. A type of circuit board. _____

12. This logic gate requires two high inputs in order to have a high output. _____

13. A type of logic gate. _____

14. Long-range communication device invented by Marconi. _____

15. Device for storing charge. _____

16. These limit the size of current in a circuit. _____

17. One pin of a transistor. _____

18. A resistor whose resistance falls as it gets warm. _____

19. The unit of resistance. _____

20. Short for amperes. _____

21. These conduct electricity when they are forward biased. _____

22. Symbol for milliamps. _____

23. An electronic device with three pins: the base, emitter and collector. _____

24. Common energy source in a circuit consists of several cells connected together. _____

25. This melts readily and joins components together. _____

26. Short for light-dependent resistor. _____

27. Another name for potential difference. _____

28. This can be used to turn a circuit on or off. _____

29. A component used to make a time delay circuit. _____

30. Power is measured in this. _____

31. Components can be connected in series or in _____.

32. This changes electrical energy to motion, often used in projects to give movement. _____

33. These have two pins: the anode and the cathode. _____

34. A source of electrical energy. _____

35. If a switch is this, then current is zero. _____

36. The smallest part of an atom is the _____.

37. The value of a resistor is found by reading a series of _____ bands.

38. A complete _____ is required for charge to flow.

39. If the current is the same through two components, they are connected in _____.

40. A higher resistor will _____ the amount of current flowing.

TECHNICAL GRAPHICS

1. There are recommended ways of displaying information on different types of drawings. These are called _____.

2. The most common type of drawing paper is white _____ paper, which is available in various _____ and thickness.

3. Plastic erasers are more efficient and cleaner to use than old-fashioned _____ erasers.

4. School compasses are fine, but to draw small, accurate circles, _____ compasses are better.

5. Using templates or stencils for circles and _____ is recommended.

6. When freehand drawing, hold the pencil lightly. Move your whole _____, not just your wrist.

7. Using the soft pencil to produce _____ degrees of tone represents shadow or light.

131

JUNIOR CERTIFICATE TECHNOLOGY

8. The use of colour makes a sketch much more _____.

9. Dimensions are added to _____ drawings, as this is usually the last drawing before _____.

10. Measurements should be upright when the page is upright, or when the page is turned _____ clockwise.

11. Oblique, isometric and perspective drawings are all types of _____ drawings.

12. With oblique drawings, all measurements drawn backwards are _____ the original measurement.

13. You can go over grid lines with black marker and use it as a _____ sheet to be placed underneath your drawing paper.

14. The further away something is from the observer, the _____ it appears.

15. With both single-point perspective and _____ drawing, you begin your sketch by drawing a straight-on view of one face of the object.

16. With both two-point perspective and _____ projection, no face is straight on towards you.

17. In an orthographic projection, usually a front, side and top view are drawn, as these have the most useful _____.

18. Cutting lists, component lists, tools required, processes required, skills, plan of execution and procedural sketches can all be included in _____ drawings.

19. Draw titles carefully between _____ ruled lines.

20. For your drawing to look really well, create a _____ around it.

PROJECT

1. In your Junior Certificate project, the design folder is worth _____ per cent of the project marks and the product is worth _____ per cent.

2. The product and design folder must be finished by the date given by the _____ _____, usually the start of May.

3. Store your work in your _____ _____ as you go along.

4. You will be given a _____, which is the starting point for the project.

5. The phase after analysis is _____.

6. Ideally, design ideas should be drawn in _____ _____.

7. You should have a minimum of three to five _____ to choose from.

8. The phase after selection and justification is _____.

9. The final phase of the project is _____.

10. The main part of analysis is to ask lots of _____.

11. For _____, books, catalogues and the Internet are valuable resources.

12. _____ is working out who your customers are and what they like.

13. _____ is where lots of people get together to share ideas.

14. In selection and _____, each of your ideas must be evaluated.

15. In addition to orthographic projections, you should have a _____ representation of your final product in drawings for manufacture.

16. Balsa, plasticine, lollipop sticks and fabric are all useful for making _____ _____ or _____.

17. One reason for doing a mock model is to check your _____.

18. A plan of manufacture is similar to a _____ for baking.

19. The important thing to do in the testing phase is to describe how you _____ your product and what the _____ were.

20. You would ask 'Did my product meet the brief?' in the _____ stage.

REVISION

MIXED REVISION WORD SEARCH 1

O	D	A	O	P	T	M	R	K	E	D	S	R	I	V
U	R	H	L	E	S	E	K	L	I	F	P	E	G	A
L	J	T	L	L	T	A	E	R	T	L	R	M	I	L
K	L	L	H	E	O	V	R	E	V	V	E	M	Z	V
E	A	L	M	O	A	Y	N	T	F	M	A	A	S	D
M	V	A	I	T	G	S	F	J	W	Y	D	H	E	R
O	I	I	I	C	I	R	T	E	M	O	S	I	S	I
D	Y	O	S	O	E	L	A	C	S	L	H	P	A	L
W	N	W	N	E	D	R	P	P	R	H	E	H	B	L
V	G	D	Q	S	H	U	E	W	H	Q	E	A	A	N
S	Y	M	B	O	L	D	C	P	B	I	T	C	T	A
A	C	R	Y	L	I	C	A	T	P	B	C	K	A	W
M	R	I	L	W	N	A	F	I	I	O	K	S	D	M
G	N	I	P	O	C	H	C	N	G	L	C	A	B	W
H	B	R	E	X	U	S	O	M	W	H	E	W	O	L

1. Perspex is another name for _____. (7)
2. Another name for glue. (8)
3. Two or more metals mixed together. (5)
4. A type of saw for cutting curves, not as deep as a scroll saw. (6)
5. A type of metal commonly used in wires. (6)
6. A computer application that would be suitable to hold school records relating to each student. (8)
7. The widest dimension in a circle. (8)
8. A tool used for making holes in wood. (5)
9. This describes a material that can be drawn into wires. (7)
10. You could draw a front or side _____, which would be a 2-D front and side view of a 3-D object. (9)
11. A hand tool used for cutting metal or plastic. (7)
12. A tool used for hitting nails. (6)
13. A drawing of a 3-D object with angles drawn at 30°. (9)
14. You could use this to hit a chisel with. (6)
15. A collection of different views of a 3-D object is _____ projection. (12)
16. A type of hand tool, rougher than a file, but not as rough as a surform. (4)
17. 1:1, 1:3 and 2:1 are all examples of this. Written on technical drawings. (5)
18. A type of computer application that you could use to add columns of numbers. Microsoft Excel is an example. (11)
19. A drawing that conveys information. (6)
20. A tie is a structural member that resists this. (7)

133

JUNIOR CERTIFICATE TECHNOLOGY

MIXED REVISION WORD SEARCH 2

```
S U R X G M R F S F O G Q T G
X N V L O E O A E D Z Z U Z E
U E O M Z L T E L S B R N E A
A K E T L C O D G L T R F I R
C N M O W O M R G S I E F S C
T O W I A E E T O B K P T D R
G E M U B N N R G X Z O R L Y
R C D P N C T A M S P L O V E
P F M A R L I N E A R M T E M
E U C B R E S S O W Q S A U S
B S L U L Q S I T E H C T A R
O R K L Q H F S V A C U E C N
B V I O E R A T I R E Z Z U B
Z F M E M Y B O V O I N P U T
M O A O F U F R J W N D E L Y
```

1. The part of a project that you are given by the teacher/exam board, often a statement about a problem you need to solve. (5)
2. An electronic component that makes a noise when current passes through it. (6)
3. A strut is a structural member that resists this. (11)
4. Cam and _____. (8)
5. A wheel, often nylon, with teeth. It can be meshed with similar ones in simple or compound trains. (4)
6. These should always be worn when using power tools. (7)
7. Keyboards, scanners and microphones are examples of _____ devices to a computer. (5)
8. Abbreviation for light-emitting diode. (3)
9. Type of movement in a straight line. (6)
10. The clockwise one must equal the anticlockwise one. (6)
11. A device driven by electricity that outputs rotary motion. (5)
12. The units of force. (7)
13. A type of large, upright power drill. (6)
14. Similar to a sprocket, but a belt runs on it instead of a chain. (6)
15. _____ and pawl. (7)
16. Another word for turn. (6)
17. An input device to a computer that produces an optical image on the screen. (7)
18. The most important button on a power tool. (4)
19. The name of a structural member that resists compression. (5)
20. An electronic component with three legs: the base, emitter, collector. (10)

134

REVISION

MIXED REVISION WORD SEARCH 3

```
T V F S U R X C N B C Z Z V S
T H Q P L T I J S O J R H I C
F E E N O I T U L L O P A I R
G R M R W E R T B T A U C N O
W O E V M N E A I L K F K O L
V J T T Q I T N U R F S C L L
H M T V S T S B O E C H A R S
C P O L E A R T H X R W A A
R V Z R W I W U O O P C I M W
A R Y L C Y P I U R V E M C U
E R L A T M E K D P F C L U Q
S G N E O C H E M I C A L E Y
E T F C T L T R E V N O C A T
R A F I L E X A F Z S D N R W
S D I F U J B A M C Q I Y Z O
```

1. Common direct current source in a circuit. (7)
2. The thing that a nut threads onto. (4)
3. The type of energy stored in a cell or battery. (8)
4. This needs to be complete for electricity to flow around it. (7)
5. A type of hammer particularly used for removing nails. (4)
6. Device that contains a microprocessor as its 'brain'. It has input, output and storage devices. (8)
7. We cannot create or destroy energy, but we can _____ it to different forms. (7)
8. An office machine that can be an input or an output device to a computer. (3)
9. An abrasive hand tool or a collection of information that a computer uses. (4)
10. Another name for a scroll saw. (7)
11. A tool for cutting metal or plastic. (7)
12. Oil or grease is called this if it is used to reduce friction and wear and tear. (9)
13. He invented the radio. (7)
14. Dangerous gases cause air _____. (9)
15. The stage in a project where you check out what similar projects have been done or how similar problems have been solved. (8)
16. This is really important in the Technology Room! (6)
17. A type of saw much deeper than a coping saw for cutting ornate wood. (9)
18. This has changed a lot in the last 100 years. For example, now it can text, be mobile and have games. Alexander would be impressed! (9)
19. A type of resistor whose resistance drops when it is heated. (10)
20. You would use this type of square to check if your wood was square or to draw a line at 90° to the edge. (3)

135

JUNIOR CERTIFICATE TECHNOLOGY

MIXED REVISION WORD SEARCH 4

E	E	Q	V	B	Z	N	M	R	C	U	L	S	X	I
W	N	D	E	S	I	G	N	O	I	V	Q	L	G	G
S	O	O	L	A	C	I	N	A	H	C	E	M	D	H
U	S	O	H	H	B	V	J	I	Q	V	H	H	N	A
N	D	O	D	P	E	H	U	H	E	V	K	Z	A	I
G	X	J	L	R	O	E	S	B	N	R	T	S	H	A
X	I	K	S	X	N	R	R	L	P	N	L	G	E	N
V	V	I	Q	I	T	Y	C	O	I	D	A	R	E	U
O	O	I	B	T	P	W	A	I	T	D	G	I	R	R
N	J	R	O	C	L	O	T	H	M	O	E	D	F	I
M	U	O	V	A	I	T	N	R	S	D	M	R	D	G
T	L	L	A	T	E	M	O	E	F	P	U	Q	M	I
S	I	T	M	B	E	N	R	S	I	W	H	R	X	D
O	S	I	O	C	Q	V	F	N	A	L	P	J	D	S
L	I	Y	G	C	O	A	E	D	M	S	U	J	K	G

1. A type of gear that uses shafts at 90° to each other. (5)
2. Another name for fabric. (5)
3. When one type of energy changes to another type, we call this an energy _____. (10)
4. The type of folder you must hand up with your project. (6)
5. Drawing without using rulers, stencils or drawing tools. (8)
6. A common type of elevation. (5)
7. Type of paper with faint guidelines, sometimes used for drawing isometric or oblique drawings on. (4)
8. We should try to minimise heat _____ in the home. (4)
9. Abbreviation for medium-density fibre. (3)
10. There are two forms of this type of energy: kinetic (movement) and potential (stored). (10)
11. Material type: often hard, strong, may conduct electricity, may be attracted to magnets. (5)
12. An electronic device that converts sound energy into electrical energy. (10)
13. Converts electrical energy into mechanical energy. (5)
14. Very common softwood. (4)
15. A drawing of a 3-D object, looking down from the top. (4)
16. Stiff. (5)
17. Crank and _____. (6)
18. You probably have lots of these in your Technology Room, both hand versions and power versions. (5)
19. Used to convert wind energy into electrical energy. (7)
20. Source: trees. (4)

136

REVISION

MIXED REVISION WORD SEARCH 5

T	Y	F	A	B	M	K	L	S	C	R	E	K	L	O
S	N	S	L	O	L	E	M	I	O	N	Q	N	T	V
M	V	E	D	O	A	X	T	T	O	K	C	U	H	C
J	U	E	M	T	P	S	A	H	L	B	Z	S	T	R
I	L	R	H	P	A	P	P	L	I	E	R	S	N	
L	F	E	C	L	O	E	Y	I	K	I	W	E	P	J
A	R	F	P	L	L	L	R	E	S	I	S	T	O	R
T	K	Z	R	E	U	E	E	L	Y	E	J	N	J	M
I	T	N	T	I	G	F	I	V	Q	R	O	U	R	R
G	S	O	O	N	C	M	H	K	E	A	Y	O	O	O
I	G	O	D	O	A	T	P	V	C	D	S	C	C	W
D	E	N	D	D	I	X	I	Y	N	V	T	I	K	F
H	A	F	O	V	B	D	H	O	G	E	I	A	E	R
B	K	V	S	X	I	P	A	C	N	Y	C	V	R	P
D	D	S	T	C	I	M	A	R	E	C	K	F	E	T

1. A type of animal fabric often used to cover furniture. (7)
2. A hand tool for holding small objects. (6)
3. Mugs and plates are usually made from this material. (7)
4. We make one of these before we make our real project to help us check measurements and how the final manufactured product will look. (5)
5. The point around which a lever rotates. (7)
6. The type of electronics used in computers. (7)
7. A type of portable disk. (6)
8. It resists current. (8)
9. Type of switch usually used in a light switch. (6)
10. The material usually used in wrapping food. (7)
11. 2-D drawing of a 3-D object. (11)
12. Type of plastic often used in the Technology class. (3)
13. A type of screw used when you want the screw head to be level with the surface. (11)
14. Type of small garden creature, or something to use with a wheel. (4)
15. The key used to tighten and loosen drill bits. (5)
16. The type of force between brake blocks and wheels. (8)
17. A type of saw, so called because its blade is in a continuous band. (4)
18. Computer input device, commonly used in computer games. (8)
19. Marconi invented this. (5)
20. Bell invented this. (9)

JUNIOR CERTIFICATE TECHNOLOGY

MIXED REVISION WORD SEARCH 6

```
G F V W M C V C J T I P P P D
T R A N S P A R E N T E I X A
A M C T N P F K S L A R S A N
T L I H M Y C U D R L S T Z N
O G E C L O L C P N C P O J T
V T J T R A O P A Q U E N R W
I Z S P T O I Y H S Z C U W Q
P Y S I E E S T B L N T W L C
B F O L P A R W N O H I S A B
G N X X U D A W I E A V A I E
L A I R O T C I P T T E F R A
Y L E V E B F V M C C O E E T
B B A N D R H C E F A H P T C
U O T Z H Y Y J K X O N J A E
L W M M Z J X X A P O D X M L
```

1. Type of view or technical drawing of an object that is a bit like a picture. (9)
2. Another word for see-through. (11)
3. Not see-through. (6)
4. The type of energy in a wound spring or a weight held at a height. (9)
5. What we put in our attics or around our water cylinders to reduce heat loss. (10)
6. The name given to a bar connecting two wheels. (4)
7. The common way of communicating over long distances, before telephone and e-mail. (6)
8. Metal, plastic, fabric, ceramic and wood are all examples of this. (8)
9. The type of table we draw to show the operation of a logic gate. (5)
10. The value of a resistor is shown by a series of coloured ones. (4)
11. A small switch. (11)
12. Each one is 1.5 V. Batteries are made from them. (4)
13. This reciprocates (move up and down) in engines. (6)
14. Abbreviation for World Wide Web. (3)
15. A bike has one big one and one small one, connected by a chain. (8)
16. A sliding _____ is used to mark wood at angles other than 90°. (5)
17. A type of drawing where the object appears to get smaller as it is further away from you. (11)
18. When designing children's toys, the main question to ask is 'Is the toy _____?'. (4)
19. Gears meshed together make up a gear _____. (5)
20. To rotate around a fixed point. (5)

138

14 SYMBOLS

SAFETY SYMBOLS

Wear safety glasses.

Can be fatal.

Flammable.

Wear face guard.

Electrical hazard.

Wear breathing apparatus.

INFORMATION SYMBOLS

Recycling.

Wheelchair access.

Information.

Woolmark.

MECHANISMS SYMBOLS

Reverse motion linkage mechanism.

Push-pull linkage mechanism.

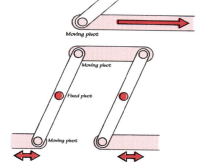

Bell crank linkage mechanism.

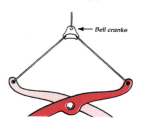

Parallel motion linkage mechanism.

Cam and follower mechanism.

Crank shaft mechanism.

Crank and slider mechanism.

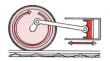

Ratchet and pawl mechanism.

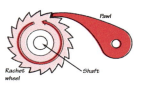

JUNIOR CERTIFICATE TECHNOLOGY

Driver, driven and idler gears.

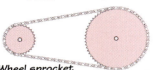

Chain and sprocket mechanism.

Worm and wheel mechanism.

Bevel gears.

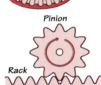

Rack and pinion mechanism.

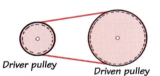

Driver and driven pulley going in same direction.

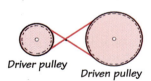

Driver and driven pulley going in opposite directions.

COMPUTER SYMBOLS

Macintosh Wastepaper Bin.

Microsoft Recycle Bin.

Paint software: spray can.

Paint software: paint can.

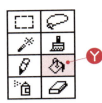

ELECTRONIC SYMBOLS

Electronic symbol: cell.

Electronic symbol: battery.

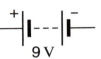 

Ohm's Law triangle.

Electronic symbol: LDR.

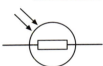

Electronic symbol: thermistor.

Electronic symbol: diode.

Electronic symbol: LED.

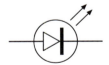

Electronic symbol: transistor.

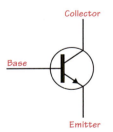

Transistor legs layout.

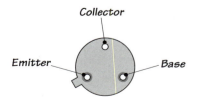

140

SYMBOLS

Electronic symbol: capacitor.

Electronic symbol: light bulb.
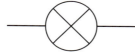

Electronic symbol: buzzer.
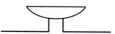

Electronic symbol: speaker.

Electronic symbol: motor.
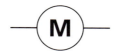

IC pins layout.

Electronic symbol: SPST switch.
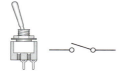

Electronic symbol: SPDT switch.
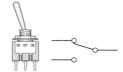

Electronic symbol: DPST switch.
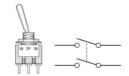

Electronic symbol: DPDT Switch.
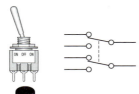

Electronic symbol: push to break switch.

Electronic symbol: push to make switch.
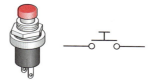

AND gate: truth table and electronic symbol.

A	B	Q
0	0	0
0	1	0
1	0	0
1	1	1

OR gate: truth table and electronic symbol.

A	B	Q
0	0	0
0	1	1
1	0	1
1	1	1

NOT gate: truth table and electronic symbol.

Input	Output
0	1
1	0

NAND gate: truth table and electronic symbol.

A	B	Q
0	0	1
0	1	1
1	0	1
1	1	0

Ammeter symbol.

Voltmeter symbol.

DRAWING SYMBOLS

First-angle orthographic projection symbol.
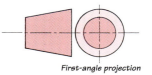

JUNIOR CERTIFICATE TECHNOLOGY

GRID PAPER

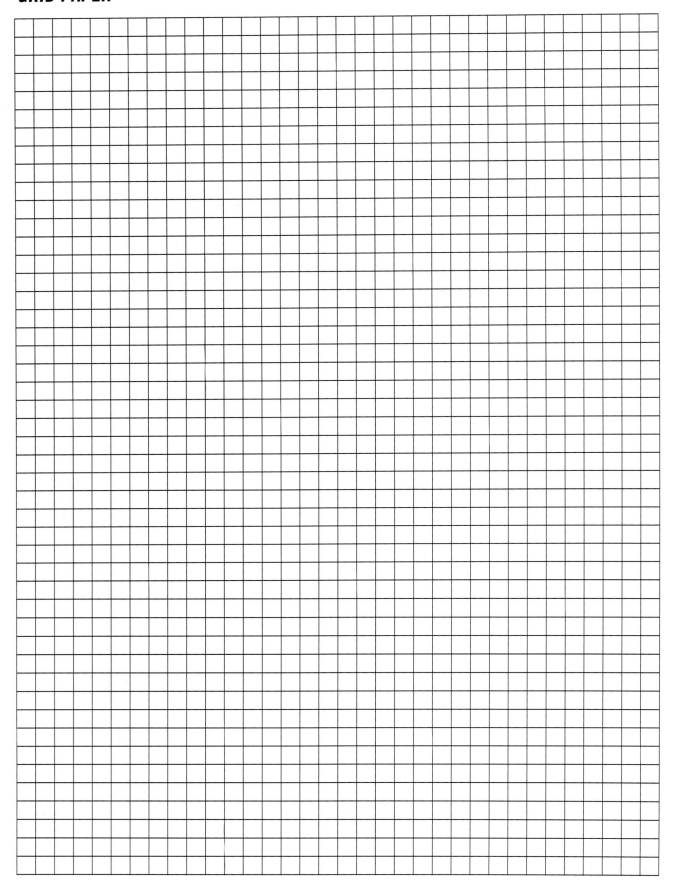

SYMBOLS

ISOMETRIC PAPER

JUNIOR CERTIFICATE TECHNOLOGY

OBLIQUE PAPER

SYMBOLS

COPPER STRIPBOARD LAYOUT PAPER

GLOSSARY

A

Abrafile: Looks like a coping saw, but files through sheet metal. Very good at cutting curves and round shapes.
AC (alternating current): Charge flows in different directions from an AC source.
Alloy: A substance made up of two or more metals.
Ammeter: A test instrument used to measure current in an electric circuit.
Analogue signal: Signals that vary in a continuous manner.
Analysis: The phase of the project where the brief is analysed and questions are asked.
Anodising: Coating one metal with another.
Anticlockwise moment: A force that tries to turn a lever anticlockwise.
Artefact: An object produced by humans, usually a tool or an ornament.
ATM (automated teller machine): A bank machine.

B

Balsa: A very soft hardwood, often used for models or for filling small gaps.
Band saw: A power saw with an endless toothed steel-band blade.
Beam: A long piece of wood, metal, etc. used as a rigid part of structures.
Bevel (or mitre) gears: Connects two moving shafts that meet at right angles.
Biodegradable: Can decay/rot naturally over time.
Bolt: A screw with no point. Used with a nut.
Bore: To make a hole in a material.
Brace: A tool to turn a bit by hand.
Bracket: An L-shaped support projecting from a wall, as in to hold a shelf.
Bradawl: Tool for making small holes in wood before screws are put in and before drilling.
Brief: The starting point for a Technology project.
Brittleness: How easily a material shatters.

C

CAD (computer-aided design): Software for drawing advanced technical drawing, e.g. drawing plans for a house, drawing a car engine.
CAM (computer-aided manufacturing): The process of using specialised computers to control, monitor and adjust tools and machinery in manufacturing.
Cam: Mechanisms used with followers. They are used to change rotary motion (cam) to linear motion (follower).
Cantilever: Bracket for supporting balconies, shelves, etc.
CD-ROM (compact disc read-only memory): A read-only form of storage with a capacity of about 600 megabytes.
CD-RW (compact disc read write): A CD that can be written on.
Centre of gravity: The point in an object from where the whole body weight appears to act. If the centre of gravity is low, the object is stable. If it is high, the object is unstable.
Chemical energy: Stored in food, coal, oil, petrol and electric batteries.
Chisel: A hand tool for making small cuts and getting into recesses.
Circuit: A path or loop of components put together in different ways, connected by wires. The path starts and finishes at the power source.
Clamp: A tool that holds two or more pieces of material together. Same as a cramp.
Clockwise moment: A force that tries to turn a lever clockwise.
COM: Common, e.g. the common leg on a lever microswitch.
Component: Electronic devices like resistors, capacitors, diodes, etc.
Compression: Being pressed into less space, being flattened by pressure.
Computer input device: A device used to input information from the user to the computer, e.g. keyboard, mouse, scanner.
Computer output device: A device used to get information to the user from the computer, e.g. monitor, printer, speakers.
Computer storage device: A device onto which information can be stored from a computer, e.g. hard disk, floppy disk, CD-ROM, DVD.
Conductor (electrical): Material that allows an electric current to pass through it easily. Usually metal.
Conductor (heat): Material that allows heat to pass through it easily.

GLOSSARY

Coping saw: Hand saw used for cutting curves in wood, with a narrow blade in tension.
Corrosive: Harmful, caustic substance that can corrode or eat away, e.g. acid.
Countersunk: Sloping hole, sunk into material.
CPU (central processing unit): The part of the computer that does all the work, or the 'brain' of the computer.
Cramp: See 'Clamp'.
Crank and slider mechanism: Mechanism often used to rotate the wheels of steam trains, composed of a crank, a slider and a connecting rod.
Cross filing: Used to remove waste material and to file down to a line.
Current: See 'Electric current'.

D

Database: Software suitable for storing lots of information related to a person or object, e.g. storing school information for pupils, storing insurance and tax information for cars.
DC (direct current): Charge only flows in one direction from a DC source.
Device: Something designed for a particular purpose, especially a machine.
Die: A tool that cuts threads on screws and bolts.
Digital signal: Signal that varies in a non-continuous manner.
Dimension: A measure of something, especially width, height or length.
Diode: Semiconductor device that allows the current to flow in one direction only.
Disposable: Designed to be thrown away after use.
Dovetail joint: Strong joint where the pieces of wood are shaped like doves' tails.
DPDT switch: Double pole double throw switch.
DPDTCO switch: Double pole double throw centre off switch.
DPST switch: Double pole single throw switch.
Draw filing: Done with a smooth file to give a smooth, shiny finish to the work.
Ductile: Can be drawn into wires.
DVD: Digital Versatile Disk.

E

Eco-friendly: Something that is friendly to the environment, e.g. made from recycled parts, solar powered, biodegradable, etc.
Efficiency: (Energy out ÷ energy in) x 100%, or (work out ÷ work in) x 100%.
Elasticity: How much a material can stretch without being permanently damaged.
Electric current: The flow of electrons/the flow of charge.
Electrical energy: Movement of electrons through an electrical conductor.
Electromechanical relay: See 'Relay'.
Elevation: A view of an object taken straight on from a particular direction.
Energy conversion: Converting energy from one form to another, e.g. solar energy to light energy.
Energy: Allows work to be done.
Engine: A machine that uses fuel to make something move.
Engineer: A person who plans, makes or looks after machines, roads, bridges, etc.
Evaluation: The phase in a project where the final solution is judged and its success or failure is analysed.

F

Feedback: When the output is fed back into the input in CAM.
Ferrous metal: Metal containing iron, attracted to magnets.
File (computers): A collection of information that a computer uses.
File (tools): A tool to shape wood, plastic or metal and smooth edges, curves and holes.
Fixed resistors: Colour-coded components that resist the flow of current through a circuit. The amount that they can resist it is fixed.
Follower: Reciprocates, i.e. goes up and down, following the rotation of a cam.
Fossil fuels: Fuels that formed over millions of years from fossils, e.g. coal, oil, gas and peat.
Fossil: Plant and animal remains.
Fret saw: See 'Scroll saw'.
Friction: A force that opposes the motion of a body when it is in contact with another body.
Function: The action that a particular item does, how it works, what its job is.
Fuse: A short, thin piece of wire placed in something electrical, which melts or 'blows' if too much current passes through it.

G

Gear: Toothed wheel that can drive other such wheels.
Gigabytes (GB): One thousand megabytes.
Glass paper: Ground glass stuck onto strong backing paper.
Glaze: To cover with a smooth, glossy surface. This is how you finish ceramics, e.g. mugs.
GM (genetic modification): Crops in which scientist have placed a gene extracted from a different living plant, animal or person. This

creates new varieties of plants that could not have been created by nature.

Guillotine: Uses a shearing action to cut heavy sheet materials.

H

Hacksaw: Hand saw for cutting straight lines in metal.

Hazard: A possible source of danger.

Hydraulic: Using the energy stored in compressed oil.

I

Idler gear: Gear placed between the driver gear and driven gears. The idler gear only changes the direction of the driven gear.

Insulator (electrical): Material that does not allow electricity to pass through it easily. These are usually plastic.

Insulator (heat): Material that does not allow heat to pass through it easily.

Integrated circuit: A tiny electronic circuit on a single computer chip.

Isometric drawing: Pictorial drawing done with horizontal lines drawn at 30° angles.

J

Junior hacksaw: Small version of the hacksaw.

K

Kilobyte (KB): One thousand bytes.

L

Laser: An apparatus with a strong, narrow beam of light used to cut materials, send messages, etc.

Latch: The output value changes when the input changes, and stays at the new value even if the input changes back.

LCD (liquid crystal display): Special display systems for use with computers and digital watches.

LDR (light-dependent resistor): Component whose resistance is high in darkness and low in brightness.

LED (light-emitting diode): Device with coloured top that gives off light when current flows through it.

Lever: A rigid body that can rotate around a fixed point, called a fulcrum.

Logo: A name, symbol or trademark designed for easy and definite recognition.

Lubricant: Oil or grease used to reduce friction in moving parts.

M

Magnet: An object, such as a piece of iron, steel, etc. that can draw iron (or ferrous metals) towards it.

Malleable: Can be stretched or shaped by hammering or by pressure from rollers.

Mallet: Like a big, wooden hammer.

Mechanical advantage: Load ÷ effort.

Megabytes (MB): One million bytes.

Microcomputer: A small computer (PC) that fits on a table or desk and can be used at home or at school.

Microprocessor: The integrated circuit that controls a microcomputer.

Microwave: 1. Type of radio waves. 2. Short for microwave oven, an oven in which food is cooked very quickly by microwaves entering the food.

Mine: A hole, usually under the ground, from which coal, gold, tin, etc. are dug.

Moment: Something that tries to turn a lever. Moment = force x distance from the fulcrum. For a lever to be balanced the clockwise moment must equal the anticlockwise moment.

Monitor: An instrument like a television screen on which the results of computer programs can be shown.

Motor: A machine that changes electrical power into rotating movement.

Multimeter: Test instrument or tool used to measure voltage, current and resistance by changing setting.

N

NC: Normally closed.

NO: Normally open.

Non-renewable energy: Energy from non-renewable sources, e.g. oil, gas, coal, peat, nuclear.

Non-ferrous metal: Metal that contains no iron.

O

Oblique drawings: Pictorial drawing with horizontal lines drawn at 45° angles.

Ohm's Law: V = I x R (i.e. voltage = current x resistance).

Opaque: Light cannot pass through.

Operating system: Software that runs on your computer to let it run other software, e.g. Windows 98 is an operating system for PCs.

GLOSSARY

P

Painting: Coating a surface with a coloured substance.

Pincers: Used to pull out small nails and to cut the heads off small nails.

Piston: A mechanical device that moves in and out.

Plan: A view of an object drawn from above.

Plane: Tool to remove waste wood when the amount is too thin to be cut with a saw.

Plastic memory: The way thermoplastics remember the shape they first were.

Pliers: A gripping hand tool with two hinged arms and serrated jaws.

Plotter: Like a printer, but especially for drawing. Used by CAD software.

Pneumatic: Using the energy stored in compressed air.

Polarity: Some circuit components have positive and negative sides and only work if they are connected in a certain way. These components have polarity.

Pole (power source): A moving wire in a switch that can make contact with one or more throws.

Pole (switch): A moving wire in a switch that can make contact with one or more throws.

Polishing: Making smooth and glossy by rubbing.

Potential divider: Using resistors to divide up a voltage to get a lower voltage.

Potentiometer: See 'Variable resistor'.

Power: Electrical or mechanical energy. The amount of work done in a unit of time.

Power source: Circuits must have a source of electrical energy, e.g. battery, mains.

Precaution: An action that can be taken to protect against possible danger or failure.

Pressure: The application of force to something by something else by pressing directly on it.

Pulley: Wheel that transmits force to or from a moving belt that rides in a groove in its edge.

Pylon: A large vertical steel tower supporting high-tension wires.

R

Radar: A way of finding the position of objects, such as ships, etc. by using radio waves.

RAM (random access memory): A type of computer memory that holds information and programs.

Rasp: Similar in appearance to a file, but works more quickly and gives a rougher finish.

Ratchet: A ratchet is a wheel with teeth that rotate. It is used with a pawl to allow rotation in one direction only.

Recyclable material: Materials that can be broken down and used again, e.g. paper, glass, aluminium.

Recycle: Breaking down objects and materials to reuse them.

Reed switch: A switch activated by a magnet.

Relay: This changes switching contacts when it receives an electric signal.

Renewable energy (sometimes called alternative energy): Energy from renewable sources, e.g. sun/solar, wind, wood (if replanted), water, plants.

Research: The phase of a project where books, catalogues and the Internet are searched for information relevant to the project.

Resistance: Resistors resist, i.e. try to stop or slow down, the flow of current in a circuit. The larger the resistor, the smaller the current that can flow.

Resistor: An electronic component that provides resistance to current flow.

Robot: A machine that can do some human work, often used in assembly lines, planet exploration and bomb disposal.

ROM (read-only memory): A type of computer memory.

S

Satellite: Objects that travel around planets, sending information back to Earth.

Scroll saw (fret saw): A long, narrow-bladed saw suited to cutting curves and circles in thin sheet material.

Semiconductor: Material whose ability to conduct electric current is somewhere between that of a conductor and an insulator.

Sensor: A device that converts a signal from the real world into an electrical signal, e.g. light and sound sensors.

Shear: Cutting or clipping force.

Shears: See 'Tin snips'.

Snips: See 'Tin snips'.

Software: Programs for directing the operation of a computer or processing data.

Solder: An alloy of lead and tin that melts easily and hardens again quickly when it cools, thus is ideal for joining other metals together.

Solenoid: An electronic device where a bar pulls in one direction when current flows through the solenoid and returns to its original position when the current stops.

Space probes: Objects sent into space unmanned, sending information back to Earth.

SPDT switch: Single pole double throw switch.

Spreadsheet: Software suitable for putting information in table format, especially handy for doing calculations on the tables, e.g. adding up columns.

JUNIOR CERTIFICATE TECHNOLOGY

SPST switch: Single pole single throw switch.
Steel wool: Looks like a Brillo pad. Used to finish an edge of acrylic.
Structural failure: When a structure collapses or breaks down.
Structural member: A part of a structure. These work together like a team, every one being either in tension or compression.
Structure: Something that provides support and maintains its shape under a load, e.g. buildings, chairs, skeletons, etc.
Strut: A part of a structure in compression for keeping two objects from coming closer together. A strut is in compression, e.g. a pillar supporting a roof.
Surforms: Cross between a file and a plane. Removes material with a pushing action.
Switches: Allows one to control current flow in circuits. They are usually used to turn things on and off.

T

Tap: A tool for cutting an internal screw thread.
Telescope: An instrument used for detecting distant objects, e.g. a radio telescope.
Tenon saw: Hand saws that are good for cutting tenon joints in wood.
Tensile strength: The maximum force a material can withstand in tension (pulling).
Tension: A stretching, straining, pulling force.
Thermistor (or thermal resistor; temperature-dependent resistor): Its resistance is high in the cold and low in the heat. They are suitable in temperature detection circuits.
Thermoplastic: Plastics that soften when heated and harden again when cooled and can be softened and cooled many times, e.g. PVC, acrylic.
Thermosetting plastics: Plastics that melt the first time they are heated and harden when cooled and cannot ever be melted again, e.g. Bakelite is used for saucepan and iron handles.
Thread: The raised rib gong around the outside of a screw, or the inside of a screw hole.
Throw: A fixed wire stopping point inside a switch.
Tie: A part of a structure in tension for keeping two objects from spreading or separating, e.g. the cross piece on a swing.
Tilt switch: A switch activated by a mercury ball free to roll to or away from a contact, making an open or closed switch.
Timber: Wood used for building and making things, e.g. furniture and wooden toys.
Tin snips: Used to cut thin sheet metal with a shearing action.
Tongs: Used to hold hot material.
Toxic: Poisonous.
Transistors: Electronic devices with three legs – emitter, base, collector. A small voltage across the base-emitter junction causes a larger current from the collector to the emitter.
Translucent: Light can pass through, but objects on the opposite side are not clearly visible, e.g. coloured acrylic.
Transparent: See-through, e.g. clear glass.
Triangulation: The use of triangles in a structure.

U

Units: Energy = joules (J); power = watts (W); resistance = ohms (Ω); current = amps (A); voltage = volts (V); capacitance = farads (F); force = newtons (N); pressure = pascal (Pa) or BAR.

V

Valve: Mechanical device used to control the flow of liquid or air.
Variable resistor/potentiometer: A resistor whose resistance can be varied.
Varnish: A type of paint that provides a hard, glossy, waterproof, transparent coating.
Velocity ratio: Distance moved by effort ÷ distance moved by force.
Veneer: A thin sliver of wood, used to coat a manufactured wood or to make plywood. The veneer is usually an expensive wood, e.g. oak.
Vice: A tool used to hold materials firmly.
Voltage: The higher the voltage in a circuit, the more power there is to drive the electrons.
Voltmeter: Test instrument used to measure voltage.

W

Washer: A metal disc with a hole in its centre, used to spread load spreading under a screw or bolt head.
Wire: Long, thin object for electric current to pass through, with copper (conducting) cores and a PVC (insulating) covering.
Word processor: Software suitable for writing reports and regular text, e.g. Microsoft Word.
Work: Force x distance.
Worm and worm wheel: Mechanism comprising a gear (worm wheel) and a worm, used to make a fast motor turn something at a much lower speed.

X

X-ray: A powerful, invisible beam that can pass through opaque substances.

INDEX

A
abrafile	33
acid rain	11
adhesives	2, 40
alloy	23
ammeter	83
analysis	116
AND gate	89

B
band saw	36
batteries	77
beams	50
bearings	50
blow moulding	39
bolt	35
brace	34
bradawl	34
breadboard	85
brief	116
bulb	82
buzzer	82
bytes	73

C
cam and follower	60
cantilevers	50, 61
capacitors	81
cell	77
centre punch/dot punch	32
ceramic	26
chisels	32
chuck	37
compass	31, 100
composites	26
compression/pressure	49, 51
computer	71
computer-aided design (CAD)	73, 101
computer-aided manufacture (CAM)	66, 73
computer input devices	71
computer output devices	72
computer storage devices	72
conductor	77
coping saw	31
copper stripboard	86
countersunk	35
cramps/clamps	32
cranks	60
current	76

D
darlington pair	81
design folder	115
development	103
digital electronics	89
dimensions	102
diodes	80
dividers	31
dovetail joint	41
dovetail saw	31
dowel joint	41
drawing board	101
drill	34, 36, 37, 38, 63

E
efficiency	65
effort	57, 58, 65
electrical conductor	23
electrical insulator	23
electricity	2, 76
electric scroll/fret saw	36
electroplating/anodising	42
elevation	105
energy	16, 65
environment	11, 51
evaluation	120

F
fabric	22
file (computer)	73
file (tool)	33
finger joint/comb joint	41
555 timer	83
force	48, 57
fret saw/scroll saw	31
friction	49, 65
fulcrum	58
fuse	78

G
gears	62, 63, 64
genetic modification (GM)	6
glass paper	34
gravity	48, 51
guillotine	31

H
hacksaw	31
halving joint	41
hammer	32
hand tools	30
hardware	71
hardwood	24
hatching	102
hinges	36
hot wire cutter	31
hydraulics	66

I
inclined planes	58
insulator	77
integrated circuit (IC)	82
Internet	71, 73
inventions	5
inverter/NOT gate	89
isometric projection	104

J
jigsaw	36

L
lap joint	41
latch	90
lathe	37
LDR	81
LED	80
levers	58
linkages	59
load	57, 58, 65
logic gates	89
logo	73
lubricant	49

M
machines	57
machine tools	36
mains electricity	77
mallet	33
marking gauge	30
marking knife	30
manufactured wood	24

JUNIOR CERTIFICATE TECHNOLOGY

materials	22
mechanical advantage	58, 60, 64
mechanisms	57
metal	23
micrometer	30
microprocessor	71
milling machine	37
mock model/prototype	119
moisture sensor	81
motor	82
multimeter	83

N

nail punch	33
nails	35
NAND gate	90
nut	35

O

oblique projection	104
Ohm's Law	78
operating system	72
OR gate	90
orthographic projection	105, 106

P

PC	71
perspective	104
single-point	105
two-point	105
pictorial drawings	104
pilot hole	35
pincers	33
pixels	74
plan	106
planing	2, 38
plastic	25
pneumatics	65
potential dividers	79
power sources	77
power tools	2
press moulding	39
printed circuit board (PCB)	86
protractor	100
pulleys	64

R

rasp	33
ratchet and pawl	61
recycling	12
relay	83
rendering	101
research	117
resistor	78
rivet	35
robotics	66
robots	71

S

sanding	33
satellites	8
sawing	2, 38
scale	102
screwdriver	36
screws	35
semiconductor	77
set square	100
shadow	106
shear	49
sliding bevel	30
snips/tin snips/shears	31
software	72
softwood	24
soldering	3, 40
spanners	36
speaker	82
split pins/cotter pins	35
springs	61, 62
steel wool	34
stencils	100
strip heater	38, 39
structures	47
strut	51
surforms	33
switches	84

T

tenon saw	31
tension	48, 50
testing	120
thermistor	81
thermoplastic	25, 39
thermosetting	26
tie	50
timers	82
tolerance	79
tongs	32
toothed belts	63
torsion	49
transformer	78
transistor	80, 81
try square	30
T square	101

U

units	83

V

vacuum forming	39
variable resistor	79
vice	32
voltage	76
voltmeter	83

W

washers	36
wood	24
working drawings	106